THE HISTORY OF LIVE M
VOLUME I: 195

This volume is dedicated to Jenny McKay

The History of Live Music in Britain, Volume I: 1950–1967

From Dance Hall to the 100 Club

SIMON FRITH
University of Edinburgh, UK

MATT BRENNAN
University of Edinburgh, UK

MARTIN CLOONAN
University of Glasgow, UK

EMMA WEBSTER
University of Glasgow, UK

Routledge
Taylor & Francis Group

LONDON AND NEW YORK

First Published 2013 by Ashgate Publisher

2 Park Square, Milton Park, Abingdon, Oxon OX14 4RN
711 Third Avenue, New York, NY 10017, USA

Routledge is an imprint of the Taylor & Francis Group, an informa business

First issued in paperback 2016

British Library Cataloguing in Publication Data
The history of live music in Britain. from dance hall to
  the 100 Club.
  Volume I, 1950-1967 : – (Ashgate popular and folk music
  series)
  1. Concerts–Great Britain–History–20th century.
  2. Popular music–Great Britain–1951-1960. 3. Popular
  music–Great Britain–1961-1970. 4. Music–Social
  aspects–Great Britain–History–20th century.
  I. Series II. Frith, Simon, 1946-
  780.7'8'41'09045-dc23

Library of Congress Cataloging-in-Publication Data
The history of live music in Britain / by Simon Frith ... [et al.].
    p. cm. – (Ashgate popular and folk music series)
  Includes bibliographical references and index.
  ISBN 978-1-4094-2280-8 (hardback)
  1. Popular music–Performances–Great Britain. 2. Great Britain–Social life and customs–
20th century. 3. Great Britain–Social life and customs–21st century. I. Frith, Simon, 1946-
  ML3492.H57 2013
  781.630941–dc23

ISBN 978-1-4094-2280-8 (hbk)

ISBN 978-1-138-24849-6 (pbk)

Contents

General Editor's Preface

The upheaval that occurred in musicology during the last two decades of the twentieth century has created a new urgency for the study of popular music alongside the development of new critical and theoretical models. A relativistic outlook has replaced the universal perspective of modernism (the international ambitions of the 12-note style); the grand narrative of the evolution and dissolution of tonality has been challenged, and emphasis has shifted to cultural context, reception and subject position. Together, these have conspired to eat away at the status of canonical composers and categories of high and low in music. A need has arisen, also, to recognize and address the emergence of crossovers, mixed and new genres, to engage in debates concerning the vexed problem of what constitutes authenticity in music and to offer a critique of musical practice as the product of free, individual expression.

Popular musicology is now a vital and exciting area of scholarship, and the *Ashgate Popular and Folk Music Series* presents some of the best research in the field. Authors are concerned with locating musical practices, values and meanings in cultural context, and draw upon methodologies and theories developed in cultural studies, semiotics, poststructuralism, psychology and sociology. The series focuses on popular musics of the twentieth and twenty-first centuries. It is designed to embrace the world's popular musics from Acid Jazz to Zydeco, whether high tech or low tech, commercial or non-commercial, contemporary or traditional.

Professor Derek B. Scott
Professor of Critical Musicology
University of Leeds

Preface

This is the first volume in a projected series of three. Our aim is to provide a social history of music in Britain since 1950. The books are designed to fill an obvious gap in the academic (and non-academic) literature – there is presently no general history of British music in this period. But in writing this history, we will adopt a particular focus: we are interested in the role which live music has played in British cultural life since 1950. There are several reasons for taking this approach.

First of all, we want to shift attention in socio-economic studies of popular music from the recording industry to the business of live music. Our starting point here is that most present accounts of 'the music industry' (which are often derived from Adorno's analysis in the 1940s of 'the culture industry') over-privilege the recording sector at the expense of the sector in which most musicians in all genres have been located historically: the live arena. These books will chart the changing symbiotic relationship between the recording and live sectors in the last 60 years, a relationship that is neglected in popular music histories organised around record releases and sales charts. Among other things, this means that we will examine the key role of the promoter in musical life: the three volumes chart three eras of promotional activity. We believe that a proper understanding of the live music business is necessary for a proper understanding of the recorded music business.

The second advantage of a music history written from the perspective of live musical activity is that it draws attention to the importance of place. Live music, by its nature, must happen in a particular locality, and our second concern in these books is to look at the changing sites and venues of musical performance, from the post-war dance hall to the contemporary rock club circuit, from the state-run arts centre to the pub back room, from the coffee bar to the stadium, from the original jazz and folk festivals to Glastonbury and T in the Park. The history of live music is also a history of leisure and the night-time economy, of city geographies and holiday destinations, of fans' movements around towns and musicians' movements around and between countries. Throughout these volumes we will draw material from three cities in particular: Bristol, Glasgow and Sheffield.

Third, live music involves the state – and thus politics – much more directly than recorded music. On the one hand, live musical events of all kinds are subject to regulatory frameworks, to national laws concerning public performance, health and safety, the sale of alcohol, noise nuisance and so forth, and to the decisions of local licensing authorities. On the other hand, both national and local authorities have been active in promoting live music, building and funding venues and, through arts councils, directly supporting musical groups and organisations, and sponsoring tours and performances. A history of live music is necessarily also a history of cultural politics, and one theme that we will develop through these three volumes is that the live sector involves a complex relationship between three kinds of promoter: the state-funded, the commercial and the enthusiast. The last of these may be driven by various motives (love of a particular kind of music, bohemianism, artistic or political vision, friendship), but such musical activists will be central to our history.

It has been the orthodox view in the academy for the last 40 years or so that the live musical sector is in decline, as a matter of both economics (the sector's inability to compete with other music media in price terms) and sociology (the sector's declining role in people's everyday use of music). As Glenn Gould famously remarked in *High Fidelity* in 1966:

> In an unguarded moment some months ago, I predicted that the public concert as we know it today would no longer exist a century hence, that its functions would have been entirely taken over by the electronic media. It had not occurred to me that this statement represented a particularly radical pronouncement. Indeed, I regarded it almost as self-evident truth. (Gould 1966: 46)

Our books clearly challenge this view and it is a paradoxical effect of the digital revolution that the live music sector is now seen as particularly significant both economically (as record companies' long-established ways of money making no longer work) and sociologically (as the live musical event seems ever more important for music lovers in all genres). We intend to explain this paradox – to explain the value of live music – through a historical investigation. In broad terms we will argue that it is through the history of live music that we can grasp the changing relationship of the public and private in an era of great technological, industrial and social change. It has always been through the live – public – experience of making and listening to music that it has been most deeply embedded in people's everyday lives and in their understanding of their personal and social identities.

In telling this story we will draw on a range of methodologies and sources. We will use case studies, local ethnographies and historical snapshots. We will draw on systematic reading of the music press, archival work (especially in the previously unavailable Musicians' Union archive) and a series of interviews with promoters from a range of different musical genres, eras and locations. We will bring together material from a wide range of non-academic secondary sources – musicians' autobiographies, local histories of particular venues and fan memoirs – as well as from specialist academic studies in musicology, sociology and social and economic history. Each volume will conclude with a description of a Rolling Stones show.

We should note here three issues of scope and definition. First, our definition of 'live' music includes music on record provided by disc jockeys for dancers and audiences gathering in public places. This might seem a distortion of terms (though even the Musicians' Union eventually agreed that a DJ was a musician), but venues combining live and recorded music are an important part of our story.

Second, although popular music is at the centre of our work, we will also be concerned with the history of classical and art music performance. This is, again, because the different sectors have overlapping histories (in terms of venues, for example, or promotional practices), but also because we are interested in the ways in which people's understanding of the live musical experience is affected by the ideologies of 'high' and 'low' music.

Third, our use of the term 'musician' is very broad, as already indicated. In the live music sector the distinction between professional, semi-professional and amateur performers is blurred both in performance settings themselves and in musicians' individual careers. One of our concerns is how live music practices have changed (and have been changed by) the ways in which people and institutions understand what it is to be 'a musician' in the first place.

In this book, volume 1 of our history, we cover the period 1950–1967. The Second World War had obviously caused a huge disruption to everyday life in Britain and hence to the organisation and enjoyment of live music. The immediate post-war period thus involved attempts by the various established players in the live music world to get back to normal. In the first part of the book we examine this from three perspectives – commercial promoters, the state and musicians. By the mid-1950s, though, it was becoming clear that new social and musical forces were creating new forms of musical entertainment for new kinds of audience organised in new ways. In the second part of the book we examine the rise of 'do-it-yourself' music making and promoting, the emergence of 'the teenage consumer' and the increasing importance of the record industry in British musical culture. By 1967, a map of live music in Britain shows a very different soundscape to that of the early 1950s and in the final part of the book we will describe this by reference, on the one hand, to venues and audience experiences and, on the other hand, from the perspective of promoters and the live music business.

Acknowledgments

The research for this book was made possible by a grant from the Arts and Humanities Research Council (AHRC) (AH/F009437/1).

The book, like the AHRC project, is a collaborative work. Matt Brennan did most of the national industry interviews and archive research and drafted Chapters 1, 6 and 7. Martin Cloonan did the remaining national interviews, the archive research on the Musicians' Union and state regulation, and drafted Chapters 2, 3 and the account of the Rolling Stones in Richmond in 1963. Emma Webster did the interview and archive research in Bristol, Glasgow and Sheffield, and wrote the 1962 snapshots of those cities. Simon Frith wrote the book's final version and takes responsibility for all errors and infelicities.

We would like to thank the AHRC for its support, Derek Scott and Ashgate for being willing to take on a three-volume proposal, and all the industry people who talked to us so informatively. We are also grateful to Dave Allen, Annette Davison, Keir Keightley and Kevin Tennent for letting us read and cite unpublished research.

Simon Frith would like to thank Cressida McKay Frith for the musical accompaniment and Jenny McKay for reading and improving the manuscript and for much else besides. This volume is dedicated to her.

Chapter 1

Getting Back to Business

Many forces combine to make the present an exciting and promising moment in the history of English music. The nation is now conscious of the need for music as part of daily life and education and, with English composition at a level unknown since the end of the seventeenth century, the opportunities for making and enjoying music are fuller and more varied than ever before. (Political and Economic Planning (PEP) 1949: 211)

Most people's musical pleasures are of the simplest and relatively few can raise their level of musical understanding very much ... most youngsters to-day like jazz and little else; their elders fancy the old music hall songs best and a few sentimental parlour ballads, while beyond that their musical horizon is a desert. Some of this music is fun, some of it has charm, some of it is moving, but most of it is pretty low-level stuff and many of the dance lyrics are of an enervating 'wishing-will-make-it-so-kind' that is not much use to anybody; but, like it or not, it is the popular music of our time. (Workers Music Association 1945: 13)

Introduction

British live music in 1950 was, in many ways, still adjusting to the impact of the Second World War, which had disrupted every aspect of British life. During wartime, the raw materials used to make musical commodities were in short supply: whether it was the shellac used in 78 rpm records (the dominant recording format of the era) or the brass used to make saxophones, resources that had previously been taken for granted were diverted to manufacture military and essential goods. And British nightlife had obviously been affected by the German air raids. Buildings where music was performed were damaged, whether landmarks such as St Paul's Cathedral or specialist venues such as London's Café Anglais, a popular nightspot for dancing and jazz bands. Buildings that were not damaged directly were affected regardless, as the chaos forced many venues to close temporarily and disrupted transport and the night-time economy. But the most severe impact was that a generation of professional and aspiring musicians, as well as concert promoters, agents and others involved in British musical culture, were forced to abandon their careers and serve their country in the armed and other services.

By the time the war was over, Britain was a devastated country. In the words of historian Geoffrey Macnab, 'it was estimated that the country had lost a quarter of its national wealth, some £7 billion, and its export trade was in tatters: every last bit of energy had been depleted' (1993: 162). Live music was, of course, deeply affected by these economic problems. State regulation continued to restrict musical activity. A special purchase tax was introduced: anyone buying a musical instrument was charged a hefty 66.6 per cent in tax because instruments were considered 'luxury goods'. The dance band paper *Melody Maker* reported on the impact of the tax, lamenting its dire consequences for the fate of British music: '1) musical instruments are not luxuries, they are the tools of a man's profession; 2) musical culture in Britain will die if youth cannot afford to buy instruments; 3) in war time, instruments were necessary for morale: must morale suffer now?' (17 April 1948: 1). The government also directed British citizens working in essential industries to remain in their jobs and forbade these workers from taking musical employment through a new 'Control of Engagement Order'. As the *Melody Maker* again reported, 'the semi-pro [musician] whose daytime job is in essential industry will find it extremely difficult to obtain release from his present employment in order to become a full-time professional musician, should he wish to do so' (11 October 1947: 1).

Despite this climate of austerity in certain aspects of musical life, there was still plenty of live music to be heard. Social historian Harry Hopkins claims that by the end of the 1940s, 'in "unmusical" London alone four million seats were now sold each year for concerts, opera and ballet' (Hopkins 1964: 236), and this statistic only covers classical music. This chapter will therefore provide a map of the live music business in Britain in 1950, as entrepreneurs tried to return to their 1930s ways of working. We will approach this mapping exercise from three different angles. First, we will examine live music culture in terms of musical discourses, while describing the kinds of live music being performed at this time. Second, we will explain how the live music business worked, outlining the differences between three kinds of promoter (enthusiast, state-funded and commercial) and their dealings with venue owners, agents and managers. Third, we will review how the rest of the British music industry – broadcasters, record companies, song publishers and royalty collectors – related to the live music industry and describe how musicians interacted with the industry at a collective level, through the Musicians' Union. The chapter will thus introduce the main issues to be discussed throughout the rest of the book.

Discourses, Genres and Artists

It is not easy to provide a comprehensive overview of the diversity of live music performed in Britain in the mid-twentieth century. One way to begin is with a framework of different social worlds with music at their centre, each with its own set of practices and values. The idea of musical 'art worlds', proposed by sociologist Howard Becker (1984), is developed by Simon Frith in his book *Performing Rites*. Frith argues that, as well as interacting in different kinds of social world, musical actors also make sense of their practice discursively, sharing values and language that endow a musical experience with social meaning (1996: 26). A 'discourse' in this sense is productive; it does not simply name a pre-existing social world, but produces that world and its social institutions, professions and genres. Frith argues, in particular, that 'music is heard through three overlapping and contradictory grids' which he calls folk discourse, art discourse, and pop discourse (ibid.). These discourses represent ideal sets of values that are derived from the folk, art and pop music genres that share their names. However, when applied to practical examples, these ideal discourses quickly become complicated, compromised and conflicting. In his study of English class and culture, for example, Ross McKibbin concludes that by 1951 there were three musical publics: a small public for 'serious' music (as broadcast by the BBC's Third Programme); a larger public for 'middlebrow' music (made up of many strands including the classical music canon); and a much larger one for popular music (predominantly American popular music) (McKibbin 1998: 416). Such a listening map (which is obviously also a simplification of musical tastes) is useful in drawing attention to the confusing ways in which musical discourses are applied in practice (in BBC or Arts Council policy, for example).

For Frith, folk discourse is a set of anti-modernist values that understands the commercialisation of music as corruptive and suggests that the appreciation of music should be linked to the appreciation of its social function in creating community. Drawing on the work of folk scholar Niall MacKinnon (1993), Frith agues that the embodiment of these values can be found in British folk clubs, which 'attempt to minimise the distance between performer and audience, to provide a "different form of socialising in which active musical performance and participation [are] integrated"' (Frith 1996: 41). The folk festival is another event 'within which folk values – the integration of art and life – can be lived ... the folk festival seeks to solve the problem of musical "authenticity": it offers the experience of the folk ideal, the experience of collective, participatory music making, the chance to judge music by its direct contribution to sociability' (ibid.).

In Britain in 1950, folk discourse was certainly being applied to the various folk music and dance traditions of the country's different nations and regions, though it would be a mistake to think of any of these traditions as 'pure' or 'authentic', despite the ideological values attached to them. In his book *Fakesong*, Dave Harker (1985) explains how British folk traditions were as artificially constructed as any other genre: prominent folk song collectors, such as Francis Child in the nineteenth century and Cecil Sharp in the twentieth century, had great influence over the selection and shaping of a canon of British folk music, just as music conservatories were influential in constructing the canon of classical music repertoire. In fact, by the second half of the 1940s, the process of determining what British folk music meant was still taking place, through a revival led by organisations like the English Folk Dance and Song Society and individuals like Bert Lloyd and Ewan MacColl.

Neither was it only music that labelled itself as 'folk' that was socially organised around the values of folk discourse. In their own ways, both the British brass band movement and amateur choral societies operated by integrating musical practice with lived experience and building a sense of community (and 'Britishness'). Even musical genres that might have been understood as primarily commercial, such as jazz, could be (and frequently were) interpreted using the language of folk discourse. The New Orleans revivalist movement of the late 1940s, for example, explicitly defined itself against commercial jazz, against swing, and sought to embody in its return to 'traditional' instruments and playing practices an understanding of 'real' jazz as the celebration of community. In the words of Charles Fox, writing in *The PL Yearbook of Jazz* in 1946 (in which 'real' jazz is described as a form of folk music throughout):

> The jazz of New Orleans was a natural growth, springing out of the life and needs of a comparatively limited community. Swing is a premeditated music, run as a business, with its control in the hands of cultural illiterates who virtually dictate the forms which popular music shall take. (McCarthy 1946: 41)

Folk discourse may have manifested itself most clearly in genres that define themselves with the 'folk' word, but as a set of aesthetic and social values, it can be found in varying degrees across many musical worlds. The same can be said of art and pop discourses too.

According to Frith, the source of art discourse lies in the history of the bourgeois art world and the development of the nineteenth-century high/low cultural divide found in classical music aesthetics (Frith 1996: 36). Frith argues that the organising institution of art discourse is the academy, 'the music departments of universities, conservatories, [and] the whole panoply of formal arrangements and practices in which classical music in its various forms is taught and handed down the generations' (ibid.: 36). With respect to live music, the central bourgeois music event is the concert, where 'music's essential value is its provision of a transcendent experience that is, on the one hand, ineffable and uplifting but, on the other, only available to those with the right sort of knowledge ... only the right people with the right training can, in short, experience the real meaning of "great" music' (ibid.: 39).

In mid-twentieth-century Britain, various institutions, including universities, conservatories, the BBC and the newly formed Arts Council of Great Britain (established in 1946). supported the view that certain kinds of music and music-related performing arts – symphonies, opera, ballet and chamber music – were to be privileged above other genres (particularly folk and pop). Due in no small part to the Arts Council (to be discussed further in the next chapter), British classical live music performance indeed found itself in a period of remarkably good health by the end of the 1940s, despite the fact that such key venues as the Queen's Hall in London and the Free Trade Hall in Manchester had been bombed and forced to close during the war (PEP's 1949 *Enquiry into Music* identified 'the general shortage and the many inadequacies of halls' as the major problem facing live classical music after the war (1949: 33–5)). Pre-war London-based ensembles such as the London Symphony Orchestra and the London Philharmonic had been joined by major new orchestras such as the Philharmonia in 1945 and the Royal Philharmonic Orchestra in 1946. Important ensembles had been established in other areas of Britain as well, such as the City of Birmingham Orchestra (founded in 1920, it became a full-time orchestra in 1944, changing its name to the City of Birmingham Symphony Orchestra in 1948) and the Scottish National Orchestra (founded in 1891, it became a full-time orchestra as the SNO in 1950). The annual Edinburgh International Festival had been launched in 1947 in collaboration with Glyndebourne, which slowly came back to operatic life in the late 1940s, staging the premieres of Benjamin Britten's *The Rape of Lucretia* in 1946 and *Albert Herring* in 1947.

The Arts Council itself had been formed as a consequence of wartime efforts to encourage the arts, which included through the Council for the Encouragement of Music and the Arts (CEMA) a policy of providing funding not only for London-based musical activity, but also for music – both locally produced and touring concerts – in smaller provincial towns. But if, by 1950, Arts Council support meant that London now 'had the chance of becoming the musical centre of Europe' (PEP 1949: 14), funding for art music outside of London had declined to the extent that the first Arts Council-commissioned report on opera and ballet stressed the need for more support to allow national ensembles to tour the country (Witts 1998: 229).

Frith's third musical discourse is pop, the discourse rooted in the commercial music world. As Frith argues, 'its values are created by and organised around the music industry, around the means and possibilities of turning sounds into commodities – musical value and monetary value are therefore equated, and the sales charts become the measure and symbol of "good" pop music' (1996: 41). In the logic of pop discourse, live music events sell 'fun' and 'escape from the daily grind' (ibid.: 41–2). The supply of commercial music available in 1950s Britain was wide-ranging, despite the privations of post-war austerity, with the influence of American popular music being particularly prevalent. Popular music from the USA made its impact via star performers on major record labels as well as in featured songs from hit Hollywood films and Broadway musicals (*Oklahoma!* and *Annie Get Your Gun* opened in London's West End in 1948 and were both still running in 1950) and through dance-floor fads. Other forms of popular music were particular to Britain, such as songs from the music-hall and variety tradition and from British film and theatre.

It is difficult to measure the popularity of different kinds of popular music in Britain during this period, as there were few sales figures available to chart the industry and, as business economist Terry Gourvish (2009) has demonstrated, those that existed were unreliable. There was no systematic information about ticket sales in the UK at this time, for example, just the occasional news story about shows that had (usually according to their promoters) done exceptionally well (or poorly).[1] It is

---

[1]   Hopkins claims that 'between the Convertibility Crisis [1947] and the Devaluation Crisis [1949], *Oklahoma!* cheered up 2,200,000 British citizens', but does not give a source for his figures (Hopkins 1964: 107).

no easier to extrapolate the relative popularity of live performers from their record sales since no vaguely reliable British record sales chart existed until November 1952, when one was compiled by Percy Dickens for the first time in the *New Musical Express*. It is, however, possible to say something about the popular success of songs (as against performers or records): Radio Luxembourg, the BBC's main continental rival, broadcast a 'Hit Parade' show of songs from 1948 onwards.[2] This was based on the sales of sheet music rather than discs, a reminder that at this time it could still be assumed that it was songs (performed by numerous recording artists) that were popular rather than specific recorded performances made by specific artists. If Frank Sinatra did well with 'Goodnight Irene' on Columbia Records, for instance, then other recording companies would quickly release their own versions of the song recorded by one of their own contracted artists, and it was still unusual for one version to prove vastly more popular than another.[3] To give an indication of what kinds of song were popular in 1950, the table below (Table 1.1) lists all of the number one songs for that year according to Radio Luxembourg.

The most striking feature of this chart is how clearly it demonstrates the dominance of American popular songs in Britain. With the exception of 'The Harry Lime Theme' from the British film *The Third Man*, all of the number one hit songs of 1950 were first popularised by Americans (and, apart from the Italian song 'You're Breaking My Heart' and 'Hop Scotch Polka', originally a British music-hall song by Billy Whitlock, written by Americans too). Some songs became popular via Hollywood films ('My Foolish Heart') or musicals ('Bewitched, Bothered and Bewildered'); others were popularised by star American performers and then covered by British artists: for example, 'Dear Hearts and Gentle People', sung by Bing Crosby, but covered in Britain by Billy Cotton, and 'Music! Music! Music!', sung by Teresa Brewer and covered by Petula Clark.

The most popular stage acts in 1950 were also a mix of American and British musicians. In the live setting, however, a crucial distinction was made between instrumental musicians and singers. The vast majority of professional instrumental musicians in both the USA and the UK were members of their respective musicians' unions and, following a long-standing dispute between the US union (the American Federation of Musicians (AFM)) and its British counterpart, American instrumental musicians were not allowed to perform in the UK and vice versa. By contrast, singers had historically been denied membership in musicians'

---

[2]   For a good account of sporadic British music charts prior to 1948, see Nott 2002: 207–8.

[3]   Philip Ennis documents the market transition from audiences buying songs without significantly discriminating between who sang them to gradually valuing a specific version of a song recorded by a single artist in his book *The Seventh Stream* (1992: 239–40). Although his research is limited to record sales in the USA, the British recording industry operated similarly; hits were songs rather than records, and every record company felt the need to have its own version of the popular songs of the day.

Table 1.1   Number 1 Songs 1950

Week ending	Song title	Weeks
7 January	You're Breaking My Heart	2
21 January	Hop Scotch Polka	1
28 January	The Harry Lime Theme	4 (returned for 3 weeks from w/e 18 Feb)
4 February	Dear Hearts And Gentle People	2
11 March	Music! Music! Music!	6
22 April	(If I Knew You Were Comin') I'd Have Baked A Cake	1
29 April	My Foolish Heart	11
8 July	Bewitched, Bothered and Bewildered	8
9 September	Silver Dollar (Roll, Roll, Roll)	7
28 October	Goodnight Irene	4
25 November	Rudolph The Red-nosed Reindeer	6

(Chart compiled by Smith 1999)

unions on both sides of the Atlantic, and instead belonged to unions for variety artists and entertainers. The result was that, despite being popular in the UK via their recordings, very few American instrumental musicians performed live in the UK during this time – with the important exception of performances at American military bases – while American singers did visit and tour the UK (accompanied by British instrumentalists), sometimes with remarkable effect. Danny Kaye's debut at the London Palladium in 1948, for example, was:

> a personal triumph such as the British music hall had not seen for a quarter of a century. Next day, Danny Kaye had become the talk of the town. *The Times* printed his photograph on its back page; Cabinet Ministers flocked to the stalls; Royalty went round to the dressing-room. Ticket spivs reaped a rich harvest from queues that stretched around the building. Standing-room tickets changed hands at £3 and stalls from anything up to £20. (Hopkins 1964: 108)

The most popular British bandleaders in 1950 had been playing professionally since well before the Second World War. Dance-band performance was a long-term career for these men; rather than operating in a system of producing a hit at a young age and enjoying early success before fading in popularity, they were instead part of a musical tradition where experience was valued and reputations were built over long periods of time. Even with the interruption of the war (in which several of them served while others played in bands to entertain the troops), many bandleaders had steadily increased their standings over the years, to the point where they achieved their peak popularity only after having played for several decades. The BBC was also of great importance to the success of a bandleader: securing a broadcasting contract was the best way of publicising the band at a national level.

Three examples help to illustrate this career model. Trained as a pianist, Geraldo formed his first band in 1924 and was popular up until the Second World War, when he was appointed to supervise the bands division of the Entertainments National Service Association and became director of bands for the BBC (Augarde 2004). After the war, Geraldo continued to enjoy great success not only as a bandleader but also as a manager and booking agent, supplying orchestras for cruise liners, dance halls, theatres and restaurants. Billy Cotton was a contemporary of Geraldo, forming his own dance band in 1925 and gaining fame throughout the 1930s. After entertaining the troops with his band throughout the war, Cotton was offered a regular Sunday morning show on the BBC's Light Programme in 1949. *The Billy Cotton Band Show* 'quickly became a Sunday lunchtime institution' (Wills 2004). Trombonist Ted Heath played in many dance orchestras (including Geraldo's) before forming his own band in 1944 and growing in popularity as a bandleader in his own right. A regular poll winner in *Melody Maker*, Heath was considered to have the best swing band outside the USA.

So far we have been discussing folk, art and pop discourses and their corresponding music worlds as if they can be clearly distinguished, but for most musicians this is certainly not the case. They occupy musical worlds that use elements of all three discourses. A good example of this (to which we have already referred) can be found in the jazz world, in London's jazz club scene. In 1950, British jazz was mainly divided between 'traditional' New Orleans and Dixieland music and 'modern' bebop and progressive music. Each style had its own representative venues and events. On the one hand, 'hundreds of clubs, operating in pub back rooms, working men's institutions, drill halls and palais were formed to accommodate the legion of revivalists and their following' (Godbolt 1984: 268). Leading British trad jazz musicians such as Humphrey Lyttelton, Ken Colyer and Chris Barber played at a cafe on 100 Oxford Street, which was variously known as the Feldman Swing Club, the London Jazz Club and the Humphrey Lyttelton Club. Modern jazzers gathered at London's Club Eleven, which was formed by and regularly featured musicians such as Ronnie Scott and Johnny Dankworth.[4] Both club scenes were created by groups of enthusiasts (performers and fans) who came together to hear music not heard on the radio or promoted by record companies or music publishers, a kind of music not often reflected in the sales charts (folk discourse). At the same time, these were not just folk-like communities. These scenes were led by musicians, the best of whom possessed impressive technique and musicianship and performed a harmonically and rhythmically complex music

---

[4]   Club Eleven was highly influential during its short existence from 1948 to 1950, but closed down at the end of April 1950 following a police raid (*Melody Maker*, 29 April 1950: 1, 6).

by any standards, a music that was being championed in its recorded form by critics (in *Gramophone* and *Melody Maker*, for example) seeking to have jazz recognised as an art form. And most of these new jazz spaces (and certainly the ones that survived) were commercial enterprises, which attracted audiences looking for entertainment. The post-war jazz club, the first expression of a new British live music culture to come, drew on all three musical discourses at once.

A similar argument could be made about the post-war folk club (and we will return to these developments in Chapter 4). The only further point to make here is that these overlapping discourses (articulated across all music worlds) relate to the interaction of amateur and professional music making. The vast majority of musicians performing live music in the UK were enthusiasts or semi-professionals rather than full-time musicians. This may seem counter-intuitive given the development of mass mediated music in the first half of the twentieth century; as James Nott has argued, the period between the First and Second World Wars 'saw a huge shift away from private performance in the home and a rapid increase in the public performance of live music. The general public became listeners rather than performers, reflecting the growing commercialisation of popular music' (2002: 100). Despite this, however, music making remained a popular amateur pastime and, crucially, the music performance world was one with a significant overlap between the amateur and professional spheres. Sometimes these two groups worked in harmony to create live music events, as when amateur choral societies performed alongside professional orchestras in concerts. At other times, however, there could be resentment from professional musicians (not to mention aggravation in the Musicians' Union) that amateur or semi-professional ensembles were willing to perform for cut rates or for free. This was the case for many military bands, community brass bands and dance bands. Nott points out, for instance, that 'price cutting had always been prevalent among dance musicians because of the large number of semi-professionals willing to offer their services for less than professional rates' (ibid.: 143).

There are also important gender distinctions to consider when examining the worlds of amateurs and professionals. There were 13,700 professional musicians working in England and Wales in 1951 (Ehrlich 1985: 235).[5] As in most professions in the UK, the career of musician was dominated by men, who outnumbered women approximately three to one. Although music was actually an easier career for women to pursue than most other professions, it was nevertheless a difficult environment in which to advance. In 1912 the London *Standard* reported on the inaugural concert (for charity) at the Shaftesbury Theatre of the Orchestra Femina, made up of women players only:

> Another important excursion into man's field of labour is to be made by the other sex in its new-born activities. Thousands of women, it is true, have for years earned their livelihood solely by playing in more or less important institutions

---

[5]   Unfortunately, Scotland and Northern Ireland are unaccounted for in Ehrlich's data.

up and down the country. But they have always had the humiliating experience of playing second fiddle in every sense of the term to some mere male rival, while among the more complicated, or, rather, less graceful instruments of the orchestra, they have been wholly unrepresented. (Quoted in Fifield 2005: 93)

The idea that only certain instruments were 'appropriate' for women was deep laid. As a commentator in another London newspaper, the London *Opinion*, wrote a few years later:

Neither Sir Henry Wood, Sir Thomas Beecham, nor Landon Ronald has any objection to lady violinists, violas or cellists playing in the orchestra if, and when, it be found necessary, but I understand that any idea of having lady wind instrument players is out of the question. I am glad myself. I cannot imagine anything more ungraceful or unwomanly than seeing a girl struggling with a huge brass instrument like the trombone, for instance. Women can do much that men can, but they will never be able to sing baritone, become soldiers, or blow wind instruments – unless it be their own trumpets! (Quoted in ibid.: 95)

There is no doubt that this attitude was still widespread in the classical music world in 1950, as was the belief that the professional symphony orchestra was a masculine institution in which women were not particularly welcome. When the newly established Royal Opera House sought to recruit instrumentalists for its orchestra in 1946, in competition with the equally newly established Philharmonia and Royal Philharmonic Orchestras, its leader 'went looking for women players' and thereby incurred 'a reprimand from his union' (Lebrecht 2000: 69). As for the more established orchestras:

'The LSO was very macho,' recalls the cellist, Bob Truman ... 'A lot of drinking, a whole lot of butching it up with the boys.' And of course they were all boys – even in the early 1970s. (Morrison 2004: 185–6)

Parsonage and Dyson describe similar prejudices in the jazz world: 'females were often paid less than men and were subject to persistent discrimination by critics, employers and even the Musicians' Union', although there is plenty of evidence that 'women were active as musicians in jazz and dance bands both alongside men and in all-female groups as well as in the position of bandleader', the most famous of whom was Ivy Benson, who led all-female bands known variously as the Rhythm Girls, Ladies Orchestra and Showband (Parsonage and Dyson 2007: 129).

In the profession of teaching music, however, women outnumbered men by over three to one; the gender ratio of musicians and music teachers combined was thus a fairly close 52:48 split in favour of men (Ehrlich 1985: 235). When one considers that many music teachers probably performed in public, if only at a local level, there was probably something closer to an equal male/female split, at least in classical performance. But this is to raise another gender issue. For male musicians (as for men in other trades and professions), women could be regarded as 'amateurs' because they did not share the male necessity for work – they were home makers rather than breadwinners – and their entry into the music profession was therefore likely to undercut pay rates (a particular issue in the post-war periods, when men sought to return to occupations in which women had been employed in their absence). During the First World War, for instance, when orchestral musicians in London's Stoll Theatres went on strike in demand of a 50 per cent pay increase (assuming they were in a strong bargaining position because of the shortage of male players), they were sacked and replaced by women instrumentalists (payed at the original rates). A total of 2,000 women applied for the jobs in Stoll's seven halls (Fifield 2005: 94). While nothing so dramatic happened in the Second World War, there is no doubt that for many in the music profession, getting back to business after 1945 meant getting back to a male business.

The Live Music Industry

As we have shown, British live music in 1950 was plentiful, varied and best understood as a series of different but overlapping social worlds. We will now turn our attention to a different set of issues that emerge from the study of live music as a business. Live music of all sorts was promoted with all manner of motivations: for profit, for political purposes, for fun, and sometimes for all these reasons at once. In this section we will examine the different kinds of people involved in the business of live music, particularly venue owners, promoters, agents and managers.

By 1950, national touring circuits had been re-established for both popular and classical musicians. Such tours were organised around three kinds of venue. First was the *music hall and variety theatre circuit*. Although the heyday of the music hall predates the advent of cinema, music halls and variety theatres continued to be significant for live music in Britain until well after the Second World War. Second was the *dance hall and ballroom circuit* and, in particular the ballroom chains Mecca and Rank, which had been important leisure venues since the 1930s. Finally, there were *concert halls and town halls,* which, while not a centrally operated circuit, were unified in other ways, mainly as venues for orchestras and choirs, both state-funded and amateur community ensembles. We will examine each of these circuits in turn.

British entrepreneurs began competing for dominance in a burgeoning commercial live music touring market in the mid-nineteenth century. The history of British music halls clearly demonstrates that there is nothing new about a small number of conglomerates owning vast swathes of British live music venues: in the late nineteenth century, businessmen such as Oswald Stoll, Edward Moss, Richard Thornton and Frank Allen made their reputations by acquiring chains of variety theatres and music halls which helped them gain an upper hand in negotiations with artists. In 1899, these four venue owners agreed to form a syndicate to consolidate their power. According to Dave Russell, the new Moss Empires syndicate, with Stoll as managing director, was 'basically a booking cartel designed to reduce labour costs by offering performers guaranteed advanced bookings in return for reduced fees' (Russell 2004).[6] This made artist unions such as the Musicians' Union (competing unions representing musicians founded round the turn of the century merged to become the Musicians' Union in 1921) and the Variety Artists Federation (founded 1906) all the more necessary to negotiate fees on behalf of performers. Stoll-Moss was not the only theatre syndicate: another key venue owner in the early twentieth century was Sir Walter de Frece, whose circuit was taken over by Charles Gulliver's London Theatres of Variety (LTV) in 1919. Despite its name, this company also owned theatres in the provinces, and in 1928 LTV's circuit was bought by Sir Walter Gibbons, who aimed to establish the General Theatres Corporation (GTC) as a nationwide circuit of music halls, with the London Palladium as its flagship venue (Murphy 2004a).

The popularity of music halls declined as cinemas began to displace other forms of mass entertainment, especially after the advent of sound films in the late 1920s, and yet the subsequent history of cinemas is entangled with the history of live music: not only did cinema development impact on musical employment (thousands of musicians in cinema pit orchestras were made redundant by the introduction of sound films), but cinemas themselves were crucial spaces for live music into the 1950s and 1960s. The Gaumont chain, for example, offered variety acts as well as films on its programmes and its cine-variety policy meant that its new cinemas in the 1930s and 1940s were built with stage facilities and dressing rooms (Eyles 1996: 114–15). As with music halls, business conglomerates did their best to consolidate ownership of British cinemas and create nationwide film circuits. In addition to buying music halls, Gibbons also invested in cinemas, and it was not long before GTC as a whole was bought by the rival Gaumont-British Picture Corporation (Murphy 2004a).

J. Arthur Rank got into cinema ownership relatively late in the game, after buying his first film house in the late 1930s. He became the biggest cinema circuit owner of all during the Second World War, when, according to Richard Davenport-Hines (2004), 'partly by the chance deaths of his nearest rivals, Rank acquired control of the Gaumont-British ... production company (1941) and of the exhibitors Odeon Theatres (1942)'. The Odeon chain was to play a significant part in the emergence of a new generation of concert promoters in the 1950s, who began by staging music shows in cinemas on Sundays and then did deals for concerts on other nights:

> I worked out a deal with the Rank Organisation, whereby if we booked a theatre on a Tuesday, say, and they had a movie playing there, I convinced them that if people wanted to see the movie on a Tuesday, they would go on a Wednesday or Thursday. I guaranteed them that the money they estimated they would

---

[6]   Stoll left this syndicate in 1910; Stoll Theatres re-merged with Moss Empires in 1960.

take, they would take more with the concert. And the first one was the Odeon
Hammersmith. (Davison 2010)[7]

Dance halls and ballrooms were also crucial to the British live music business.
Although the Rank Organisation is best known for its role in development of
the British film industry, by the 1950s it also operated a substantial number of
ballrooms and dance halls. However, the biggest such chain was owned by Mecca,
which grew under the leadership of Carl Heimann. Heimann joined the firm Ye
Mecca Cafés in 1924 working as a waiter, but quickly moved up the ranks to
become catering manager for dance halls and convinced the company to begin
acquiring and managing its own halls (Nott 2004). Throughout the 1930s, Heimann
developed the dance hall division of the company along with Scottish entrepreneur
Alan Fairley; by 1946, they were joint chairmen of the new Mecca Ltd; in the
1950s, they were rivalled only by Rank (whose ballroom circuit was known as Top
Rank) in market share of the British dance hall circuit.

The story of concert halls is different from that of music halls and dance halls,
primarily because the former served as key venues for classical and art music in post-
war Britain and involved both state-subsidised and commercial concert promotion.
The development of concert halls and town halls where music could be performed
became an important feature of British urban history in the nineteenth century:

> As concert-going became ever more popular in England, concert facilities began
> to be provided by local governments as a public amenity. And as music – for
> example, that of Elgar – was becoming increasingly a matter of national identity,
> its performance became a matter of political expediency. Moreover, the choirs
> [of various towns] were, like the town halls themselves, symbols of civic pride …
> The municipal hall frequently became the chief place of musical entertainment
> in the town, housing a great organ and a festival choir, all reflecting new-found
> wealth and pride. (Forsyth 1985: 140)

Such halls often had resident or affiliated choirs, orchestras or other musical
ensembles, and also received touring musicians from elsewhere. After 1946, certain
concert halls, opera houses and orchestras also received national state support via
the Arts Council. From its inception, the aim of the Arts Council was to 'increase the
accessibility of the fine arts to the public' and while this policy effectively excluded
both amateur and popular music from Arts Council support, there was, nevertheless,
still some overlap between the worlds of state-subsidised and commercial music:
many town halls were available for hire by commercial promoters and while it is
tempting to ascribe particular styles of music to each circuit – to say, for instance,
that star singers dominated live music performance in variety theatres, while big
bands mainly stuck to the dance hall circuit and classical repertoire orchestras only

---

[7] Tony Smith recalls his father, John Smith, getting into national promotion through
the same route (Smith 2010).

played concert halls – in reality there was a degree of crossover in terms of what kind of music was performed in what kind of venue.

In addition to the touring circuits so far described, a more seasonal network of live music venues included seaside piers and summer holiday camps. The most important British resort chain was owned and managed by Billy Butlin, a self-made businessman. Butlin opened his first holiday camp in 1936 and quickly expanded his business, attracting holiday makers partly by instituting concerts at the camps which featured variety theatre and radio stars (Reid 2004). Although Butlin's camps were sequestered during the war to house servicemen and women from the Navy and the Air Force, Butlin turned this to his advantage by offering to build further camps (with state funds) for the military during the war; once the war ended, he bought the new camps back from the government at a fraction of what it cost to build them and quickly turned them into additional holiday resorts – an interesting example of public/private partnership. By 1947, not only was Butlin a millionaire, but he also claimed to spend £4,500 per week on live dance music at his camps, making him a significant concert promoter as well as Britain's biggest holiday caterer (*Melody Maker*, 23 August 1947: 4). He also began to promote ballroom dance festivals both on and off the campsites (in Earl's Court in London, for example – see *Melody Maker*, 31 January 1948: 1).

To summarise, by the time the Second World War ended, a small handful of companies controlled a substantial portion of the important venues for British live music. Considering that ownership was being consolidated in British music-related industries as well, in hotels, restaurants, the theatre and London's West End clubs, it is clear that by 1950 a significant amount of live performance was controlled and managed by a relatively small number of players.[8]

In order to create their live music events, venue owners had to work with promoters, agents and managers.[9] According to Dave Laing, the term 'promoter' describes 'the person or company responsible for the physical organisation and presentation of a concert or festival, which can be taken as the minimum requirement for what a promoter does', and this definition would certainly have held true in 1950 (Laing 2003: 561). The promoter is also generally the person or company that carries the financial risk in a live music event, putting up the money for not only the artist's fee but also other costs such as venue hire, production, ticket sales and so on. The word 'impresario' was also in use to describe this role in this period, although it was perhaps used more frequently with reference to classical music and theatre. The two terms seem to have been used interchangeably in *Melody Maker* when referring to the promotion of dance bands, jazz combos and singers.[10]

---

[8]   By 1948, three-quarters of all theatre seats in London and the provinces were owned by A.S. Cruickshank and Prince Littler (Croft 1995: 212).

[9]   They might also deal with artists directly, though this was unusual.

[10]   *Melody Maker* used both the terms 'promoter' (e.g. 19 July 1947: 5; 3 July 1948: 2; 14 January 1950: 1) and 'impresario' (19 June 1948: 1; 14 January 1950: 1) to designate

Table 1.2   Live music events 1950

	Enthusiast promoter	State-funded promoter	Commercial promoter
Folk discourse	George Webb's Dixielanders: Red Barn Public House, Barnehurst, Monday evenings in 1948	No state funding for folk worlds in 1950	Kathleen Ferrier: concert at the Royal Albert Hall, 18 May 1950
Art discourse	Glasgow Cathedral Choral Society performing Handel's *Saul*, Glasgow Cathedral, 19 December 1950	Royal Philharmonic Orchestra at Usher Hall, Edinburgh, 27 August 1950	Jay Pomeroy's New London Opera Company: *Tosca* at Cambridge Theatre, London, performed through October 1947
Pop discourse	Amateur dance bands performing throughout UK	No state funding for pop worlds in 1950	Frank Sinatra at the London Palladium, 10–23 July 1950

For the purposes of this book, we will make a distinction between three kinds of promoter: the *enthusiast* promoter, the *state-funded* promoter and the *commercial* promoter. In this model, the enthusiast promotes because they want to, because they enjoy the music; commercial considerations are a secondary motivation if at all. The state promotes live music via subsidy and for policy reasons – educational, cultural, social and economic. The commercial promoter puts on concerts to make money. There are noteworthy parallels between these three categories and the folk, art and pop discourses discussed in the previous section. But if discourses are sets of aesthetic and social values that define particular musical worlds, the three types of promotion describe business organisations. To illustrate this, we can map live music events onto a grid. In Table 1.2 we have done this for live music events from 1950 (or thereabouts).

The table above can be used to understand the historical dynamics of live music promotion in Britain. It is worth noting that the examples may in fact fit into more than one box, just as specific musical events can draw from more than one discourse. George Webb's Dixielanders occupy the 'folk discourse/enthusiast promoter' box, for example, because the early British trad jazz movement drew predominantly, but not exclusively, from folk discourse; Webb began promoting his Monday evenings jazz nights at the Red Barn primarily as an enthusiast, although as they became more successful over time, various members of the band, including Humphrey Lyttelton and Webb himself, moved into commercial models of promotion. Similarly, Kathleen Ferrier, who occupies the 'folk

---

individuals responsible for the business of organising, presenting and financially backing concerts and tours.

discourse/commercial promotion' box, was one of Britain's most successful classical singers, but also incorporated folk songs into her concert repertoire. The Glasgow Cathedral Choral Society was an amateur, enthusiast choir, but its concert of Handel's *Saul* featured the Scottish National Orchestra, which received state subsidies from 1950 onwards. The gridlines of the table should therefore be read as permeable rather than fixed, although the table remains useful as a way of making sense of the different discourses and promotional business models at play in any given live music event.

After the promoter, the second significant figure in the live music business is the agent. According to Donald Passman, it is the agent who, in conjunction with the performer's management (if applicable), books the tour and 'makes the deals with the promoters (which includes the job of picking promoters that will put on the show professionally and not disappear with [the] money)' (2004: 354). The agent represents the artist and negotiates the performance fee, as well as scheduling the artist's touring itineraries and influencing decisions regarding appropriate venues and ticket prices.

Passman is generalising from contemporary commercial practice. Historically the role of the agent emerged as music-making opportunities changed. As a performer in the mid-nineteenth century, Clara Schumann:

> Rented the pianos and had them moved and tuned, rented the halls and provided for lights and heat, had tickets printed and distributed, arranged for advertising in newspapers and on posters – and then appeared, beautifully gowned in concert attire, to play, as though this was her sole care. (Bowers and Tick, 1987: 269)

By the end of the nineteenth century, the music economy was such that, in William Weber's words, 'the independent concert agent' had become a more dominant figure than 'the self-managing musician' (Weber 2004). The changing role of the agent in the British classical music world is well illustrated in Christopher Fifield's study of the dominant classical music agency in Britain in 1950, *Ibbs and Tillett* (2005).[11] Its origins lay in a concert and music agency opened by George Dolby above the offices of the music publishers Chappells in 1858 (among other things, Dolby organised Charles Dickens' 1866 reading tour), and Fifield shows in illuminating detail how its activities evolved, as the company organised rehearsals and repertoire, took on the role of 'protecting' its clients from direct approaches from local music societies, sought to correct false press stories, determined the distribution of free tickets, inflated tickets sales for publicity purposes, organised recording sessions and broadcasts for visiting artists from abroad, solicited concert programme retail advertisements for its domestic artists' latest releases and, in general, moved from being a nineteenth-

---

[11]   The 1953–4 *Concert Artists (Classical Music) Directory* lists 13 agencies, all based in London. At that point Ibbs and Tillett had 45 acts on its books. The next biggest company, Harold Holt, had nine acts (Fifield 2005: 300–1).

century to a twentieth-century music business. Throughout this period, though, 'the argument persisted about whether an agent should act as an impresario or (as John Tillett strongly believed) as a service industry' (Fifield 2005: 299). George Dolby's successor, Narcisio Vertigliano, who took over the company in 1880, had used it to develop child prodigies and performing stars. When Robert Ibbs and Peter Tillett broke away from him in 1906, they followed a different strategy:

> Right from the start, Ibbs and Tillett's unbending view was that they were running a booking agency and artists provided a service to the client, whether music club, choral society or concert organization, at the lowest possible price. (Ibid.: 40)[12]

This was still company policy in 1950 (John Tillett duly turned down the chance to act for Yehudi Menuhin), but whether this pre-war way of working could survive was beginning to be questioned. Terry Slasberg, whose career in the classical concert agency business began in the post-war period (with Ingpen and Williams), suggests that it was at this moment that:

> Music changed almost overnight and was never to be the same again. The standard of performance had gone into orbit; and suddenly, also, there was 'Presentation'. No longer were we treated to a mere musical event with musicians appearing on stage in evening dress, playing, and then disappearing into the night like spirits. The 'Classical Concert' had become 'A Show', with performers worthy of the name of 'Entertainers'. They were personalities who began to be stars. (Slasberg 1993: 5)

For agents taking on such stars, they, rather than the people paying for them to perform, were the clients (and their agents might also therefore function as their managers). In the classical music world, then, the roles of agent, promoter and manager can be confused by different accounts of who is whose client. Understanding these roles in popular music practice is equally complicated. In 1950 (as now) it was not uncommon for a single person to work as manager, agent, promoter, venue owner and, indeed, musician, often all at the same time. The brothers Bert and Stan Wilcox, for instance, were the leaseholders of the London Jazz Club on 100 Oxford St in 1950 and promoted shows at their own venue as well as at others across Britain. The bandleader Geraldo managed his own business affairs and also booked other bands in restaurants, hotels, holiday camps and cruise liners. These are just two of many examples of professionals in

---

[12]   It is interesting to compare the role of agents – or 'concert caterers' as they were known in the late nineteenth century – in providing musical acts for working men's clubs. They also sought to provide a musical service at the lowest cost and saw the clubs as their clients, but in this context were accused of exploiting musical labour – see Taylor 1972: 67–8.

the live music industry wearing several hats at once, a form of multi-tasking that could be said to define this business sector.

There was also the complicating factor that the roles of manager, agent, promoter and venue owner were organised differently in different popular music worlds. The promoter and dance band agent Maurice Kinn thus noted in *Melody Maker* his frustration at the discrepancy in expectations of variety artist agents, who, he claimed, 'do no more in general for their artistes than obtain the engagement', and the dance band agent, who 'is expected to book the date, arrange the billing, publicity, photographs, hotel accommodation, train reservations or coach bookings and transport of instruments. In some cases dance-band agents act as accountants, and in many instances financiers to their bands' (18 June 1949: 3).[13]

There were no strict rules, formulas or entry requirements for a successful career in the live music industry, and much of an individual's success depended on how they could innovate and carve out a unique professional niche for themselves. In order to better understand what such a career looked like in practice, we will take a closer look at three of the most powerful figures in British showbusiness at this time: Val Parnell and the brothers Lew and Leslie Grade.

Val Parnell was probably the most powerful British live music promoter in 1950, even though his area of promotion was primarily limited to music hall and variety. Parnell began working at the age of 13 in the offices of Sir Walter de Frece's music hall circuit. When London Theatres of Variety took over de Frece's venues, Parnell stayed on to manage 10 provincial theatres for the company. According to Robert Murphy, 'finding he was unable to book top acts because of the competition of the more powerful Moss Empires circuit, Parnell responded by booking a greater number of acts for shorter turns, thus providing a show which ran faster than those of his rivals. He was later to use the same "high-speed variety" technique – though this time with big names – to revive the fortunes of the London Palladium' (Murphy 2004). Through a series of acquisitions and expansions, the Gaumont-British Picture Corporation eventually acquired not only the LTV circuit but also Moss Empires. Parnell worked as assistant to George Black in managing the circuit and played a significant role in ensuring the continued economic viability of music hall and variety as it faced competition from the growth of the cinema industry. When Black died in 1945, 'Parnell succeeded him as managing director of Moss Empires and director of GTC in charge of their variety halls', controlling an unrivalled network of halls and theatres across the country (ibid.). By 1950, following his success with Danny Kaye, he had established what was, for the moment, an effective survival strategy for the provincial theatres on the Moss Empire circuit (which in the immediate post-war period had been unsuccessfully relying on nostalgia for pre-war acts): he took around Britain 'an influx of American stars' (Robinson 2007: 71–5). This dependence on American acts was to play into the hands of his rivals, the Grades.

---

[13]   Kinn went on to buy the ailing music paper *Musical Express and Accordion Weekly* for £1,000 as it was about to go bust, and to relaunch it, with editors Percy Dickins and Ray Sonin, as *New Musical Express* in March 1952 (Hutchins 2000).

Lew Grade and his brother Leslie entered showbusiness later than Parnell.[14] Lew began his career as a professional dancer, but left the stage to work at the Joe Collins agency in 1935. His younger brother Leslie followed Lew's career choice and the two of them eventually formed their own agency, which represented acts on the music hall and variety theatre circuit. Like J. Arthur Rank, the Grades made their biggest advances by remaining cool-headed during the chaotic times of war, even when Lew had to serve in the military – Leslie ran the agency on his own for several years. According to their biographer Hunter Davies, one way of advancing was by taking risks: when venue managers were reluctant to gamble on uncertain shows, the Grades would 'jump from being an agent, even an exclusive agent, into becoming partly responsible for the show itself, acting as agent-cum-impresario. Having put together a package, arranged the star and the supporting acts, Leslie and Lew would then go to the theatre management and offer to share the show. The agreement was usually to share all proceeds, 40/60 in the agent's favour' (1981: 83). This meant that the Grade Agency paid for all the acts and publicity while the management only paid the theatre's overheads, but it also meant that the Grades reaped much greater profits than agents who merely booked engagements.

The brothers displayed similarly aggressive tactics in their investments, and through a series of astute acquisitions of competitors who struggled during the war, they built up the Grade Agency until it was the second largest in Europe, rivalled only by the Foster's Agency, which had become the biggest by linking up with William Morris in the USA, 'which had always given them an enormous advantage' (Davies 1981: 120–1). Foster's had dominated the agency industry for so long with its film and theatre roster that it was blind to a growing audience demand to see a new kind of public icon: the recording star. Leslie's son, Michael Grade, recalls how his father adapted to this shift in 1948:

> Val Parnell used to book the Palladium and the Moss Empires circuit and he was very, very thick with a man – because he used to play golf with him – called Harry Foster. The Foster's Agency was the big agency … who had Danny Kaye and all the American stars who came through the Morris office, straight to the Palladium and Lew and my father couldn't break that thing to get at the Palladium … Eventually a new agency built up in America called GAC [General Artists Corporation of America] with a guy called Buddy Howe, who had been a dancing act that Lew and my father had booked … And he became the agent for all the new recording stars that suddenly emerged. From Frankie Laine, Johnny Ray, Nat King Cole.[15] All those people would work through GAC. Because of my father's relationship with Buddy Howe

---

[14] Bernard Grade, Lew and Leslie's other brother, was involved in showbusiness, but changed his name to Delfont and worked as an impresario rather than an agent.

[15] Grade and Davies both exaggerate the extent to which GAC monopolised the representation of recording artists: the Foster's Agency represented the Ink Spots, one of the most successful recording artists of the period.

they broke the Foster's/Moss Empires – Harry Foster/Val Parnell golfing cosiness – because Val needed these acts ... And that's how they got into the Palladium. (Grade 2009)

As the Grades' career demonstrates, the roles of agent, promoter, venue owner and manager could overlap – being an artist's agent did not preclude one from promoting the artist's shows as well (and if the agent happened to own a venue where the show could happen, so much the better).

Music Business and the Musicians' Union

Live music may have been the primary source of income for the majority of professional musicians in 1950, but the music industry as a whole was made up of other interrelated sub-industries. The most important of these were broadcasting (radio and now TV), song publishing, recording and royalty collection. All of these will be explored in much greater detail in Chapter 6, which will focus on the rise of the recording industry as it came to dominate the other music sectors between 1950 and 1967. For the moment, we will simply describe each of these core sub-industries as they looked in 1950.

Since its inception in 1922, the BBC had had a monopoly over British broadcasting. No other radio company was allowed to broadcast from within the UK and the BBC therefore wielded extraordinary power in the dissemination of music. The BBC's charter dictated that its broadcasting, including music programming, was to serve as 'a means of education and entertainment', and it was accused by the British press of not catering enough to public taste, despite the fact that the majority of its music programming in the 1930s was 'dance music' and 'light music' (Briggs 1961: 357–8; Nott 2002: 59–66). During the 1930s, entrepreneurs circumvented the BBC's radio monopoly by using powerful transmitters to broadcast advertiser-supported programmes from continental Europe aimed specifically at British audiences. The most successful of these were Radio Luxembourg and Radio Normandie, both programming mainly popular music. During the Second World War, the American Armed Forces Network further threatened the BBC's control of the airwaves, and the BBC itself changed its own programming policies to better satisfy the listening interests of servicemen and women.

By 1950, the BBC had divided its radio broadcasting into three strands. According to senior staff at the BBC, the Light Programme provided 'best quality and popular entertainment' (Briggs 1979: 60); the general interest Home Service was designed to 'reflect the life and community in which we live ... the broad middle strand of the BBC's broadcasting' (ibid.: 63); and the Third Programme was envisaged as broadcasting of 'a high cultural level, devoted to the arts, serious discussion and experiment, which would 'provide an intelligent alternative at peak hours' to the Light Programme (ibid.: 66).

Due to the needle-time agreement with the Musicians' Union and the licensing agency Phonographic Performance Limited (PPL), the playing of records on the BBC was restricted and most of the music it broadcast was performed live on air.[16] The BBC was therefore not only a significant employer of live musicians but was also massively influential in establishing the reputations of bandleaders, featured singers and variety artists as well as classical artists and orchestras, via contracts that could range from a one-off broadcast concert to regular weekly shows hosted by the same performing ensemble. The medium of television would prove to be another great influence in publicising performers, but in 1950 TV was still an expensive luxury item owned by a tiny minority of the population.[17]

In the orchestral world the BBC was significant not just as a broadcaster but also, through its funding of its own orchestras, as a competitor:

> The licence fee was a gold-mine that enabled the BBC easily to outbid everyone else for the top musicians, frequently paying twice the rates offered elsewhere. But this enormous subsidy also allowed the BBC to undercut the ticket prices of commercial promoters, and still mount adventurous, well-rehearsed programmes that were too uneconomic for the private sector to contemplate. (Morrison 2004: 70)

After live music and broadcasting, the next important sector of the music industry was recording. The British record industry in 1950 was essentially a duopoly of two companies: Decca and EMI. The industry had enjoyed a great boom in its early years up until the end of the 1920s, but suffered along with the rest of the economy when recession hit in 1929. Decca and EMI took advantage of the hard economic times, buying out their struggling competitors, to the point where in 1950 they controlled the vast majority of the British recording market.[18] The record industry was boosted by the arrival of new recording formats at the end of the 1940s: 12" long-player and 7" single vinyl records replaced the expensive and fragile format of the 78 rpm shellac disc. James Nott shows that if one combines the sale of gramophone players with that of gramophone discs, the gramophone industry had become the most economically important sector of the musical instrument industry (replacing piano manufacture) in the inter-war period (Nott 2002: 32). It is more difficult to assess whether the money spent on records exceeded the money spent on live music in 1950 – reliable data does

---

[16] 'Needle-time' was a reference to the fact that records were played using a needle stylus. The needle-time agreement therefore imposed a limit on the amount of time records were allowed to be played in a broadcast. The use of pre-recorded material was regarded by the Musicians' Union as a threat to the employment of musicians performing live.

[17] The BBC had just over 125,000 TV licence holders in 1949 (Briggs 1979: 241).

[18] When the first British record sales charts were published in *New Musical Express* in November 1952, EMI and Decca held a 100 per cent share of the chart via their licensing agreements (Gourvish and Tennent 2010: 190).

not exist. It seems unlikely, however, if only because it was not until later in the decade that the record industry came to be seen as the dominant player in the British music economy by the other music business sectors.

Leading British music publishers such as Boosey and Hawkes, Chappell and Novello had gone through dramatic changes in fortune after record sales and broadcasting impacted negatively on the sales of sheet music in the inter-war period. According to Nott, 'by the end of the interwar period, successful music publishers were more likely to gain their revenue not from the sales of sheet music, but from fees collected on the performance of their works. Public performance, either "live" or via radio and cinema, was now vital to success' (2002: 114). Despite this, an indication of the continued importance of music publishers was the fact that, as we have seen, the only British music sales charts in 1950 were still based on songs and sheet music rather than records. The publishing industry was also in the news after the Second World War when it was accused of payola for song-plugging, allegedly bribing bandleaders, venues and the BBC to play songs so they would become hits (*Melody Maker*, 16 August 1947: 1). One report suggested that music publishers stood to 'save' £100,000 annually once stricter anti-song-plugging regulations came into force at the BBC (*Melody Maker*, 10 April 1948: 1). Song-plugging proved to be a difficult practice to eradicate, however. In 1950 new reports emerged with allegations from bandleaders that the BBC and music publishers had made a 'secret pact' to allow it to continue (*Melody Maker*, 8 July 1950: 1).[19]

Song royalties in Britain were collected and distributed by various agencies set up to pay copyright holders for music used in broadcasting, recording, sheet music or live performance. The first of these was the Performing Right Society (PRS), formed in 1914 (following the 1911 Copyright Act) to collect royalties on behalf of copyright owners of songs – be they composers, songwriters or publishers – for the public live performance or broadcast of songs. The second was the Mechanical Copyright Protection Society (MCPS), formed in 1924 to collect royalties for the same copyright owners anytime their song was mechanically reproduced on record pressings, film soundtracks and so on. Finally, PPL was formed in 1934 to collect royalties on behalf of owners of recordings (as opposed to songs) whenever the record was broadcast or played in public.

---

[19] Of course, music publishers' attempts to influence BBC playlists didn't always involve collusion with BBC producers. In 1962, for example, Johnny Marsden, Promotion Manager at Boosey and Hawkes, circulated this request to his network of friends and contacts: 'My friend, will you help by requesting this artiste [Kay Wilson] and song ['Goodbye My Love'] to be included in any of the following Record Programmes currently featured over the air: Housewives' Choice, Family Favourites, Pick of the Pops, Jack Jackson's Record Roundup, The David Jacobs Show, 12 O'Clock Spin, Saturday Club.' Thanks to Richard Witts for this information – he found a copy of the letter in the BBC archives, which suggests that the Corporation was well aware of such wiles.

The various licensing agencies each had an interest in the business of live music (live venues, for example, had to be licensed by the PRS) and all had been formed institutionally by conflicts over the distribution of the various kinds of live music income. The PRS' long-running dispute with film exhibitors in the years when silent films were accompanied by live musicians, for example, had a long-lasting effect on both its music licensing arrangements and its relations with the Musicians' Union (Davison 2013), but it is also true to say that the Musicians' Union was the music institution which in this period depended most on live music. From the perspective of labour relations, the live music industry made money not simply out of music, but also out of musicians, and like other British work forces, musicians had unionised in order to leverage power when negotiating with employers. By 1950, various organisations had formed representing the interests of musical entertainers besides the Musicians' Union, including the Variety Artistes' Federation (which included popular singers), the Dance Band Directors' Association (1936), the Songwriters' Guild (1938), the Composers' Guild of Great Britain (1944) and the British Academy of Songwriters, Composers and Authors (1947). Alongside these the Incorporated Society of Musicians (1882) was the professional body representing classical musicians, music teachers and music organisations. The Musicians' Union was, though, the most powerful of these various organisations and we will examine it in detail in Chapter 3. For now we will briefly consider its influence in 1950 on radio programming, the playing of recorded music in public and international touring.

The Musicians' Union had not always been so powerful. In the early twentieth century there were several competing unions representing musicians, including the Amalgamated Musicians' Union and the London Orchestral Union of Professional Musicians. These two merged into a single collective known as the Musicians' Union in 1921, but even then the Union had difficulty unifying musicians across different genres and work situations. James Nott identifies many problems that the Union encountered in the inter-war period (2002: 143–4). One was a disparity in aims and attitudes between classically trained musicians and dance-band musicians. Another was disagreement about the status of musicians as real 'workers' by other trade unions. In addition, the abundance of amateur and part-time musicians made it all but impossible to create a 'closed shop' system – the means by which unions traditionally exert power by controlling all labourers with a particular set of work skills – thus rendering the Union less effective in negotiating better fees from employers or protecting live musicians from the competition of radio and recording.

The Union found it particularly difficult to mobilise dance-band musicians. As Nott describes, 'in September 1930 a "Dance Section" was established in the London branch of the Musicians' Union', but collapsed after only a year (2002: 145). Several other attempts to organise dance bands failed until finally a Dance Band Leaders' Association was established in 1936, as a separate entity from the Musicians' Union. In fact, one of the few successes the Union had with regard to the dance-band profession was controversial even amongst dance-band musicians themselves. As Moore (2006) documents, in the first half of the 1930s, the Union became increasingly opposed to foreign musicians performing in the UK (although protection of British musicians' jobs had always been part of the Union's raison d'être), and by the mid-1930s, the increased tension between the Musicians' Union and the AFM led the Union to object to any American dance musicians performing in the UK.

In 1945 restrictions on American dance bands were in place, but American popular culture dominated the UK regardless, not just via Hollywood films, musical theatre and imported recordings, as in the 1930s, but also now following the impact of US soldiers stationed in Britain during the war, an 'occupation' which according to Jon Savage had a particular effect on the spread of American popular culture amongst Britain's youth, with American popular music making 'the most dramatic impact' of all (Savage 2007: 416). The popular swing dance known as 'jitterbugging' became a national obsession, and in a rare exception to the restrictions on visiting dance bands, Glenn Miller and his American Air Force Orchestra was allowed to entertain British audiences as well as American service people in 1944. As Savage notes, that year 'Miller played seventy-one concerts to nearly a quarter of a million listeners in the United Kingdom' (ibid.: 417).

By the end of the 1940s, the Musicians' Union was facing other challenges. Perhaps the greatest threat to the employment of British musicians was the dizzying tide of innovation in music-related technology. Although it may seem odd in retrospect, the Union fought a campaign against the rising popularity of electric organ keyboards, fearing that a single amplified organ player could potentially replace an entire dance orchestra. In a *Melody Maker* article entitled 'MU "Electric Organ" Dispute May Affect Liner Bands', it was reported that 'strong action may follow a Musicians' Union Executive Committee meeting … if the Union does not receive assurances from the Cunard White Star Ltd, that the electric organ recently installed in the "Queen Elizabeth" will not ultimately be used to replace the twenty musicians at present employed in the ship's orchestras' (16 April 1949: 5).

Recording technology was also perceived as a major threat to the employment of musicians, as evidenced in an article written by the Union's assistant general secretary, Hardie Ratcliffe,[20] provocatively entitled 'We Must Beat the Record!':

> A show-down will come before long. Musicians throughout the world – particularly those providing dance music – will be forced to fight broadcasting and recording interests. The issue will be whether musicians are to control the recorded music they make or leave control to those with the money-bags. Musicians must beat the record – or go out of business! (*Melody Maker*, 15 November 1947: 4)

---

[20]   Ratcliffe was Assistant General Secretary at the time of writing the article; he was elected General Secretary of the Musicians' Union the following year.

Ratcliffe's diatribe against the recording industry was prompted by news of a similar struggle occurring in the USA between the AFM and the recording industry. The AFM's president, James 'Caesar' Petrillo, had successfully led his union in a long strike against the recording industry between 1942 and 1944: American union musicians refused to play on any kind of recording until an agreement was reached with record companies to pay royalties into a fund that would sponsor union musicians across the country to give concerts in their own communities (Wald 2009: 132–4). As Wald notes, the American strike was also aimed at radio broadcasters, who would be forced to employ live musicians on air due to the absence of pre-recorded music. Petrillo's 1944 agreements with the record companies were now coming to an end and he was once again in the news threatening a new strike. In Britain the Musicians' Union, facing similar concerns, was helped in its negotiating position with record companies and radio by the knowledge that previous strikes in the USA had been successful. As a result, in May 1947 the Musicians' Union struck a deal with British record companies ensuring that 'the competition of a musician's recorded work with his live performance is to be rigidly controlled and compensated' (*Melody Maker*, 17 May 1947: 1). However, these agreements came just prior to the arrival of two revolutionary recording formats: the vinyl 33⅓ rpm LP and the 45 rpm single. These new formats were introduced to the US record-buying market in 1948 and would begin to be sold in Britain by 1950. Their impact will be discussed further in Chapter 6.

The third technology which the British Musicians' Union resisted was broadcasting, both the established BBC radio and the quickly growing popularity of television. Briggs explains that most music broadcast on the BBC was performed live rather than from records:

> BBC music, classical or popular, had never depended on current commercial gramophone records or discs to the extent that most other broadcasting systems had depended upon them ... There had been strictly enforced restrictions on 'needle time' even during the war, and a new agreement further limiting use had been signed with the Musicians' Union in May 1946. (Briggs 1979: 730–1)

The Union treated television as a 'completely separate field of employment from sound broadcasting' and was still trying to come to an agreement on how the use of music should be regulated in TV broadcasts.

Evidence of the power of the Musicians' Union in negotiating with the BBC – whose music programming at this point depended on the employment of unionised musicians – can be seen in an example from 1948, when the Musicians' Union threatened to call its musicians on strike as the result of a 'ten-months fight with the B.B.C. for better broadcasting conditions and increased fees' (*Melody Maker*, 24 January 1948: 1). The Dance Band Directors Association backed the strike, which banned radio broadcast relays from theatres and music halls, with plans to extend the ban to hotels, restaurants and dance halls (*Melody Maker*, 3

January 1948: 1). In April 1948, *Melody Maker* reported under the sensational headline 'M.U. Bans Television' a further extension of the strike to include television broadcasts (3 April 1948: 1). Although the dispute between the BBC and the Musicians' Union dragged into 1949, it was ultimately a success for the Musicians' Union, and improved conditions and fees were agreed (*Melody Maker*, 31 July 1948: 1; 7 May 1949: 1).

The battleground on which the union continued to be most effective, however, was in preventing American dance bands from performing live in the UK. As we have already discussed, the Musicians' Union had been arguing since the 1930s that one of its duties was to prevent foreign labour from replacing British jobs in music, whatever the public demand for US music, and it successfully lobbied the Ministry of Labour to continue to deny work permits to foreign musicians wishing to perform in the UK. On some occasions it was possible to arrange a reciprocal exchange in which a dance band from another European country was granted work permits so long as a similarly sized British band was allowed to perform the same number of concerts in that country. But it was the 'threat' of American musicians that most mattered to the Musicians' Union, and the relationship between musicians' unions in the UK and the USA continued to be strained. Singers were not affected by the ban, meaning that Frank Sinatra, Nat 'King' Cole, the Ink Spots, Ella Fitzgerald and other American singers (as well as numerous actors and variety performers) did come to the UK to perform, albeit with British accompanists rather than their usual American backup bands. On rare occasions, famed American instrumentalists were also granted work permits as 'variety entertainers'. Such was the case with Duke Ellington, who played a season at the Palladium and toured Britain in this guise, accompanied by the American singers Kay Davis and Ray Nance (*Melody Maker*, 19 June 1948: 1).

The effect of the ban on American dance bands will be explored in greater detail in Chapter 3. Suffice it to say here that the success of the Musicians' Union's policy had the unintended (but unsurprising) effect of fuelling ever greater public demand to see American musicians perform live in Britain. It also meant that British musicians were self-conscious about their ability to play musical styles that originated in America. As one *Melody Maker* article put it, 'because no American jazz bands had been allowed to visit the UK since 1934, British jazz musicians were pre-occupied with whether British jazz was as good as American jazz, but were unable to know without seeing the Americans perform live' (31 May 1947: 4).

Conclusion

By 1950, the dominant players in the live music industry had successfully routinised several aspects of the industry that had begun developing in the first half of the century, from national touring circuits to live broadcasting. As we have seen, many of the industry's leading players managed to survive pre-war recession and post-war austerity by seeing off or absorbing their competitors. These included companies such as Mecca, Rank, GTC, EMI and Decca, as well as individual entrepreneurs such as Val Parnell and the Grades, who between them seemed by the middle of the century to have a controlling grip on the British music industry. This was also a time when many of Britain's most popular dance-band leaders had reached the peak of their career and these established figures in British live music, in the industry and on stage, seemed on the verge of perfecting a particular model of the music business (first given shape well before the war) in which live performance was at the heart of the modern music economy. This was the model strongly supported by the Musicians' Union, which had, it seemed, fought back the tides of both technology and Americanisation that were threatening to develop a model of the music business that was entirely different.

The truth, however, is that the music establishment's apparently powerful position was deceptive. As the 1950s progressed, it would become clear that the live music business could not get back to normal if that meant getting back to the ideal economy envisioned in the 1930s. There were new social, musical and commercial forces that did not fit into established ways of doing things (and there were, in consequence, new opportunities for those breaking into the industry). A prolonged period of change in British live music had begun, the roots of which – the do-it-yourself organisation of jazz clubs, the growing popularity of recording stars and the youth appeal of American dance music – were already showing in 1950.

Chapter 2
Live Music and the State

Over the last few years the streets that once rang with music had become oddly quiet. The guild of 'Waits and Musicians' still operated in Newcastle – 'no fiddler, piper, dancer upon ropes, or others that went about with motions or shewes' could perform without a licence – and during the American war the Common Council cracked down on subversive ballad singers. In 1781 they even passed an order forbidding singing-clubs in public houses. (Uglow 2007: 121–2)

By the provision of concert halls and suitable civic centres, we desire to assure to our people full access to the great heritage of culture in this nation. (Labour Party Manifesto 1945, quoted in Sinfield 1995: 189–90)

Introduction

One of the most familiar pieces of post-war British popular music folklore concerns the 'rock'n'roll riots' that supposedly accompanied the British showings of the film *Blackboard Jungle*. The film featured Bill Haley and the Comets' 'Rock Around the Clock' and, in the words of Wikipedia (summarising common knowledge):

> marked a watershed in the United Kingdom. When shown at a South London Cinema in Elephant and Castle in 1956 the teenage audience began to riot, tearing up seats and dancing in the aisles. After that, riots took place around the country wherever the film was shown.[1]

These 'riots' can be understood from a variety of perspectives. They mark, for example, an early example of what would become routine moral panics about teenage musical behaviour and there is no doubt that the press exaggerated the violence and damage involved, thus, in turn, putting pressure on local authorities to prevent trouble by banning the film altogether, the policy pursued by Bristol, Liverpool, Warrington and Carlisle.[2] As Humphrey Lyttelton noted at the time:

---

[1]   Wikipedia's cited source is a throwaway comment by Dick Hebdige (Hebdige 1983). Hebdige gives no sources. In popular accounts, audience responses to *Blackboard Jungle* (shown on the ABC circuit) and *Rock Around the Clock* (shown on the Gaumont circuit later the same year) are treated as a single set of events.

[2]   See Martin and Segrave 1993: 32–6; Rogers 1982: 16.

'All that the much-publicized rock'n'roll riots have amounted to is a handful of youngsters getting up and dancing in or outside cinemas, often at the instigation of enterprising newspaper reporters' (Lyttelton 1958: 69). This view was confirmed by a customer at a Saltaire Gaumont showing of the film *Rock Around the Clock*:

> The performance I attended was full to capacity with a fair sprinkling of Teddy Boys in the audience. A row of policemen was standing along the way at the back of the stalls. The patrons were clearly present for the music only and made this apparent by a collective groan whenever the film cut away from it to concentrate on some fatuous piece of dialogue. Occasionally one of the bolder Teddy Boys would entertain the rest of us with a spot of jiving in the aisle while the floor beneath us reverberated to the massed tapping of feet. The atmosphere was entirely good-humoured and, as far as I could tell, the policemen were not called upon to arrest anyone. Since they were all young, perhaps they were too absorbed in the music themselves. (Quoted in Eyles 1996: 143)[3]

From the perspective of live music history, though, there are two other points that are interesting about these events. First, the disturbances occurred when sections of the film's audiences tried to jive in cinema aisles and the resulting trouble reflected the problem of staging musical events in unsuitable venues in which issues of health and safety (no blocking the aisles) came into conflict with the point of the music (jiving). In this case the music was being provided by a recording on a film soundtrack, but the conflicts involved were to become commonplace in the subsequent promotion of live music. In October 1963, for example, Glasgow councillors cancelled an upcoming Gerry and the Pacemakers gig after 100 seats were damaged during a Beatles concert in the city's Concert Hall and by 1965 the council was banning all groups with 'disorderly' fans, while in the neighbouring town of Hamilton magistrates banned 'beat groups' following disturbances at a Rolling Stones gig in May 1964.[4]

Our second point is the concern of this chapter: the 'riots' were a problem for local authorities; they had the power to prevent them by stopping such musical events from happening at all, through their ownership or licensing of venues. This might seem a banal assertion, but it is because such local authority interference in musical activities is so familiar to promoters and audiences alike that it is important to understand its roots and consequences. How and why did music become a matter for state control?

---

[3]   Eyles suggests that although some local managers did decide not to show the film, Rank 'thought any property damage and adverse publicity worth enduring to have a film that drew in such large audiences' (Eyles 1996: 143). When Bill Haley toured live in the UK for the first time in 1957, at least 14 of his 24 performances were booked into cinemas, which suggests both that their owners were not actually much concerned about potential riots and that there remained a shortage of suitable venues for rock'n'roll shows.

[4]   See Martin and Segrave 1993: 130, 328; and Wyman 1991: 257.

To understand the role of the state in the history of live music, we need to make two kinds of distinction. On the one hand, the state both regulates live music (through a variety of legislation) and promotes it (providing venues, facilities and investment). On the other hand, the state is significant at both a national and a local level. But while such distinctions are analytically necessary (and this chapter is organised around them), they are not clear-cut. Historically, the state's interest in live music as regulator and promoter is a policy consequence of a single ideology: in the nineteenth century, the 'rational recreation movement' was concerned to discourage some kinds of (disreputable) working-class leisure activity while simultaneously encouraging other (uplifting) kinds.[5] State music policy has been implicated ever since with ruling-class concerns about urban leisure, public gatherings and class culture. At the same time it is misleading to treat local and national government as discrete: local state regulation of music usually involves the enactment of national legislation, while national policy on live music necessarily depends on local interpretations of how the law should be applied.

Live Music in an Industrialised Society

The origins of the modern regulation and promotion of culture by the state can be located in the processes of industrialisation. As Britain moved towards being a largely urbanised, class-divided society, traditional patterns of leisure were subsumed by new ones (of which the music hall may be the paradigmatic case).[6] New leisure habits were subject to increasing official concern; 'undesirable' activities that could not be outlawed were instead 'licensed'. The modern system of licensed entertainment – of which music is a key part – thus evolved as an expression of bourgeois anxiety about working-class leisure.

Alcohol consumption occupied a key role in urban leisure from the start and its importance here is enhanced by the fact that drinking as a pastime had long accompanied musical entertainment. As Milestone notes:

> Since the Restoration there had been 'free-and-easy' musical performances in taverns and tea gardens, which increased greatly in variety and number as taverns and public houses became larger, and more lavish and commercial ... From the beginning of the eighteenth century, inns were developing as the prime venues for entertainments such as balls, assemblies, plays, lectures and concerts. (Milestone 2007: 297)

---

[5] See Bailey 1978; Cheshire 1974; Cunningham 1980; and, for Scotland, Brown 1996.

[6] According to Bailey (1978: 150): 'The Victorian music hall qualifies as a prototype modern entertainment industry, not just because its capital investment allowed economies of scale which secured it a mass paying audience, but because of the thorough-going commercialisation which accompanied it and affected all facets of its operation.' Its performers were 'reconstituted as a full professional labour force'.

By 1800, it was common practice for English musical clubs and societies to meet in pubs, and as the century unfolded, music was used more and more by publicans to promote their business.[7] For nineteenth-century reformers, music was positioned as both saviour and sinner. Its redemptive powers meant it could be regarded as an exemplary form of improving recreation; its sinful nature was encapsulated by the risqué music hall songs which when accompanied by a surfeit of alcohol became the *bête noire* of moral campaigners. For Methodists, moralists and, later, the Salvation Army, hymns were encouraged; bawdy tavern songs could thus be drowned out.

Such concerns were reflected in legislation. From the mid-nineteenth century onwards, the state was increasingly called upon to intervene in workers' leisure activities and in so doing politicians came to understand that the promotion of appropriate forms of leisure could be as effective as clamping down on those deemed illicit. By the time our history begins, the UK had been subject to more than a century of state regulation and promotion of musical life.

National Regulation

There are senses in which the term 'national regulation' is a misnomer in the UK. Setting aside the fact that it has four component parts – England, Northern Ireland, Scotland and Wales – each with varying degrees of autonomy from the rest, there has never been a national body overseeing the regulation of all live music in the UK, and this chapter largely draws upon the experience in England and Wales.[8] Historically, live music promotion has been affected by a variety of laws and regulations. Many of these have concerned alcohol, but other significant regulatory areas are health and safety, planning, immigration and labour law. In addition, the ways in which live music has been regulated have been significantly mediated by local interpretations and implementations of licensing regimes. National legislation on the sale and consumption of alcohol has, nevertheless, provided the basic framework within which the everyday regulation of live music takes place and this must be our starting point.

The key concept here is licensing. An obvious point to make, but those entering the domain of music and entertainment licensing (whether as promoters or academics studying promoters) do so at their peril. Even the most casual observer is likely to be struck immediately by the plethora of Acts of Parliament determining what may and may not be done in which premises at what times and with which people. In addition, rationality or coherence is not always at the forefront. As Butterfield notes:

---

[7]   See, for example, Clark 2000: 164; and Milestone 2007: 297.
[8]   Scotland has never required separate licences for the provision of music and dancing.

> Unfortunately there is no consistency in the Acts of Parliament. Each piece of legislation lays down different requirements for applications, various grounds for refusing an application or revoking a licence. This means anyone involved in licensing has to refer to a wide range of publications in an effort to find the answer to a query. (Butterfield in Webster, Leib and Button 2007: xi)

In 1933, Isaac Foot MP told the House of Commons that: 'There is no part of our law more intricate and difficult than that which deals with licensing' (House of Commons Debates, 8 December). In 1960, Rab Butler, the Home Secretary, suggested that this mess of legislation covered three key areas: general licensing laws, permitted hours and regulations covering registered clubs (House of Commons Debates, 28 November), which may have been true but did not do much to disentangle the various different principles according to which licences, permissions and registrations might or might not be granted. Indeed, one of the main inspirations behind the 2003 Licensing Act (which we will discuss in detail in volume 3 of this series) was a desire to reshape in a coherent way the myriad of licensing laws that had been passed by Parliament since the eighteenth century.

We do not have space here to go into the history of licensing in detail, but it is necessary to describe its basic structure. The origins of the modern licensing system can be traced back to Edward VI, who in 1552 passed an Act which 'introduced the three distinct forms of control which are the basis of modern licensing: the power of selection, withdrawal and the imposition of conditions' (Kolvin 2004: 2). In 1606 James I attempted to license alehouses specifically, passing two laws, the second of which was an 'Act for Repressing the Odious and Loathsome Sin of Drunkenness' (ibid.: 3–4). In 1618 he issued the Newmarket Proclamation, which contained the first mention of licensing hours.

Licensing was, then, from the beginning concerned with the control of alcohol sales and consumption, although it could be applied to other kinds of public activity – in 1708, for example, the Sunday Observance Act gave authorities the right to grant licences for concerts on a Sunday, provided that the music performed was suitable for the Sabbath – and the licensing system continued to evolve (or be tinkered with) throughout the eighteenth century as alcohol sales burgeoned to the extent that England was said by an 1824 observer to be 'sodden with gin' (Kolvin 2004: 7). By the mid-nineteenth century, when concern about the new urban working class focused on their leisure-time drinking, passing new licensing laws was the obvious legislative response, leading to the development of an ever more complex web of regulations, which was more or less liberal depending on whether moralists or brewers had the dominant parliamentary voice at any one time. An early example of liberalisation was the Beershop Act of 1830, which allowed ratepayers to brew and sell beer, one of the competitive factors in the development of singing saloons. These offered in essence a form of variety and were the precursor of the music halls.[9] In 1843 the Theatres Act sought to establish

---

[9]   See Bailey 1978: 28–9.

a distinction between these saloons (with alcohol) and theatres (without), but discrepancies soon emerged.

The next significant piece of legislation from our perspective was the 1890 Public Health Acts Amendment Act, which empowered licensing justices to grant music, singing and dancing licences. Cheshire explains that outside London:

> music-hall licences were [now] issued by licensing justices or local authorities under powers derived either from special local Acts or by adoption of Part IV of the Public Health Amendment Act 1890. The latter also allowed the licensing authority to attach conditions to licences. The attached conditions were intended to prohibit profanity, improper dress, striptease, or any poster or advertisement likely to be injurious to morality. (Cheshire 1974: 92)

This was the national framework within which significant variations developed over the next 50 years between the policies of different local licensing authorities. In 1943, for example, Mass Observation noted in one Northern England town a clear distinction being made between customers singing round a piano (not requiring a licence) and a musical event (which did): the local Chief Constable had issued a letter to local licensees in the 1930s banning them from employing singers or variety artists (Mass Observation 1943: 256). But it was London that was most consistently treated differently. Kolvin describes the 1949 Licensing Act as:

> a substantial liberalising measure ... in relation to certain parts of the metropolis. The Act provided for the grant by the justices of a special hours certificate to hotels and restaurants with a music and dancing licence, and to registered clubs with a music dancing certificate. (Kolvin 2004: 12)

Although this act was applicable only to inner London, Kolvin describes it as 'the forerunner of the modern night time economy' and the 1961 Licensing Act extended the 'special hours certificates for premises providing music and dancing ... to the nation as a whole' (Kolvin 2004: 13).

The piece of legislation with the greatest implications for music in the post-war period (until the reforms of 2003) was undoubtedly the 1964 Licensing Act. This established a dual regime covering the sale of alcohol on and off licensed premises. And it introduced Public Entertainment Licences (PELs), to be issued by local authorities which could set their own fees for the administration of the system and attach their own conditions to the licence in accordance with local circumstances.

PELs were required for all businesses offering 'music and dancing or other entertainment of a like kind' to the public (an exception was made for private members' clubs). The licences were administered by local authorities on an annual renewal basis. In order to obtain a PEL, premises had to meet certain standards with regard to issues such as the fire risk, air conditioning, air-filter changes and door staff. The operating conditions attached to PELs would 'allocate terminal trading hours and capacity limits and impose measures to control noise emission' (Hadfield 2006: 40).

The PEL system also established the 'two in a bar' rule. Performances involving no more than two musicians were exempted from this licensing requirement.

Above all, though, the Act reinforced the connection between music and drink (in this respect there was a direct relationship between the PEL and Special Hours Certificates established in the 1961 Act – concern had often been expressed that late-opening premises were ignoring the requirement to provide entertainments).[10] The 1964 Act allowed premises with a PEL to open beyond the standard closing time. To get a late licence (until two in the morning or three in London), 'it was necessary for applicants to prove the sale of alcohol was going to be ancillary to dancing or serving food' (Hadfield 2006: 51). This legislation was to have a profound effect on the economics of live entertainment as music was now increasingly promoted in licensed premises.

Overall, the period between 1950 and 1967 can be seen as one in which alcohol licensing laws were gradually modified while the regulation of live music continued to be shaped by a licensing regime for which it was not a central concern. Despite its strong association with alcohol and a recognition that music and dancing were likely to take place outside the 'standard' opening hours of licensed premises, live music was seldom the focus of legislation and not until the rise of free festivals and, later, raves did the state seek to legislate for music-related activities in their own right. But what we have also tried to establish here is a sense of the legal situation in which all promoters had to operate by the 1950s, a situation that was bureaucratically complex and determined for good or ill by the local mediation of national laws.

Local Regulation

Notions of locality have become important in popular music studies in recent years as researchers have sought to illustrate the distinctive contribution place makes to popular music history.[11] Their point, put simply, is that where we live has a significant impact on our musical experiences and it is not coincidental that non-academic local histories of bands and venues have become something of a growth industry in recent years.[12] All these histories sooner or later recount tales of run-ins with the local licensing authorities.

The local is the place where national legislation is implemented: 'in England and Wales, the development of licensed premises has long been subject to three

---

[10]   Thanks to Phil Hadfield for this point and for his assistance with this chapter.

[11]   For the pioneering work on music and locality, see Cohen 1991; Finnegan 1989; and Shank 1994.

[12]   See, for example, Allen 2009 (Portsmouth); Brocken 2010 (Liverpool); Jones 2009 (Bristol); Fields 2009 (Glasgow); and Firminger and Lilleker 2001 (Sheffield).

primary forms of municipal control: planning, public entertainment licensing and liquor licensing' (Hadfield 2006: 39). This is the essential characteristic of licensing: national legislation and guidance is adapted to local circumstances. 'Licensing is a matter for local control depending on what is necessary in an individual case to promote the licensing objectives' (Kolvin 2004: x). And because national legislation is open to local interpretation, the degree to which it is enforced has been to some extent dependent on key local individuals, chairs of licensing authorities or chief constables, who can therefore occupy an unexpectedly significant role in the music history of particular towns or regions.

The origins of the modern system of local government can be traced back to the 1835 Municipal Corporations Act, which followed the extension of the franchise in the 1832 Reform Act and 'further encouraged a change towards more democratic administration from within the town' (Milestone 2007: 295). By the 1840s, it was already clear that licensing was developing differently across the country. Music halls in London, for example, were defined and regulated differently from those in the rest of the country. It is also important to note, though, that local initiatives could have national effects. As Bailey points out:

> Before the 1850s it had been only in London and a twenty-mile radius of its centre that a music and dancing licence had been required in addition to a liquor licence. In 1851 Birmingham introduced music licences, and the rest of the country gradually followed suit. (Bailey 1978: 162)

Local licensing authorities applied their powers according to a variety of principles. For example, following a production of *Le Nation* (which featured the Can-Can), the Alhambra Theatre in Leicester Square had its application for a licence renewal refused, presumably on moral grounds (Pearsall 1973: 35).

The 1878 Metropolitan Board of Works Act brought in new safety requirements, the costs of which many halls could not afford when they were applied by especially zealous local officials. This became a particular problem in London after the power of licensing music halls was transferred from magistrates to the new London County Council (LCC) in 1889. The LCC took to this task with some relish and had soon:

> won itself a reputation for the stringency of its licensing committee; it had a further powerful sanction to hand in its fire and safety regulations which ... caused the closure of many smaller halls unable to afford the alterations necessary to meet them. (Bailey 1978: 162)

Licensing is an intervention in free trade and local authorities are often therefore in effect mediating between different business interests. In late nineteenth-century London, theatre owners 'fought for greater regulation of their more lucrative rivals in music halls which, they claimed, were little more than "glorified pubs"'

(Hadfield 2006: 14). In 1892 the Select Committee on Theatres and Places of Entertainment recommended that:

> there should be three classes of licences; one for theatres proper, where smoking and drinking would not be permitted in the auditorium; one for those music-halls which are now sometimes called Theatres of Varieties, and one for concert and dining rooms.

Theatres of Varieties could put on ballets and plays without a licence provided that they lasted no more than 40 minutes and had no more than six performers. These recommendations were enacted in 1912.[13]

It should be clear from even this potted history of late nineteenth-century licensing policy that the effects of local regulation were not just short term (on immediate licensing decisions) but had longer-term effects on promotional practices. Bailey notes that 'it was the provinces that produced entrepreneurs like Moss, Stoll and Thornton, who built up big syndicates that began to take over the London halls [hit financially by LCC regulations] in the 1890s' (Bailey 1978: 149). Through their combined ownership of local venues and control of licences in the commercial leisure sector, local authorities by the end of the nineteenth century had a great deal of power in determining the entertainment provided for their citizens.

By 1913 Charles E. Hands was complaining in the *Daily Mail* that the LCC had deliberately sought to make the music halls safe for the middle classes and was thus taking them away from the working class: 'The County Council, as soon as it came into existence, set itself to purify popular amusements, and as soon as it got to work the big central music-halls were purified' (cited in Cheshire 1974: 52). Not that the regulators had it all their own way. In 1866 it was reported that 26 music halls in London were providing theatrical entertainments without a licence. By 1900 it was estimated that there were 150,000 illegal performances a year (ibid.: 93).

As the twentieth century progressed, live music in Britain was thus provided under conditions subject to a great deal of local variation. During the 1920s, for example, Leyton Council banned jazz and one step from its halls and Wallasey Liberal Hall got a licence renewal only with the proviso that no saxophones were played by visiting jazz bands.[14] By 1952 Newcastle was banning a Johnny Dankworth/Nat King Cole gig on the simple grounds that 'jazz audiences are rowdy' (*Melody Maker*, 10 February 1952: 6).

We have spent some time on the history of licensing in order to establish three points. First, by the 1950s, it was taken for granted that social problems associated with urban leisure were best addressed through a licensing system. Second, this meant in practice that local authorities were responsible for both defining and

---

[13]   See Cheshire 1974: 93.
[14]   See Godbolt 1984: 45; and Hustwitt: 1983: 12.

addressing what these problems might be. Third, promoters were well aware that their business depended on understanding how local licensing authorities operated. All these factors were apparent in the reception of *Blackboard Jungle* and *Rock Around the Clock* that we described at the beginning of the chapter. In general it is clear that the licensing system is so deeply embedded in the British way of doing things that all new developments in public musical activity are subject to local authority responses that vary greatly from area to area. Adrian Horn describes, for example, the complexity of local regulations that faced the juke-box business in the 1950s.

In Lancashire, for instance, the Blackburn Hundred maintained separate registers for music licensing, singing and dancing, where radio, piano and radiogram were specifically noted, and the Kirkdale Division Petty Sessions music and dancing register 1949–61 refers to 'coin-operated phonograms'. Local licensing did not happen evenly over the country, though; instead, interpretations of the law were subject to local and regional peculiarities. In 1956 it was reported that: 'There is [a] legal problem – the attitude taken by local licensing authorities. The Justices' view of this music appears to vary from place to place. Some areas hold that a music licence is required for a juke-box, whether it is in a public house or a milk bar.' Applications for music licences 'very often hinged on local bye-laws and the interpretation of those laws, and on the attitude of the local chief constables' (Horn 2009: 163).

In some cases (Horn's examples are Manchester and Doncaster) magistrates simply refused to allow juke-boxes in certain premises; in others the issue was whether the juke-box would provide a suitable form of entertainment – at a Morecombe magistrates application hearing, police representatives stressed that any music played on a Sunday should be suitable for that day – orchestral music rather than dance.

Underlying most magistrates' and chief constables' concerns was the belief that juke-boxes or, rather, the venues that housed juke-boxes were potentially sites of juvenile delinquency. As Horn notes, juke-boxes first appeared in Britain in fairgrounds, and 'fairgrounds and arcades were regarded as magnets for deviant male youths' (2009: 29). This association remained powerful in some police forces.

The 'old guard' had fixed views on what they saw as the 'seediness' and degeneracy involved with amusement arcades and these were frequently used as arguments within local magistrates' courts against granting music licences to café and snack bar owners (Horn 2009: 164–5).

This leads us to perhaps the most fascinating aspect of licensing law in this period. In the 1950s, public authorities were increasingly worried by the emergence of a new kind of urban public gathering, young people meeting in venues *which did not sell alcohol* and which therefore were not subject to the usual licensing regime. As Horn shows, the juke-box industry in the 1950s placed its machines not in pubs but in 'milk and snack bars' which were at that point seen as more 'modern and glamorous'. 'In the late 1940s and 1950s teenagers perceived pubs as old-fashioned, lacklustre and dreary, and frequented by old men playing outdated pub games' (2009: 181).

We will discuss the emergence of a new youth music culture further in Chapter 5. The point we want to stress here is that the youth musical venues that developed in the 1950s and 1960s – milk bars, coffee bars and the clubs that variously and in quick succession named themselves as jazz or folk or blues or rock (Liverpool's Cavern Club is a good example) – did not sell alcohol and were therefore unlicensed. Moreover, as the smarter promoters and venue owners quickly realised, if they became membership clubs, then the police had no right of entry or supervision. Sheffield's Club 60, for example, which opened in October 1960, 'was non-alcoholic and only sold coffee and soft drinks'. The local police didn't much like it and occasionally got special authority to mount a raid to check membership cards, but, as a members-only club, Club 60 fell outside the usual jurisdiction of the local licensing magistrates.[15]

Similar clubs could be found in most British cities at the beginning of the 1960s, but the resulting tensions between local authorities' anxiety about youth morals and their lack of regulatory control of youth venues were felt most intensely in Manchester. In the 1950s, Manchester had not been regarded as a particularly repressive city for young people. Whereas police in Huddersfield, for example, found ways to close the local jazz club down – 'they could usually do this by invoking the fire regulations, and claiming the premises were unsafe'[16] – the more metropolitan Manchester developed a thriving jazz scene. Perhaps local concern grew because of the sheer number of musical venues by the end of the decade – Lee suggests that there were at least 200 'beat' clubs in the city by the early 1960s (2002: 67), but the crucial change seems to have been the appointment of J.A. McKay as Chief Constable in 1959. McKay believed both that the police had a duty to enforce moral standards and that morals in Manchester had become particularly lax under his predecessors.[17]

McKay soon turned his attention to Manchester's night life. Local MP Sir Robert Cary had voiced his own concern in a House of Commons debate (on

---

[15]   See Hale and Thornton 2002: 11.

[16]   Jackson 1968: 121. Jackson notes the gap between the police/media perception of what was happening in Huddersfield's jazz club and the reality: 'The other-reality of the press picture – as if a Soho enclave of prostitution, drugs, violence had been found in Huddersfield – was such that even the crowd's [club members'] parents didn't connect them with the "six men and two girls" [described in the local newspaper account of a police raid]. "They were all talking about it at t'mill. My mother asked me if I'd seen it, about where they'd found them girls, and I said 'yes'. She didn't think I was one of them".'

[17]   A *Police Review* article in 1963 noted that whereas there were only three prosecutions of men for homosexual importuning in the four years before McKay's appointment, in the four years following there were 486 (cited in Chapman 1968: 10). McKay's belief that the police should seek to counter moral decline was to be shared by his even more notorious successor, James Anderton, Chief Constable of Manchester from 1976 to 1991.

29 November 1960) about Manchester clubs 'in which, I am certain, the most unwanted and despicable things are happening', but for McKay, the problem was the limited authority he had to deal with such venues: 'frustrated by a lack of formal powers, Manchester police turned to the more underhand grass-roots tactics of covert surveillance' (Jackson 2008: 290). McKay's Annual Reports drew attention to the problems they found – drug taking, sexual immorality, havens for runaways – as 'he pushed to change local licensing laws, making extensive use of the press to publicize the "coffee club menace"'. The result was a clause in the Manchester Corporation Act 1965 (which came into force in January 1966) giving 'local police powers to supervise and control leisure venues associated with young people' (ibid.: 209–10). Under McKay, Manchester rigorously applied all licensing laws, but the 1965 Act was the basis of his impact on local music. In Lee's words, it 'granted the Manchester Police far-reaching powers in controlling and curtailing clubs ... no-one could [now] own, operate or run a club without explicit police permission' (Lee 2002: 80). The police got the power to object to the issuing of licences on various health and safety grounds, to revoke existing licences and to enter premises without a warrant. Lee reports that some clubs decided to close in the run-up to the Act and that:

> The summer of 1966 was the time of the movings on and the herdings, of being shunted around from place to place and music being stopped. As 1966 gave way to 1967 only a handful of venues were left and they shied away from confrontational practices such as holding all-nighters ... by 1968 only two city centre venues catered exclusively for young people, the Magic Village and the Twisted Wheel. (Lee 2002: 82)

For Manchester historians like Lee, the point of this story is that a particular policeman's puritanism had profoundly negative effects (lasting at least a decade) on a local music scene. From our perspective, the significance of the entertainment clause in the Manchester Corporation Act is as an example of how the licensing of music venues came to involve other concerns than the control of alcohol. McKay's anxieties about young people's drug taking and sexual behaviour were to become familiar in both parliamentary and local authority responses to the rock music culture that developed in the late 1960s and early 1970s. His bill may have been a local initiative, but it had a national resonance. The 1967 Private Places of Entertainment (Licensing) Act 'enabled [all] local authorities to introduce a system for licensing clubs and for prosecuting those who permitted offences to be committed on the premises' (Jackson 2008: 304).

Local Promotion

The Arts Council of Great Britain (ACGB) was established in 1946. This was undoubtedly the most significant post-war political decision for the state promotion of music, but it was important in part simply because the state nationally had never been so directly involved in the arts before. As Keynes noted when the Council was being set up: 'I do not believe it is yet realised what an important thing has happened. State patronage of the arts has crept in. It has happened in a very informal unostentatious way – half-baked if you like.'[18]

Half-baked perhaps, but its policies, in consequence, both drew and depended on a long history of local state interest in musical activity.[19] One of the first funding applications the ACGB had to consider, for example, was for support for the first Edinburgh International Festival (which was planned for 1947). It duly offered £20,000, but on condition that £40,000 'should be provided from other sources before the project is launched' (Crawford 1997: 4). Those other sources were private donors to the Festival Fund and Edinburgh City Council, and this kind of combination – council, local authority, philanthropy – became the norm of ACGB music funding policy. This was not just pragmatic. Local authorities had established the principles for the state support of music, and we will therefore begin our discussion at the local level.

Once again, a handy place to start is with the Municipal Corporation Act of 1835. Henceforth, one way in which local authorities could express civic pride was through the provision of cultural events. In part this meant the building of civic facilities, of which the town hall was the paradigmatic example. As Milestone notes, there was often a cultural element to this:

> As the century progressed, halls designed specifically as suitable venues for popular, though culturally respectable, activities were increasingly in demand, and it became necessary for towns to provide performance spaces other than those traditionally provided, and restricted, by the church ... In many places the new town hall presented the ideal venue. (Milestone 2007: 298)

The town hall thus became a symbol of both a town's commercial wealth – it was rich enough to afford it – and local market failure – commercial interests had failed to provide the facilities local citizens needed and the council was stepping in:

> No town hall was considered complete without its great hall, and so the use of this space for concerts provided an important direct link between the citizens and the municipality, achieving a political, as well as moral and artistic, mission. (Milestone 2007: 299)

Town halls were built alongside municipal museums, art galleries, parks and, later, libraries, but the ideology that drove the grander plans of municipalities did

---

[18] This much-quoted remark was originally made by Keynes in a BBC broadcast in 1945 – see Wolf 2010: 83.

[19] As PEP noted at the time, 'the greater part of the public money spent on music comes from local sources' (PEP 1949: 210).

not necessarily determine the ways their venues were actually used. Milestone's account of Stalybridge Town Hall (built in 1831) provides a good example of the resulting tensions. She describes how the building went in and out of favour with musicians and promoters, depending in part on the availability of more appropriate premises, but also reflecting its general limitations for most kinds of music making. She notes that while it was always envisaged that the Stalybridge Town Hall would host music, 'no provision for the needs of the performance was considered ... In [nearby] Ashton the town hall seemed to provide for all musical needs, whereas in Stalybridge, at this time, it certainly did not' (Milestone 2007: 312–13).[20]

As we move further into the Victorian era, the provision of civic facilities comes to be driven not just by civic pride but also by the argument that the social questions posed by an urban working class should be addressed culturally. In Dave Russell's words, 'to most middle-class Victorians it was axiomatic that music should be more than artistic experience or a form of amusement'. Its role was to instil discipline, morality, devotion to God and, often, temperance. 'The view of music as an object of social utility and balm for society's many evils remained extraordinarily common until at least 1914' (Russell 1997: 23).

Participation in music was seen to counter the influence of the demon drink, while at the same time helping to smooth class relations. Russell charts the development of 'people's concerts' in the 1840s and 1850s, which were privately sponsored events promoted by such organisations as the Glasgow Total Abstinence Society or the Leeds Rational Recreation Society, but which put political pressure on local authorities to build suitable civic buildings – examples are the St George's Halls in Bradford and Liverpool and the Colston Hall in Bristol.

From its opening in 1867, the Colston Hall became the focal point of the musical life in the city. George Risley, who was appointed cathedral organist in 1875, began from that time to imitate the Monday Popular Concerts held at the Crystal Palace, with similar concerts at the Colston Hall. In the 1880s and 1890s, he expanded his activities to include popular concerts on Saturday nights as well, which were less 'high brow' than the Monday concerts. These were extremely well supported, playing to large audiences in the winter months (Mellor 1976: 220).

By the end of the nineteenth century, the local state was involved in music promotion in a variety of ways, from the building of new facilities to the provision of municipal organists and the staging of concerts 'on the rates'. As Russell notes, while often having their roots in various sorts of philanthropic and/or religious/

[20] PEP's 1949 *Enquiry into Music* concluded from its extensive survey of Britain's concert halls (and their inadequacies) that 'nearly all the defects come about through the halls not being built with the needs of music in mind. In fact the better halls in the country are better simply because the advice of local music societies was sought before they were built'. As the report also points out, though, most 'modern' municipal halls had by necessity 'been designed for a variety of purposes, especially dances, which is the most remunerative use to which a hall can be put' (PEP 1949: 36).

moralist movement, by the late nineteenth century 'some of the most impressive [local musical] events were those backed by a degree of municipal patronage' (Russell 1997: 45). Such patronage (and use of rate payers' money) was not unopposed. Conservatives and many Liberals saw no need for local authorities to enter into competition with private entertainment providers, and it is at a local level that we first see the arguments that would become familiar in later political debates about the ACGB. Local state patronage of musical activities was justified by two suggestions: that the music supported was good for people and that (probably for just this reason) it was not being produced by commercial interests.[21] And, of course, at the heart of these arguments was the understanding that some music was more elevating than others.

Simon Gunn has detailed the significance of musical institutions in the development of high culture (or what in the last chapter we called 'art' discourse) in Manchester, Leeds and Birmingham in the second half of the nineteenth century: 'Firstly, they effected the transposition of classical music from the semi-private realm of club and society to a public sphere of art deemed representative of the urban community as a whole ... The second significant feature of classical music as a component of high culture was its status as a non-profit activity ... the highest forms of music in the provincial cities were seen as autonomous of the market.' Gunn points to a resulting tension:

> On the one hand, the institutions of the Hallé and the [music] festivals were intended to represent the urban community as a whole, rather than a narrow county or urban elite. Music was to be opened up to the anonymous 'public', made accessible to substantial, if not all, sections of the population. On the other hand, the inherited association of classical music as part of polite culture meant that despite its transposition from the private to the public sphere it retained an aura of exclusivity This exclusivity in fact remained essential to the construction of classical music as a cornerstone of high culture. The cultural status as well as the financial viability of the principal musical institutions was fundamentally dependent on the identification of the concert-hall with urban 'high society'. (Gunn 2000: 140–2).

The contradictions described here afflicted ACGB policy from the start, as we shall see, but the immediate effect of the ideology of high culture was that audiences had to be convinced of 'the superiority of music that had no function

---

[21]   Such justifications for national state expenditure on music were clearly articulated by PEP in 1949: 'We are aware that all these recommendations call for an increased expenditure of public money, and this at a time when economy is being demanded. But the total sum being spent on music to-day is small when compared, for instance, with the vast expenditure in physical welfare. Music, and indeed all the arts, have the power to refresh, invigorate and inspire, and money wisely spent on them is a national investment' (PEP 1949: 210).

other than aesthetic', which meant 'a new concert-hall regime'. As Gunn notes, 'the discipline of collective silence in public was a relatively new phenomenon', but the combination of the increasing professionalism of musical performance, the developing status of the conductor, the emergence of music criticism and the use of programme notes created the idea of 'serious' music needing an attentive and educated listener:

> By the later nineteenth century the music hall was represented as the social and cultural obverse of the concert hall, the former identified with brash vulgarity and commercialism; the latter with refinement, decorum and disinterestedness. (Gunn 2000: 146–54)[22]

If the concert hall required decorum, it could also be argued that the appreciation of concert hall music was both a means of social discipline and a source of social status. Such music became embedded in 'respectable' working-class culture, in the choir and brass band movements, for example, with significant consequences for professional musicians: one of the better gigs for the nascent London Symphony Orchestra (LSO) at the beginning of the twentieth century was 'an engagement to play for the mighty choral society in Huddersfield … in return for "£125 and a substantial meat tea"' (Morrison 2004: 38). In the 1930s the economic recession in the north of England thus had consequences for London-based classical musicians:

> There was real hardship among those who worked in the pits and mills. If they couldn't pay their 'subs', the choral society couldn't afford to hire professional musicians – and certainly not players whose return train fares from London also had to be covered. (Morrison 2004: 82)

Another kind of example of municipal support of classical performance can be found in the history of the Bournemouth Symphony Orchestra. This emerged from the decision of Bournemouth Council to appoint Dan Godfrey as Municipal Bandmaster in 1893, with the job of providing music on the pier. Because several of his players were double-handed, playing string as well as well as wind, he had the nucleus of an orchestra. In 1897, following the public success of Godfrey's concerts of light, classical and military music on the pier and in the Winter Gardens, his group became the Bournemouth Municipal Orchestra, the first state-funded permanent orchestra in Britain.

As the twentieth century progressed, municipal authorities became increasingly important for local concert culture. Birmingham Council's support was essential for the foundation of the City of Birmingham Orchestra in 1920, as was Liverpool Council's support for the survival of the Liverpool Philharmonic from 1942, while 'Glasgow was the first local authority to give regular support to an independent

---

[22]   For similar developments (and tensions between art and commerce) in London in the nineteenth century, see McVeigh 2007.

orchestra and for over twenty years has been the largest guarantor of the Scottish National Orchestra' (PEP 1949: 50). In Manchester the Hallé made unsuccessful calls for help from the local council during the First World War, but by the 1920s was receiving its support for the provision of municipal concerts. During the Second World War, it had funds from CEMA as well from Manchester City Council, and this mix of support from local and central state became essential to its post-war survival – by 1947, ACGB and Manchester Council funding for the orchestra were roughly equal.[23]

Local government support of music was further legitimated by the 1948 Local Government Act, which allowed local authorities other than counties and parishes to use the rates system to support the arts, and the 1951 Local Government Act, which allowed them to provide various sorts of entertainments including music. By 1950, not only was the local state subsidising the provision of live music, but there was an expectation from central government that it would do so. In 1953 Sir Kenneth Clark, by then Chairman of the ACGB, reported that 'municipal patronage is taking a large and increasing share of the cost of providing the arts' (quoted in Beale 2000: 79), and by the 1960s, further evidence of the continuing importance of local government support for music can be seen in a 1966 PEP report.

PEP surveyed 29 local authorities and on this basis estimated an annual local authority spend on the performing arts of £2.75 million, including around £1.5 million on music, within which spending on venues accounted for around £500,000. By comparison, at this point the ACGB spent about £2.25 million annually on music, including opera and ballet (PEP 1966: 3). PEP noted that a clear picture of musical activity in Britain was not possible without consideration of both public and private sectors, and added that statistics were further complicated by variations in local accounting procedures and areas of responsibility: 'expenditure on music and other performing arts does not necessarily come under only one heading … brass bands and other open air performances are often the responsibility of a Parks Committee rather than the Entertainments Committee' (ibid.: 9).

The PEP report concluded that, in general, councils were neither particularly enthusiastic for nor particularly opposed to spending money on the arts. If there was a widespread feeling that the provision of music was a luxury, there were also significant local variations in the importance given to music education, in the use of an entertainments officer and in the influence of the local orchestra: 'in the case of both Manchester (home of the Hallé) and Glasgow (home to the SNO), the orchestral society in effect runs the musical life of the town' (PEP 1966: 39).[24]

The PEP report assumed that the music that matters in this context was music in the classical tradition. From a local authority perspective, it seems, popular music was either a matter for commercial market forces or, in its youth cultural aspects,

---

[23]   For Birmingham, see Gunn 2000; for Liverpool, see Henley and McKernan 2009; and for Manchester, see Beale 2000.

[24]   PEP seems to be discounting here the contribution of the BBC Scottish Symphony Orchestra to Glasgow's musical life.

a problem to be addressed rather than an activity to be supported. In practice, though, as we will discuss further in Chapter 4, rock'n'roll, skiffle and beat music were not entirely unsupported by local councils. In many small towns, schools and youth clubs were the only places in which young musicians could perform and these venues were central to local live music scenes, just as larger municipal halls were for bands that attracted larger audiences. Allan Williams, manager of the Beatles when they 'became the undisputed number one rock'n'roll beat group on Merseyside during those first few months of 1961', notes how dependent they were on such venues:

> They sound like meeting places for Labour Party conventions, dull and forbidding – Hamilton Hall, Latham Memorial Hall, Blair Hall, the Aintree Institute. These were the places the Beatles featured before trekking back to Hamburg. (Williams 1976: 203)

National Promotion

In 1940 the wartime coalition government agreed to put funds into CEMA, which had been set up in 1939 by a charity, Pilgrim Trust, to provide support for the visual and performing arts as a means of boosting morale during wartime. CEMA was concerned both to preserve 'the highest standards in the arts of music, drama and painting' despite the disruption of war and to encourage the 'widespread provision of opportunities for hearing good music and the enjoyment of the arts generally' (HM Treasury memorandum, cited by Hewison 1995: 33). When the ACGB was established in 1946, it was clearly the peacetime successor to CEMA, not simply in terms of people (Keynes chaired both organisations) but also ideologically. In Robert Hutchison's words, 'the initial assumptions and constitutional position of the Arts Council were almost identical to those of CEMA' (Hutchison 1982: 16). On the one hand, this meant a continuing stress on preserving 'the highest standards' of the arts and broadening access to them; on the other hand, it meant retaining the arm's length principle under which an organisation could be funded by central government but did not report directly to ministers or Parliament. Even for a Labour government, the idea of a Ministry of Culture seemed decidedly un-British.

In some respects, though, it is misleading to see the post-war reorganisation of CEMA as the ACGB as seamless. During the war, the government had also supported the Entertainments National Service Association (ENSA). ENSA's task was to provide entertainment for the troops, both in Britain and on front lines, and from mid-1940 this also meant cheering up war workers: 'every factory on an approved list of over a thousand now had one or two ENSA parties every week, generally performing in the canteen during lunch breaks' (Calder 1971: 429). ENSA not only provided comedians and variety performers, but also had a classical music division and a disc-lending service supporting the creation of local gramophone clubs. In parallel to CEMA's chamber concerts in factory canteens, from 1943 ENSA promoted Symphony Concerts for War Workers, and there was a clear sense among observers at the time that the usual divisions between different kinds of music and audience were breaking down. Sir Malcolm Sargent (who in 1944 took over as conductor of the BBC's Proms, now held in the Royal Albert Hall following the destruction of Queens Hall's in a bombing raid) suggested that thanks to CEMA and ENSA, people were being attracted to classical music for the first time 'because it had been made available to them in the places they have been in the habit of visiting in search of entertainment – theatres, music halls, and cinemas' (quoted in ibid.: 431).

It was this sense of a common culture that was lost with the transformation of CEMA into the ACGB.[25] The new Council was asked to take on ENSA activities when its Ministry of Labour subsidy came to an end in 1946 and, as Mary Glasgow, then Secretary-General of the ACGB, explained to Keynes:

> We said we thought the Council would be perfectly prepared to take over, provided it was clearly understood that our ways were not ENSA's. The variety entertainments would cease; the gramophone recitals would cease (if only because we have no records and it is now impossible to get them); the cheap symphony concerts at one shilling a head would cease and so would the free music clubs which ENSA has been running. (Quoted in Hutchison 1982: 90)

What Mary Glasgow meant here by 'our ways' is well captured in a minute of the Council's discussion of a request in 1948 from the Variety Artists' Federation for support for a tour of 'high-class' variety entertainment:

> Sir Kenneth Clark doubted whether such entertainment could be considered as coming within the objects of the Council laid down in the Charter and pointed to the difficulty of establishing a controlling standard in work of this kind. (Quoted in Hutchison 1982: 90)[26]

Such an attitude didn't just mean that the Arts Council only supported 'high' art but also that it concentrated on the need to 'improve the standard of execution of the fine arts' at the expense of the requirement in its Charter 'to increase the

---

[25] There is considerable debate among historians as to the reality of this 'common culture', although whether CEMA's activities are celebrated or mocked seems to depend on the ideological outlook of the historian – what facts there are certainly do not speak for themselves. For different views, see, for example, Croft 1995; Hayes 1999; and McKibbin 1998.

[26] Hutchison also found in the ACGB minutes reference to an unlikely and uneasy correspondence between Mary Glasgow and Butlin's Holiday Camps, which was looking for support for performances it was promoting by the San Carlo Opera Company (Hutchison 1982: 97–8).

accessibility of the fine arts to the public'. For a while in the 1940s, the Council continued to support ENSA-type projects, working with the Miners' Welfare Commission, for example, 'to bring music and drama to the coalfields' (one such venture involved the Covent Garden opera chorus and four soloists touring South Wales in 1948)[27] and although in these years the Arts Council promoted fewer concerts than CEMA (875 in 1946–7 as against CEMA's 4,583 in 1945), it did give increased financial assistance to music societies (though in the same year this only amounted to £2,700 in support of 427 concerts: PEP 1949: 90–1).

What cannot be disputed is that Keynes despised amateurs[28] and that the 1948 Local Authorities Act gave the Arts Council an excuse not to involve itself in local musical promotion. As Robert Hutchison persuasively argues, accessibility was reinterpreted as availability (CEMA's experiments 'in suggesting that the arts can become a part of daily life' were dropped) and under the leadership of W.E. Williams (who became Secretary-General in 1951), the ACGB developed an explicit policy of 'sustaining the best possible standards of performance at a limited number of institutions' (Hutchison 1982: 99). This meant abandoning any attempt to 'spread' cultural opportunity and instead focusing on 'raising' artistic standards. In 1952 the Council withdrew support from the local Arts Centres that had been developed with the support of CEMA because, in the words of Mary Glasgow, it 'wished to reserve its formal association for a select number of professional undertakings' (quoted in Croft 1995: 210).

From our perspective, then, the impact of the Arts Council on live music in Britain was contradictory. For popular and amateur music making, it seemed, at least in the period covered in this volume, largely irrelevant;[29] however, for professional classical music organisations, it quickly became vital for their survival. In comparison with what was available from the state in other European countries, the public subsidy of music in Britain was small, and the ACGB was more concerned with supporting existing orchestras and music companies than directing their music policies (it was not in the business of commissioning work or determining programmes, for example, unless in exceptional circumstances, such as the 1953 Coronation). Nonetheless, as Richard Morrison suggests, the Council 'would quickly come to dominate every facet of serious culture in Britain' (Morrison 2004: 96). An orchestra like the LSO soon benefited from ACGB financial support, but, in return, had to meet the Council's criteria of good financial governance and, like all recipients of ACGB funds, became dependent on the Council not just economically but also for its model of the role of a state-subsidised orchestra in public life.

---

[27]   Griffin 1999: 283–4.

[28]   In Kenneth Clark's words, Keynes was not 'the man for wandering minstrels and amateur theatricals' (quoted in Wolf 2010: 83).

[29]   Although grants continued to be made through the National Federation of Music Societies until 1955, such support was primarily 'to mitigate the costs of professional conductors, soloists and players, rather than to stimulate amateur activity itself' (Wolf 2010: 86).

Cultural historians seem to agree that the ACGB in 1950s was a very conservative organisation and that music was its 'most conservative unit' (Witts 1998: 162). In part this was an effect of its funding model. By choosing to fund a limited number of organisations that were then dependent on continuing Council support, there was little financial opportunity for newcomers ('the Arts Council waited 35 years before making any substantial cuts in the companies that it supported': Hutchison 1982: 70). And by giving its support to organisations rather than directly to artists or through its own promotions, the Council was not in a position to act as a champion for works or movements that challenged the arts establishment. Nor was it ideologically inclined to. As Sir Kenneth Clark put it: 'We know that certain writers, composers and artists go through bad times, but an Arts Council must not become a charitable organisation' (quoted in Hutchison 1982: 105).

Except, perhaps, for the small coterie of metropolitan art and music world grandees who served as its committee members. The second source of the Council's conservatism lay in its model of governance. Its 'arm's length from government' meant an arm's length from Parliament, from political parties and from any democratic or representational responsibility. In practice the Council's policies were made by much the same sort of people who had always been benefactors of the arts in Britain, but who were now displaying their largesse and prestige with state funds. Hutchison calls this group 'the English opera class' and the close ties between the ACGB and Covent Garden were apparent from the outset.[30] Throughout the 1950s, opera accounted for 25 per cent of Arts Council expenditure and by 1960–1 'over 50% of the Council's financial resources were going to grant-aid the two main opera and ballet companies' (Hutchison 1982: 35, 63). In 1966 PEP calculated that if the Royal Opera House and Sadlers Wells were excluded, then the Council spent about two-thirds of what local authorities did on music; if they were included, the figure rose to twice as much (PEP 1966: 46).

There is no doubt that in the 1950s the Arts Council brought stability and a new kind of professionalism to orchestral and opera life and established a structure for live classical music provision in Britain that is still recognisable, but it did so in a way that (unlike CEMA) took for granted the separation of the classical and popular music worlds and did its best, it seems, to ignore contemporary cultural and technological changes. It took the election of a Labour government in 1964 to begin to alter its ways. Responsibility for the Council was moved from the Treasury to the Department of Education and Science, and Jennie Lee, the first person to assume the role of Minster for the Arts, was able to double the funding made available to the ACGB between 1965 and 1969. Her White Paper, *A Policy for the Arts* (published in February 1965), set in place a number of significant policy changes. More money was made available for the support of individual artists; the Council was encouraged to invest in buildings; the importance of regional initiatives was reasserted; and the White Paper recognised that jazz and

---

[30]   See Lebrecht 2000: 38–47.

other popular forms of music, along with radio, television and advertisement, 'can carry a cultural aspect' (Hewison 1995: 122). When the Council's Royal Charter was renewed in 1967, references to the high arts were dropped and the range of artforms that could receive funding extended. Separate Arts Councils were established for Wales, Scotland and Northern Ireland and henceforth funding regimes for music increasingly diverged. It was within this new bureaucratic and funding structure that the cultural changes of the 1960s would eventually have their effect on national music policy.

Conclusion

In its 17th Annual Report (published in 1962), the ACGB paid tribute to its 'priority institutions' (the 'limited number of power-houses of music, drama, opera and ballet') for being:

> The trustees of high artistic standard, the main line of defence against the debasement of values in public entertainment. (Quoted in Wolf 2010: 87)

As Wolf goes on to show, in its championing of high art institutions as a kind of bulwark against 'public entertainment', the ACGB not only excluded the amateur and the popular from its remit but also art that was – or sought to be – 'commercially successful' (Ibid: 90).

In part this policy was justified in terms of market failure: state funds should only be invested in activities or events in which commercial companies had no interest because they were unprofitable. The state supported that which the market did not. Keynes himself saw no objection to helping commercial organisations with uncommercial projects, but this policy had been abandoned (in the face of parliamentary criticism) by 1950 and, in any case, most of the ACGB's administrators and committee members took for granted that the value of high art lay precisely in its independence of any commercial associations. As Wolf notes:

> the exclusion of professional, but commercial, activities was considered a fundamental part of the Arts Council's outlook from early in its existence, and was enshrined in its explicit and exclusive support for 'not-for-profit' activities. (Ibid: 91)

The Council's Standard Music Agreement made this clear: 'only properly constituted companies not conducted or established for profit, and bodies functioning under charitable trusts, are eligible for association with the Council'.

> In this way, entering the 1960s, the Arts Council had an ideological justification for ignoring the promoters of popular culture. Offering them assistance would –

no doubt conveniently – have been seen as an improper use of tax revenues for profitable purposes. (Wolf 2010: 91)

And it would also have threatened the Council's high cultural self-satisfaction.

It was only with the arrival of the Conservative governments of the 1970s and 1980s that the ACGB's disdain for commercial arts promoters was challenged, and only in the 1990s, under the New Labour government, that the function of the state funding of the arts was defined explicitly in terms of support for the cultural industries rather than for culture.[31] In the 1950s and into the 1960s, the distinction between the state-subsidised and the commercial music sectors was taken for granted.

However, this was an oversimplification, and in conclusion to this chapter, we will therefore make three further points.

First, even high cultural institutions cannot escape the effects of market forces. Classical music promoters who did not get state subsidies had to seek other solutions to market failure, to the brutal fact that with the post-war rise in the costs of live music production, box office returns were increasingly inadequate. From this perspective, the most interesting art music promoter in the 1950s was John Christie at Glyndebourne. For reasons that according to most commentators lay in Keynes' long-standing antipathy for his old Etonian contemporary, Glyndebourne was not considered by the Council to be a 'power-house' and was therefore not in receipt of significant Council support until 1967.[32] Christie therefore had to seek alternative ways to supplement ticket sales and can be seen as the pioneer (at least in Britain) of various methods of expanding the financial returns from live opera, methods that were soon adopted by both other classical music organisations and by commercial promoters generally: the festival (the Edinburgh International Festival was originally a Glyndebourne initiative, designed in part to help fund its first post-war productions), sponsorship (by John Lewis and the Peter Stuyvesant Foundation, for example), priority subscribers (its supporters club), value-added tickets (dinner included), merchandise and branding (Glyndebourne wine), deals with broadcasters (opera from Glyndebourne was televised in 1951), and the sale of expensive advertising-filled programmes. Christie even had to address the problem of secondary ticketing (or, in his terms, 'black market tickets'): within days of tickets being on sale, they would be advertised for resale in the personal column of *The Times*.[33]

Second, the most important national state organisation for British musical culture in this period was not the ACGB but the BBC. And the BBC had to have a direct relationship with commercial music companies (hence, for example, the

---

[31] For detailed discussion of these changes, see Cloonan 2007.

[32] The 1967 grant was for its touring programme. Glyndebourne had received £25,000 from the Council in 1951, but that was for its contribution to the Council-promoted Mozart programme at the Festival of Britain (Hughes 1981: 172, 248).

[33] See Hughes 1981: 155, 175, 178–9, 231, 244.

problems of plugging and payola already described). There may have been much in common between the thinking (and, indeed, personnel) of the Arts Council and the Third Programme, but the Third Programme only accounted for part of the BBC's music output (and for a miniscule fraction of its listeners). Light Programme policy is therefore more interesting to study when considering how a public organisation impacts on commercial music practices.

In his 1957 memoir, Ted Heath is revealing both about the importance of the BBC for his band's success and about the problems of dealing with the Corporation's musical values. Heath formed his own band in 1944 only when he had a firm offer of several months' broadcasting ('a band, I knew, had to have broadcasts') and the band's success was guaranteed when it was booked for a BBC series called *Top Ten* (originally scheduled for six weeks, the programme eventually ran for 27). Heath actually lost money on these shows (he paid his musicians more than the BBC rate) but they were important in establishing his band's name and value as live performers (Heath 1957: 63–6). Then the BBC:

> turned its back on me. We were to have no more broadcasts. The Heath style of music, I was told, was too aggressively modern. The BBC's Listener Research organization had established that my kind of music was deplored by middle-aged listeners to whom it was incomprehensible. (Heath 1957: 82–3)

At this point, Heath 'had no intention of allowing the BBC to dictate my music policy' and, in any case, his band lacked the singers necessary if he were to 'commercialize my style of orchestration' (Heath 1957: 83). By 1950, though, it was clear that his 'progressive policy' was no longer commercially viable:

> Having decided that a *volte face* was essential, I went the whole way. Swing was out; the new Heath commercial approach was in. Latin-American costumes were hired and I booked a vocal group. (Heath 1957: 92)

He also put under contract the singer Lita Roza who, as was necessary for acts seeking broadcasts, duly took the BBC's 'routine test'. She failed. '"Miss Roza", opined the BBC, "possessed an insignificant amount of vocal talent"' (Heath 1957: 93–4). She took the test again; she failed again. Heath suggests that she was stymied by the BBC's 'anti-microphone complex', by its belief that without electrical help 'crooners … had no vocal substance whatsoever', by its fear of being criticised for broadcasting too much sentimental 'slush'. Eventually Heath arranged for Roza to have a demo recording session with Decca Records (to whom the band was contracted) and used the resulting record to persuade the BBC that she could, indeed, sing (ibid.: 94–5).

Heath's experience is interesting as an example of the complex relations between commercial and non-commercial judgements in the BBC's popular music policy. Lita Roza was not, it seems, judged by the BBC according to her potential popularity or sales – as she would have been by a record company or publisher

– but by a more nebulous concept of musical 'quality', while Heath's band was judged unsuitable for broadcasting as a result of listener research. The BBC's commitment to public service meant that, unlike the ACGB, it did see its musical policy as involving a form of representation, as taking account of the interests and tastes of all sectors of the public.[34] This meant, as we shall see, that the BBC was centrally important for the emergence of new audiences in the 1950s and 1960s for whom the ACGB was irrelevant.

The final point we want to make here is that for music promoters going about their daily business, the role of the state as regulator as described in the first part of this chapter is much more significant than its role as promoter. The state concern for public order, that is to say, has more effect on what promoters can and cannot do than the state concern for cultural uplift (even if these two concerns are ideologically related). It is misleading, though, to think of this as necessarily involving some sort of tension between what 'the people' want (and what commercial promoters therefore want to give them) and what the state allows them. 'Good order' is also a requirement for a successful live music event or venue for its promoter and, indeed, for most audiences. As Peter Bailey argues, by the end of the nineteenth century, the moral campaign for rational recreation had been to a large extent subsumed into the successful commercial construction of orderly consumption, of 'fun without vulgarity'. Bailey coins the term 'entertainmentality' for 'this modern amalgam of open ended invitation and schematized conformity that well served the emergent modern leisure industry' (Bailey 2011: 131).[35] Ted Heath illustrates what is involved here in his account of persuading Val Parnell to give the Ted Heath Band a Sunday slot at the London Palladium:

> Val didn't turn the idea down flat; on the other hand, he didn't fall over himself to welcome it. He'd *heard* about swing fans. They were, he felt, more than a little on the rowdy side and given to jitterbugging and other noisy and even destructive forms of exhibitionism. I argued that our supporters weren't a bit like this, but Val had visions of his beloved Palladium being disrupted by unruly behaviour. At last, he agreed to allow us to put on fortnightly concerts – but on one condition: I was to make reparation for any damage done to the carpets and fittings. (Heath 1957: 79 emphasis in original)

We will return to the problem of audiences, promoters, venues and changing ideas of entertainment in later chapters.

---

[34] A 1943 broadcast, for example, featured Cyril Blake's Negro Orchestra (its members all from the Caribbean) playing 'Negro Spirituals and Folk Songs', the latter almost certainly including early examples of calypso. See Cowley 1985: 89.

[35] See also Till 2004.

A Snapshot of Bristol in October–November 1962

For people going out in Bristol in late 1962,[1] the leading music venue was the Council-owned Colston Hall (c. 2,000 capacity).[2] The West of England's foremost concert promoter at the time, Charles H. Lockier, promoted touring 'package' shows there, usually in association with national promoters.[3] Highlights included: Phil Everly, Frank Ifield, Ketty Lester, Dean Rodgers, the Vernon Girls and the Terry Young Five (Thursday 1 November; admission 8/6–17/6); in collaboration with agent Tito Burns, Bobby Vee and the Crickets (Sunday 25 November); with promoter Harold Davison for a 'twice-nightly' show featuring The Dave Brubeck Quartet (Friday 30 November; 6.30 pm and 8.45 pm); and another twice-nightly starring Cliff Richard and the Shadows (Saturday 8 December; 6.30 pm and 8.45 pm; 1st house: 12/6–17/6, 2nd house: 15/--17/6).[4]

One particularly memorable show promoted by Lockier at Colston Hall included Little Richard with Jet Harris and Sam Cooke, and featured a 'personal appearance' by Gene Vincent (Monday 15 October). An article the following day reported that:

> The sight of half-a-dozen hapless patrons standing in one of the aisles searching for their seats 45 minutes after the advertised time of starting suggested that the team of ushers was not a strong one. Certainly towards the finale, with scores

---

[1] Bristol in the early 1960s was undergoing a population boom and many new flats and amenities were built as the city underwent redevelopment. In November 1966, the Mecca chain opened up the New Entertainments Centre in the city centre, home to a dozen licensed bars, the 2,000-capacity Locarno Ballroom, an ABC cinema, an ice rink, bowling lanes, a casino, a nightclub and a multi-storey car park. Only the ice rink and the cinema survived the demolition of the complex in 1998. The cinema closed in 1996 and was converted into a nightclub in 2000, originally called Rock; it is now the O$_2$ Academy Bristol.

[2] The Beatles first performed at the Colston Hall on 15 March 1963 as part of the package tour headlined by Tommy Roe and Chris Montez.

[3] Two years previously at Colston Hall, the sold-out 'Groups Galore' shows, created by Brian K. Jones, featured six of Bristol's top young rock'n'roll groups (including Paul Raven, later Gary Glitter), all managed by Jones, which allowed Bristol's youth to enjoy some homegrown rock'n'roll talent.

[4] Tickets were available via post from the promoter, Lockier's Ltd, or from the venue, and occasionally from Lewis's Travel Bureau.

of over-enthusiastic and misguided fans struggling to join Little Richard on stage, it was clear that the stewards were outnumbered. This was a time when discretion was more important than valour and the swift exit of the star averted a more serious situation, as customers and staff swapped blows.

Also of note at the same gig was the non-performance of Gene Vincent, who arrived in the country without a Ministry of Labour work permit and so was denied the opportunity to perform. Nevertheless, Vincent apparently 'emphasised [the audience's] loss and disappointment by regaling us with a few minutes of "Be-bop-a-lu-la" from the centre gangway'.

Rock'n'roll's popularity was growing in Bristol in 1962 in smaller venues as well, outside the city centre, and one would have had the choice of a number of dance events featuring local bands, including a members-only rock night featuring Ricky Forde and the Cyclones at a community centre in Sea Mills (Friday 23 November; 3/6); a 'Rock Dance' at the Horfield T.A. Drill Hall featuring Johnny Carr and the Cadillacs, who formed in 1958 (Saturday 24 November; 5/-); and a 'Rock Rave' at the Warmley Community Centre featuring Lee King and the Viceroys (Saturday 24 November). Rock, twist and jive dances also featured at venues such as The Beat Club and the Co-op Hall.[5]

Jazz fans were well provided for, with events from the 'Rollicking Jazz Club' at the Ship Inn and Bathurst Hotel, every Tuesday and Saturday, to the Bristol Chinese Jazz Club at the Corn Exchange, the latter promoting an 'All-Night Rave' from 11.30 pm till 6 am on Friday 5 October (admission 15/-).[6] One highlight of the folk music revival at this time was a folk song concert featuring Ewan Macoll, Peggy Seger, A.L. Lloyd, and the Ian Campbell Group, which took place at the Colston Hall on Sunday 4 November as part of the Bristol Trades Union Festival (admission 5/-). In addition to local amateur orchestras and choirs in smaller churches and halls, classical music aficionados were also catered for at the Colston Hall, with performances by the Bournemouth Symphony Orchestra (Wednesday 24 October; 3/6 – 10/6), the Philomusica of London (Wednesday 7 November), and the London Mozart Players (Wednesday 5 December), promoted by the Entertainments Committee of Bristol City Council.

---

[5]   More 'traditional' dancing was also well served, with a 'Teenagers' Ballroom Club' for beginners at the Embassy City Ballroom on Saturdays, and classes in waltz, quickstep and foxtrot 'especially for the over 30s' at the same venue on Tuesday nights. Rock'n'roll was creeping in here as well, as beginners could also attend a Latin-American dance club exclusively for under 21s which featured the 'cha-cha-cha, rock 'n' roll, paso-doble, rumba and samba' (Saturday 10 November).

[6]   The event was promoted in the *Evening Post* with a somewhat esoteric advertisement – 'Chop Chop Velly Velly Good Uncal Bonny' – that promised the Clyde Valley Stompers, Eric Allandale and his New Orleans Knights, and the Alvin Roy's Saratoga Jazz Band, and included 'Fly Lice, Crocodile Sandwiches, Chop Suey'.

References

A.H.R.T. 1962. 'Star vanishes as fans swap blows'. *Bristol Evening Post*, Tuesday 16 October.

Bristol Chamber Choir. 2012. 'Choir history'. Available at: http://www. bristolchamberchoir.org.uk/page10.html [accessed 11 September 2012].

Colston Hall. 2012. '1960s'. Available at: http://www.colstonhall.org/aboutthehall/history/history5 [accessed 11 September 2012].

'Entertainments'. 1962. *Bristol Evening Post*, Thursday 4 October, p. 5.

'Entertainments'. 1962. *Bristol Evening Post*, Friday 12 October, p. 5.

'Entertainments'. 1962. *Bristol Evening Post*, Friday 19 October, p. 5.

'Entertainments'. 1962. *Bristol Evening Post*, Saturday 31 October, p. 5.

'Entertainments'. 1962. *Bristol Evening Post*, Wednesday 7 November, p. 5.

'Entertainments'. 1962. *Bristol Evening Post*, Tuesday 13 November, p. 5.

'Entertainments'. 1962. *Bristol Evening Post*, Friday 23 November, p. 5.

'Entertainments'. 1962. *Bristol Evening Post*, Thursday 29 November, p. 5.

Townsend, P. 2007. 'Bristol's New Mecca Centre BS1'. Available at: http://www. flickr.com/photos/brizzlebornandbred/2052645881 [accessed 11 September 2012].

'Way back when in the West – a musical life'. *Bristol Evening Post*, 14 July 2008. Available at: http://www.thisisbristol.co.uk/news/Way-West-8211-musical-life/article-219259-detail/article.html [accessed 11 September 2012].

Chapter 3
Being a Musician

Every Sunday our tiny orchestra used to play at somebody's wedding. Not that we considered ourselves to be specialists in this kind of work, it was simply the only type of booking anyone ever seemed to offer us. It is true that we were once invited to submit a quotation for the annual staff dinner of a light engineering enterprise somewhere over in Plaistow, but it turned out that the firm was so enterprising that they had mistaken us for another orchestra altogether, and no sooner realised their mistake than they withdrew their offer. (Benny Green describes his musical life as a young man at the end of the 1940s – Green 1976: 24)

Slowly I build my collection of LPs until I have a grand total of eight. They sit on the windowsill beneath damask curtains, and I stare at them and feel like a king. I sit on the floor by the fireplace of my bedroom, playing them at 16 revs per minute instead of the prescribed 33⅓. I learn the solo by repeatedly dropping the needle into this spot, trying to match my notes to the player's. I become reclusive and private about my practice session and add to the isolation by creating a barrier around my record player out of a couch, an armchair, and a reangling of my bed. My room looks strange, as if the furniture's been arranged by a madman, but I climb across my bed and down into my magic circle and sit for several hours with guitars and LPs, lost in surrender to this world. (Andy Summers describes his musical life as a teenager in the late 1950s – Summers 2006: 37–8)

Introduction

In 1950 Robert Elkin edited a book, *A Career in Music*, which was advertised thus:

With the widespread interest in music which is a feature of our times, it is natural that many young people are wondering whether the musical profession or the music industry may provide them with a successful and congenial career. Many questions have to be considered in this connection, and there has been the need of an up-to-date book which should give reliable and authoritative answers to these questions. (Elkin 1950: cover blurb)[1]

---

[1]   Elkin was a music publisher and author of books about London's Queen's Hall and Royal Philharmonic. He had chaired the Music Publishers' Association and the London

The book had 12 chapters covering 12 kinds of career: solo instrumentalist, solo singer, composer, accompanist, conductor, orchestral player, music teacher, organist/choirmaster, musical instrument manufacture, music publishing, music retail (instruments, sheet music and recordings) and organisation/administration. This last chapter, written by John Denison, Music Director of the Arts Council, covered the BBC, the Ministry of Education and Local Education Authorities, the Arts Council, the British Council, opera administration, orchestral management, professional music adviser (for voluntary organisations) and entertainment management (for local authorities).

A Career in Music is a thorough, realistic and entertaining account of the musician's life as it had been experienced by a number of 'well-known specialists', but reading it today, two things are striking: first, it takes for granted that the music profession and the music industry are organised around live performance (gramophone recordings are only discussed in the chapter on retail; studio work refers to film studios); and second, it is focused exclusively on the classical music world (only the retail chapter refers to the need to know anything about popular music).

In 1950 there was not a supplementary volume covering *A Career in Popular Music*, not because there weren't such careers but because they were not institutionalised in the same way as classical careers; they did not require formal training or qualifications. Had such a book existed, its structure would have been quite similar: the soloists' chapters would have covered variety acts and the orchestral musicians' chapter would have been about instrumentalists in dance-bands, but the popular musicians' world was also serviced by retailers, publishers and instrument makers; popular music making also needed concert organisers and venue administrators. Would-be popular musicians in 1950 would also have assumed that a musical career was focused on live performance, not recording. What they might not have shared with their classical peers was the latter's sense of confidence. This is most apparent in Thomas Russell's chapter on 'The orchestral player'. He begins with a warning note:

> I cannot deny that the orchestral player's work may, in certain conditions, bring little more than frustration. In the London of today, where no satisfactory hall exists, and where the refinements of tone and ensemble, reached with so much expense of nervous effort, are dissipated and wasted amid the desert space of the Royal Albert Hall; where only hackneyed works which depress the players even more than the critics will attract the public, and where too many conductors use the orchestra merely as a pedestal to fame, frustration is common. (Russell 1950: 139)[2]

Choral Society and had travelled widely as an Adjudicator of Music Festivals. He could thus claim contact 'with every aspect of music-making'.

[2]   Thomas Russell, a viola player, was Managing Director of the London Philharmonic Orchestra from 1939 to 1952, when he was sacked for being a communist.

But he goes on to describe how employment conditions have improved since the war: 'no highly qualified orchestral player need be without regular work, and in selecting this he has a wider choice than ever before in this country'. Russell attributes the improvements in the music labour market to the rise of state funding, to the continuing classical music commitments of the BBC and, not least, to the organisational work of the Musicians' Union. He concludes that:

> conditions of orchestral playing today ... are immeasurably more attractive than they were even a generation ago, and they indicate a steady progress towards a secure and dignified profession. (Russell 1950: 158)

It is doubtful that a chapter on 'the dance-band player' would have made the same claim. Their working opportunities were not much affected by state funding, BBC support was regarded as capricious and the Musicians' Union had patchy influence in many of their workplaces. Unlike orchestral musicians, they had scant protection from market forces, with results that are well captured by Ted Heath's experiences in the late 1940s:

> Although I had a good band, I was always struggling for survival. Nowadays I have come to understand that the business part of a band is quite as important as the musical side. To put it briefly, a band has to live – and live comfortably – if it is to go on playing; musicians don't live to play, but rather the reverse ... a bandleader has to be a caterer, unless he can satisfy the tastes of a broad mass of people, he has no real chance of survival. (Heath 1957: 81)

Heath describes how his band had to adapt to changing market conditions, to modify its arrangements, adjust its set lists and 'soft-pedal on the jazz'. But he also describes how it benefited from the developing post-war recording industry:

> There is no doubt that the sales of our records had given us the little extra acceleration that had been needed, not merely in the matter of direct royalties, but in other incalculable ways. A hit record not only sells; it also creates a demand – for more records, for the band in the flesh. It is, in fact, the ancient snowball process. Or, to put it another way, nothing succeeds like success. (Heath 1957: 98)

Even when he is describing such success, though, Heath is aware of the instability of the music market; his memoir shows clearly, if perhaps unwittingly, how the life of a professional musician in the popular music world moves continually back and forth between anxiety and opportunity.

This chapter is focused on that world. We will show how musicians responded to new kinds of demand and competition for their services and we will discuss in some detail how the Musicians' Union sought to protect its members from the effects of such competition. We will thus address the question that came to the fore in this period: what is a musician anyway? First, though, we need to make some general comments about popular music historiography.

Writing Popular Music History

The history of popular music in Britain since 1950 is usually understood as a history of records and recordings. Changing trends and tastes are identified by reference to record sales charts, it is assumed that popular music culture is articulated in discs and the most significant musicians are taken to be those with the biggest hits. But to write popular musical history in this way is misleading and, in particular, does not make sense of musicians' own experiences. Most musicians make their living selling their services as performers rather than from their returns from record sales or copyrights, and a history of popular music in terms of live performance rather than record sales challenges orthodox accounts in three ways.

First, it makes clear that changes in musical taste and performing practice are more gradual and complex than is suggested by comparing lists of bestselling records. New ways of making music do not replace old ones but exist alongside them; they do not so much change the everyday soundscape as make it noisier.[3]

Second, it reminds us that musicians' lives do not begin and end with their recordings. For most artists, careers begin long before they reach a recording studio and continue long after their records cease to appear in the charts. The notion of 'overnight success', a common feature of the story told by the history of hit records, doesn't long survive a study of musicians' biographies.[4]

Third, professional musicians are, as Ted Heath suggests, remarkably adaptable, and a historian can only be impressed by their unquenchable ability to take on new styles and sounds to meet market demand. Indeed, for many musicians, adaptability is what is meant by 'professionalism'. In 1956, for example, Tony Crombie, one of Britain's most successful bebop drummers, put together a rock'n'roll group, The Rockets, with saxophonist Rex Morris, pianist Red Mitchell, bassist Ashley Kozak, guitarist Jimmy Currie and singer Clyde Ray, jazzers all. The Rockets were, in Pete Frame's words, 'the first British rock'n'roll band on the national touring circuit', and delighted their agent, Bernard Delfont: 'Seasoned troupers on their bill are saying they haven't seem anything like it, in an English act, for 20 years!'[5]

From a live music perspective, then, it is problematic to describe the arrival of rock'n'roll in Britain in the mid-1950s as 'revolutionary', as marking a definitive change of musical generations. Rather, it took its place amidst a plethora of

---

[3]   For the classic account of the continuing local vitality of supposedly passé kinds of popular music, see Finnegan 1989.

[4]   See, for example, Dave Laing's excellent account of Elton John's complex musical life before his recording career took off (Laing 2007).

[5]   Frame 2007: 195–6. Benny Green, meanwhile, joined Lord Rockingham's XI, the house band for Jack Good's rock'n'roll TV show *Oh Boy!*

other musical entertainments. As Dave Allen notes, 'when rock & roll came to Portsmouth in 1956, the Savoy Ballroom opposite South Parade Pier still offered traditional dancing to two bands and a vocal talent contest – all for 3/- – and late transport home after a midnight finish', and four years later, at the end of the decade, live music in Portsmouth 'was still dominated by light entertainment, ballroom dancing to live bands and jazz, traditional and modern' (Allen 2009: 2, 5). New sounds continued to arrive in Portsmouth during the 1960s, but 'older musicians and styles did not suddenly disappear'. Allen describes the career of drummer Arthur Ward:

> who had played with Portsmouth's Johnny Lyne Band in 1953 when they won the *Melody Maker's* national competition in Manchester. By the early 1960s, Arthur was in weekly residence at another seafront venue, Clarence Pier, adjacent to the funfair and close to the mouth of Portsmouth Harbour. Here on Saturday nights, Arthur's dance band would share the bill with the new beat groups including Johnny Kidd and the Pirates, Dave Dee and the Bostons and Rod Stewart and the Soul Agents. During the 1960s, Arthur employed two singers who had come from local beat groups, Mike Devon, who with the Diplomats supported the Beatles at the Savoy Ballroom in April 1963, and Mick Reeve who as a member of local beat group, the Talismen, won a major national competition with a feature in the national weekly, *Record Mirror*. Through the 'swinging sixties' across Portsmouth and Southsea, local musicians crossed over, venues shifted from tradition to innovation and back again and bills were often shared. Live music in Portsmouth in that period encompassed local, national and international, professional and semi-professional dance bands, 'traditional' and modern jazz, folk music, skiffle, rock & roll, vocalists, pop, comedy, beat, rhythm & blues and rock acts. (Allen 2011)[6]

Such accounts of the remarkable mixture of music that could be heard live in British towns and cities from the mid-1950s call into question one of the more common record-based assertions, made, for example, in Dave Harker's *One for the Money*:

> The period 1959–62 was the deadest phase of British and American recorded song since at least 1945 ... For adolescents it was a *desert*. Unless you lived in major city or coast, or had access to amusement arcade or fairground or made your own music, musically it was a '*bloody desert*'. (Harker 1980: 73, emphasis in original)

Switch attention from 'recorded song' to live performance and 1959–62 becomes less a desert than a landscape covered with a mass of foliage, from gnarled old

---

[6] The website http://www.michaelcooper.org.uk/C/pmsindex.htm contains a year-by-year list of live shows in Portsmouth from 1944 to 1969.

trees to newly planted seedlings. Not only were a significant number of adolescents making their own music in this period (including early versions of the Beatles and the Rolling Stones), but they also had a variety of local opportunities to serve musical apprenticeships.

What is a Musician?

The problem faced by musician organisations – whether they treat music making as a craft (like the Musicians' Union) or as a profession (like the Incorporated Society of Musicians) – is how to draw a clear distinction between musicians and non-musicians. We will discuss the particular problems facing the Musicians' Union in post-war Britain later in this chapter. In this section we outline several different issues involved in defining 'musician' as a particular occupational category. The various arguments here are further confused by the tendency of some people who make money out of music to regard other people who make money out of music as not really musicians at all (a view shared, for example, by dance-band musicians dismissing rock'n'roll stars in the 1950s and by rock musicians dismissing *X Factor* winners in the 2000s), but a historical approach does have the advantage of showing how such discourse is itself the effect of changing economic circumstances.

First, then, there is the question of what a musician actually does. There might seem to be a straightforward answer: anyone who makes music is a musician. However, matters are not so simple. When our period begins, for example, singers were not necessarily regarded as musicians. As we noted in Chapter 1, for the purposes of union membership and labour law, they were treated as 'entertainers' and were expected to join actors' unions, and one significant change in the popular music world of the 1950s was the movement of pop singers from the margins to the centre of the music business. By the end of our period, the Musicians' Union faced a very different question: was a disc jockey a musician? This topic has been the subject of heated debate on the letters pages of *Musician*, the Musicians' Union journal, since the mid-1960s and continues to be disputed to this day.[7]

What is common to these apparently disparate problems – were singers or disc jockeys really musicians? – is the assumption that a musician is someone who plays a musical instrument. Singers are therefore problematic because the voice is not an instrument like any other; deejays are problematic because a turntable is a means of reproducing rather than creating sounds. And, of course, 'real' musicians' contempt for rock'n'roll singers in the 1950s was precisely because these singers' 'voices' were heard as having been produced by studio trickery. Developments in recording technology in the 1950s thus posed in themselves a challenge to existing understandings of music making as well as underpinning

---

[7]   Deejays have been accepted as Musicians' Union members (in the 'Recording Artists' section) since 1989.

the threat that records posed to live musicians as competition. In his entertaining if unreliable 1974 autobiography, Jimmy Savile claimed to have been putting on gigs in Yorkshire with a gramophone, a primitive home-made amplification system and a box of 78s in the late 1940s.[8] What is certain is that by 1955 he was working for Mecca and providing dedicated record sessions aimed at youth (initially on Monday evenings and at lunchtimes), at which he took centre stage (rather than being hidden in the lighting control room) and could draw bigger audiences than the usual dance-bands. Savile was equally successful at the Mecca ballrooms in Ilford, Manchester and Leeds, and one can understand local dance-band musicians concluding that while he may not have been a musician, he was certainly a threat to musicians' jobs.

A second way of marking off musicians from non-musicians is by reference to their skills and qualifications. The problem here is that different musical genres value different musical skills, and qualifications (formal and informal) for one kind of music making may not be qualifications for another: conservatory-trained musicians are no more likely to be skilled improvisers than skilled folk musicians are likely to be good sight readers; rock guitarists can do things with their instruments that classical guitarists cannot and vice versa; opera singers cannot sing pop songs properly and jazz singers cannot sing arias. In fact, before the war, professional musicians in the classical and pop worlds had possessed pretty similar skills and did quite similar things with their instruments. It was usual for classical orchestral musicians to perform light music in seaside venues in the summer season, to play in cinema orchestras and film studios, to moonlight in dance bands and to be in the pit for musicals and variety shows. Indeed, Richard Morrison suggests that even in 1970 the 'bulk of the LSO's rank-and-file' consisted of 'old military bandsmen and theatre-orchestra veterans' (Morrison 2004: 204)[9] and, from the opposite perspective, until the 1950s it was a common criticism of British would-be jazz musicians that they could play arranged jazz but couldn't improvise. It was this consensus – that a musician was someone who could read music, play their instrument with correct technique and understand harmony – that was challenged after the war by the emergence of do-it-yourself music and musicians. As veteran Musicians' Union official Harry Francis puts it rather plaintively in his reminiscences on the *jazzprofessional* website:

> I can remember arguing with some of the traditional revivalists during the late '40s who seemed to think that, because many of the pioneer musicians in this field had played with poor intonation, overwide vibratos, and other crudities,

8   See Savile 1974: 27.

9   Morrison compares this LSO universe to that of a 'new breed of musicians who came onto the scene in the 1960s and 1970s', like cellist Clive Gillinson (who joined the LSO in 1970 and became its manager in 1984 before leaving to run the Carnegie Hall in 2005). Gillinson, who had a maths degree, was, says Morrison, 'cosmopolitan in outlook, numerate, well read and well connected' – unlike the LSO's veteran musicians it seems!

those who were copying them should also copy their faults. They thought me some kind of 'square' because I considered that traditional jazz players should, like the rest, take an 'A' before commencing a performance! My simple theory was, of course, that no music suffered through being played in tune! (Francis no date)

This relates to a third and even more problematic distinction: that between professional musicians and amateurs. Again there is an obvious starting point here: professional musicians make their living from music; amateur musicians do not. There are two difficulties with this suggestion: on the one hand, amateur and professional musicians often occupy the same performing music worlds; on the other hand, many musical careers involve a restless movement back and forth across the professional/amateur divide – music, unlike the other arts, has a recognised role for the 'semi-pro'.

Professional/amateur collaboration has long been a feature of classical music performance, something valued by the Musicians' Union: in the words of one Musicians' Union General Secretary, Dennis Scard: 'The amateur musician is not normally seen as a hindrance to the profession, the fact that there exists a large number of amateur musicians is welcomed by this Union.'[10] The spread across the country from the late nineteenth century of a great number of amateur choirs, youth and other orchestras, music societies and competitive music festivals led to a variety of new employment opportunities for professional musicians, paid by such amateur organisations to be conductors, chorus masters, accompanists, soloists and orchestral 'stiffeners'. In the twentieth century, concerts by local amateur music groups became a significant source of professional musicians' earnings. Such concerts had all the trappings of a professional event – using the same venues, setting not dissimilar ticket prices, performing familiar repertoire – but with the advantage of sold-out shows (to the friends and families of the amateur performers), guaranteed fees and, above all, a fixed place in the calendar – there are choirs in all Britain's major cities, for example, and in many towns that have been putting on concerts with professional soloists and orchestras each Christmas and Easter for 100 years or more.

Historical statistics gathered by Robert Hutchison and Andrew Feist for a Policy Studies Institute survey of the 'amateur arts' in the UK in 1991 suggest that the fastest expansion of local amateur choirs, music societies and orchestras happened in the period 1940–60, and we could speculate that this reflected both the process of post-war economic recovery and the impact of increased local authority support for cultural activity. It is also a good example of the continuities in Britain's musical life.

---

[10]   Quoted in Hutchison and Feist 1991: 105. In 1966 PEP estimated that around 7,000 UK musicians were full time, meaning that the vast majority of the Musicians' Union's 35,000 membership was part time (PEP 1966: 57).

One reason why there is so much amateur/professional collaboration in the classical music world is because the musical values and skills involved are shared by all participants. Many amateur instrumentalists have had the same musical training as professionals but made different career choices, and the professionals, in turn, depend for a significant part of their earnings on the fees from teaching and from instructing pupils, most of whom have no professional ambitions at all. The various organisations for different instrumentalists, such as the Incorporated Association of Organists (founded in 1927), the Society of Recorder Players (founded in 1937) or the UK Harp Association (founded in 1964), thus deliberately bring together professionals and amateurs in promoting concerts, discussions, workshops and summer schools. If such societies provide further examples of amateur performing enthusiasm providing a source of professional income, they also point to potential problems for the professionals involved. Go to a concert by a major professional orchestra (the City of Birmingham Symphony, for example, or the Royal Scottish National Orchestra) featuring a work needing a chorus. Both orchestras have attached choirs, and these singers are not only amateur but pay an annual subscription fee for the privilege of singing with professionals. This is a necessary feature of orchestra economics. If, however, that choir were to be booked to perform for a film soundtrack or television drama, it would, of course, command a fee. In this case it would certainly expect to be paid Musicians' Union professional rates and cannot be said to taking work from other musicians (the BBC Singers are Britain's only full-time professional orchestral choir). Nevertheless, as we shall see, the Musicians' Union has always been concerned about 'amateurs displacing work opportunities for professionals', especially when they are being used as amateurs, as musicians willing to perform for expenses rather than fees.[11]

Fear of displacement is even more apparent in other musical worlds, where amateurs and professionals compete to provide the same musical services. Such competition was obvious in the 1950s, for example, in the market for entertainment or dance music at weddings or company staff dinners, as described by Benny Green in the opening quote of this chapter. Here the amateur/professional distinction is even less clear-cut than it is in the classical music world. In popular music settings, 'amateur' may well describe a musician who is a would-be professional but is prepared to play for little or no reward simply to get started. This was (and remains) the norm for the British beat groups that began to perform in the early 1960s. The Beatles played an 'audition gig', for example, in Lathom Hall in Liverpool in May 1960 for nothing (they also played for a week backing a stripper for 10 shillings per night per player); their first 'professional' gig was for £10 (of which their then manager Allan Williams and a bouncer took a pound each); their fee for playing Litherland Town Hall later in 1960 was £6. In 1962 they were offered £30 a night by Arthur Howes for a slot on the Helen Shapiro tour, but nothing beyond expenses for an initial 'trial' performance with Frank Ifield. By late 1963, they were earning £800 a week from one night stands.

---

[11] See Hutchison and Feist 1991: 111.

This information is taken from the website http//www.beatlemoney.com, which collates information from all the sources it can find. The figures should be treated with caution, but the general point is clear: pop/rock bands start their careers by playing (often for years) gigs that make no reference to Musicians' Union rates. In the 1960s, musicians like the Beatles were, one could say, professionals being treated as amateurs; to put this another way, they were, in occupational terms, following the craft apprenticeship model while, in terms of the live music business, competing with established performers.

In the popular music world, 'amateur' thus often describes a semi-professional, a musician whose main earnings are not from music, but for whom music remains a profitable sideline. In the words of the Hollies (who started their career in the just the same way as the Beatles):

> As soon as you begin to play regularly for money you will be classed as a semi-professional group. To begin with you can expect very little money for your services. If you ask for more you will be told that you are lucky to get anything! Because of the booming popularity of new groups there will always be plenty ready to 'under-cut' you, when it comes to money. A semi-professional group means, in practical terms, one in which the members carry out normal jobs during the day, and perform in the evenings. At any rate, they are people who do not depend on livings as musicians. (The Hollies 1964: 37)[12]

Semi-pros may also occupy the other end of the career structure, as ex-full professionals now playing primarily for pleasure and therefore also more flexible about fees. Or they may simply be musicians who have decided against the difficulties of pursuing music as a full-time occupation. This is common in jazz:

> Chris Hodgkin at Jazz Services felt that whilst the division between 'amateur' and 'professional' was more defined in the classical world, this was not the case in jazz. What exists is a grey area of paid performing musicians who were in effect amateur, not necessarily of the highest quality nor adhering to Musicians' Union rates and conditions. Ruth Finnegan described jazz musicians in Milton Keynes as being 'practically all ... towards the amateur end of the "amateur/professional" continuum in the sense of relying on other means than jazz for their income and in their view of musical activity as basically enjoyment rather than job'. (Hutchison and Feist 1991: 113)

The same situation can be found in the folk world, where another pattern is also common: musicians who make a full-time living for part of the year (performing at summer agricultural shows and festivals) and return to their other occupations

---

[12]   Unlike most of the instant books written by (or for) successful beat groups in the 1960s, this is a surprisingly useful and informative account of the British music business in the mid-1960s.

from autumn until spring. We will return to some of these issues in the next chapter. The immediate point is that the 1950s and 1960s mark not just significant changes in the worlds of folk and jazz, and the emergence of new kinds of young musician, but also (through the commercial success of folk, jazz and young performers) new kinds of overlap between amateurs and professionals that made these terms more problematic than ever.

This relates to another way of defining a musician not by reference to what they do but to whom they work with. As Howard Becker has argued most persuasively, all artistic work is inherently collective and to be a musician is necessarily to work with other musicians and to be acknowledged by them as a musician. It is not enough for a musician to be able to play their instrument – they have to be able to play their instrument with other people; extra-musical social skills are also prerequisites for a successful musical career.[13] The historical issue is therefore how musicians' social worlds changed in this period, and this is to raise questions about hierarchies and power structures.

In his study of the working world of British pop musicians in the 1960s, Gordon Thompson notes that for instrumentalists seeking employment in the growing recording sector, 'entering session work meant knowing somebody on the inside' and becoming part of a hierarchy in which studio fixers had the same sort of power as the people who organised musicians for film soundtrack recording sessions. This had been one of the 'networks' from which women players had long been excluded:

> Even when she [Evelyn Rothwell] was accepted into the orchestra [the LSO], she was never given the plum engagements; the lucrative film sessions. 'Gordon Walker [LSO Chairman and first flute] was the fixer,' she later wrote, 'and he and others concerned preferred to engage men'.[14]

The 1950s and 1960s world of the recording studio was equally male and fixers were equally powerful. John Schroeder recalls his briefing by Norrie Paramour, recording manager of EMI's Columbia label, after becoming his assistant in 1957:

> Session musicians are booked through two 'fixers', namely Charlie Katz or Harry Benson. They will always do their best for you. You will discover the session circuit has some incredible musicians in it, and there is multiple choice with practically every instrument. As you begin to recognise individual talents you will be able to select who you prefer for the session in mind. (Schroeder 2009: 39)

Session musicians were competing with each other for jobs, but from within a privileged pool of recognised talent that gave them a kind of solidarity. Guitarist

---

[13]   See Becker 1974; and Cloonan 2003.
[14]   Morrison 2004: 186; and see Thompson 2008: 257.

Big Jim Sullivan remembers that he 'sought advantages over other guitarists as a way to maintain his competitive edge' by continually trying out new electronic devices and expanding his skills (learning the sitar, for example), but, at the same time:

> Sullivan networked with other guitarists, coming to musical compromises, sharing equipment, and covering for them when they were double booked so that they would return the favour when the same thing happened to him. (Thompson 2008: 14)

We will discuss the record industry further in Chapter 6. What we want to stress here is that in the 1950s and 1960s, recording had a major effect on the networks in which musicians worked, even if their lives continued to be focused on live performance. Morrison notes that by 1964:

> Much of the financial well-being of an orchestra depended on recording work, but the record companies contracted conductors, not orchestras, and a conductor would usually choose to record with the orchestra of which he was principal conductor. This was the commercial reality lying behind every principal-conductor appointment in every orchestra from the heyday of the classical recording industry in the late 1950s and 1960s until its sudden startling implosion in the early 1990s. (Morrison 2004: 146)

In the pop world the effects of recording can be traced through the changing implications of the word 'artist', a term which relates not just to how musical hierarchies work but also to musicians' self-perception. John Schroeder's initial job at Columbia in 1957 was 'to assess a song's potential as a Hit song in relation to our Artists' (his capitals). Success meant matching the right song to the right artist, and, as Norrie Paramour explained:

> First and foremost you have to be positive in your belief in the material you have selected to record with the Artist in question, and ensure that the Artist is equally happy with the material. Obviously, in recording material that the Artist does not really believe in, you are not going to get his best performance. However, it is very rare indeed for an Artist to disagree with his producer, who after all is his mentor and virtually has the power to make or break the Artist's career by what he ultimately produces on record. (Schroeder 2009: 38–9)

Schroeder's use of the term 'Artist' here draws attention to the most significant change in the British popular music world in the 1950s – the rise of the pop star, usually a singer (but including pianists like Russ Conway), who came to fame on record but came to dominate the live variety circuit. The first pop stars were Americans like Johnnie Ray, but British record companies soon had their own rosters of such Artists – hence John Schroeder's job at EMI. The novelty of this sort of act is captured in a book entitled *Discland. A Panorama of the Fabulous World of the Gramophone Record*, which was published as a *Daily Mirror* annual in 1956. This is:

> the book that every disc lover will want. The book that tells the astonishing story of the world of popular music and music makers. Pat Doncaster presents a galaxy of star-studded entertainment, an international parade of the top-line personalities who have created the fabulous realm of the radiogram. (Doncaster 1956: cover blurb)

These new stars were beginning to replace both traditional variety acts and dance bands in the showbiz pantheon. *Discland* is obviously aimed at a youthful readership but does not yet celebrate youth stars or youth audiences as such – indeed, the book has an article by Jimmy Young on why 'I hate heart-throbs!' and its pictures of young women (and men) competing to grab Dickie Valentine's handkerchief make it clear that this was the part of Valentine's act (at a *Daily Mirror* Disc Festival) when he was impersonating Johnnie Ray.[15]

This was the context in which Cliff Richard (one of Norrie Paramour's Artists) became Britain's biggest pop star and in which the youth audience made its presence felt on the variety circuit. Cliff's first live booking after the success of his first single 'Move It' (its sales boosted by Cliff's appearance on the TV show *Oh Boy!*) was for a week at the Metropolitan, Edgware Road (part of the Stoll circuit). The booker (a variety agent) had never heard of Cliff Richard ('the only reason I booked him was that my twelve-year-old niece said he was very good') so put 12 other acts on the bill ('in case he didn't succeed'). After a slow opening Tuesday, the theatre was packed each night with such crowds outside wanting to get in that the police were needed. Those teenagers who did get seats were not interested in the other 12 acts on the bill.[16]

But although Cliff and, even more so, his self-contained band the Shadows marked a decisive shift in the nature of live pop music, as record company Artists they had low musical status. Paramour was adamant, for example, that the Artist should never attend a mixing session or have anything to do with decisions over how their records should finally sound. Schroeder had 'to be a bit of a psychiatrist and learn how to cleverly manipulate them [the Artists] into making them feel they were providing the musical inspiration and creative input but realistically

---

[15]   A similar book, *Your Record Stars*, published around the same time by Eldon Press, did feature Elvis Presley. He is described as the 'King Of Western Bop' (29). The *New Musical Express 1956 Annual* had numerous record company ads for their 'pop' stars, an article entitled '1955 – the year that "pop" singers came into their own' (75), advice on 'Getting the best out of your records' (46) and, among the publisher and band leader Christmas greetings, one from a disc jockey, Chappie D'Amato (20). There is no indication yet that the youth market is seen as significant.

[16]   Wilmut 1985: 218.

you were getting them to do what you wanted and had in mind' (Schroeder 2009: 46–7). When pop stars were just singers, it was easy enough for everyone in the studio, producers, engineers and session musicians alike, to discount their creative input; when rock'n'roll bands and beat groups came along, studio sessions got trickier – for Cliff and the Drifters' first recording (the name was later changed to avoid confusion with the US act), two session players were also booked (a guitarist and a bassist), to be used surreptitiously if should be necessary. And when bands began to arrive with their own songs, sessions got trickier still. Cliff was allowed to record 'Move It' (written by the Drifters' rhythm guitarist, Ian Samwell), but it was released as the B-side and was only flipped after Jack Good chose it for Cliff's appearance on *Oh Boy!* (ibid.: 47–8).

This was still the recording studio power structure when the Beatles entered the studio in 1962, as Artists for Paramour's EMI colleague, George Martin, recording manager of the Parlophone label. Martin's initial attempts to provide them with material and a session drummer are well-known elements of the Beatles story and what is apparent in their successful resistance to such producer power is that they had a different account of themselves as 'artists'. In the 1960s, a new, romanticised account of music making became familiar, an account partly drawn from art schools (a significant number of British rock musicians derived their understanding of what it meant to be a 'creative' musician from art rather than music schools),[17] partly an effect of 1950s do-it-yourself music and the emphasis on authenticity and being true to oneself, and partly an effect of the rise of a new kind of music-making unit, the band, a self-contained group of musicians with a collective rather than individual personality.

Musical Careers

Musical careers depend on musical opportunities and one way to show how such opportunities changed after the war is by a comparative case study: our examples are the percussionist James Blades and the guitarist Vic Flick.

James Blades was born in Peterborough in 1901. He left school at 14, took a job in an engineering company and became an apprentice fitter. He had sung in his school choir but was encouraged to take up drumming by his uncle (a carpenter who, as a sideline, played drums in a small band at local dances). Blades was self-taught (he used a how-to-drum book), but did take some lessons in music reading. With a pianist friend, he put an advertisement in the local press: 'the Blades-Hitchborn Duo is open for engagements at dances, weddings, garden fetes and other festive occasions' (Blades 1977: 62). Later the same year, aged 21, he got his first professional music job in a circus. When that folded, he worked in cinema orchestras (the Wisbech Hippodrome, the Jarrow Empire, the Oxford Picture Theatre in Workington, the Kinnaird Picture House in Dundee, the

---

[17]   See Frith and Horne 1987.

Hippodrome in Crouch End and the Holborn Empire) while filling up his spare time in local dance groups (Jack Dixon's Modern Dance Band and Gale's Jazz Loonies). He quit the Holborn job for stints with the Hotel Majestic Orchestra in St Anne's-on-Sea and the Claribel Band on the Isle of Man before settling in a residency in 1931 with Jerry Hoey's band in London's Piccadilly Hotel. He was soon regularly employed too in London's recording and film sound studios (working, for example, with Benjamin Britten on *Night Mail*). Once war broke out, he toured for ENSA, joined the BBC's *Music While You Work* players and began to work with the wartime LSO and the London Philharmonic:

> In fact I had reached the rung of the ladder that was to lead me to the concert hall. It was with these symphony orchestras that I gained an insight into the works of the Classical and Romantic masters. These works I grew to love, as did many thousands of others who prior to the days of concert programmes in factory canteens, Naafi camps, garrison theatres and aeroplane hangars, had never heard, or at least had never taken heed of a note of serious music. (Blades 1977: 173)

In the 1950s and 1960s, Blades worked in light, symphony and chamber orchestras, with opera companies and advertising agencies making TV jingles, as a session musician for record companies and film studios, as well as starting a new career as a writer and lecturer.

Vic Flick was born in Surrey in 1937. He took piano lessons between the ages of 5 and 12 and when he was 14 bought a Gibson acoustic guitar advertised in the local newsagent so that he had something to play in the band his father was putting together to play at local church and political functions. He taught himself guitar (using the Eddie Lang guitar tutor and listening to the family's jazz records) and fashioned his own crude amplification to make himself heard. He left school at 16 and took various jobs, ending up as a draughtsman. In 1957 he answered an ad in *Melody Maker* for a guitarist and quit his job to join a band playing nightly in the Rock and Calypso Ballroom at Butlins, Skegness. When the season ended, he got occasional gigs (accompanying a striptease show touring US bases, for example) and formed a quintet with his brother (who had played in the RAF Dance Band). The Vic Alan Quintet auditioned successfully for the Eric Winston Agency and got another Butlins gig, as the resident rock'n'roll band in Clacton. He now had a broader range of musical contacts through whom he met and joined the Bob Cort Skiffle Group, which, on the back of a couple of Top 20 hits, had been booked on the bill for Paul Anka's first European tour. Anka's backing band was the John Barry Seven and when the tour was over, in 1958, Flick was invited to join them:

> From what seemed, in retrospect, the sedate, ordered existence of my suburban life with jazz clubs, weddings and dances, I was thrown into a succession of

concerts, broadcasts, television, photographic sessions and all the necessities of
'Show Biz'. (Flick 2008: 21)

Flick stayed with the John Barry Seven until 1963. It was a hard-working band,
performing on package shows and in dance halls, backing singers like Marty
Wilde and Adam Faith, playing seaside weeks, the *NME* Poll Winners Concert
and the Royal Variety Show, but Flick also began a complementary career as a
session musician. The John Barry Seven was the resident band on the new BBC
TV teen-aimed show *Drumbeat* and provided the music for the film *Beat Girl*,
the first British soundtrack to be released on an LP. By the time he went fully
freelance, Flick was one of the most in demand guitarists for recording studio
work (alongside Big Jim Sullivan). For the next decade, he could be heard on
many of Britain's bestselling pop singles as well on the soundtrack of James Bond
and numerous other British films, with the BBC Radio Orchestra and, each week
in the early 1970s, as a member of the Harry Stoneham Quintet on the *Michael
Parkinson Show*. As a fully occupied session musician, Flick rarely played in
public now, except at sea:

> One of the perks that developed in the session musicians' working lives in the
> '60s and '70s was 'the Cruise'. Shipping lines such as P & O and Cunard would
> engage 'a celebrity group' as added entertainment for the passengers and as a
> filler for use in all entertainment areas of the ship to give the other acts a break.
> (Flick 2008: 115)

Read James Blades' and Vic Flick's autobiographies together and both the
continuities and changes in British musicians' lives in the middle decades of
the twentieth century are apparent. It is obvious, for example, that a successful
career throughout depended not just on musicians' technical skills and musicality
but also on two other abilities: keeping pace with technological developments
in their instruments and making the right music business contacts (as discussed
in the last section).

    Blades' professional reputation thus depended in part on his ability to solve
the sound problems posed to the percussionist by cinema music directors, film and
other composers and recording engineers. Flick had to keep abreast of the continual
development of electric guitar design and amplification. Both musicians also
document the significance of what Blades calls the musicians' 'bush telegraph':

> I soon learned that several of the fourteen players in the Holborn orchestra were
> well acquainted with Archer Street and the methods of picking up a Sunday
> 'gig' as these occasional engagements are known to musicians. 'Go down to
> Archer Street on Saturday afternoon and look for my friend Dave Musikant,'
> Sam Belafonti, one of the violinists, advised me. By that instinct that seems to
> go with professionalism I found Dave Musikant with whom I booked a gig for
> the following evening – a Jewish wedding at La Boheme Rooms in Mile End

– a pound for the job, and 'five bob for the gear', straight music [Gilbert and Sullivan] from 8pm to 10 pm with dance music until 1 am. (Blades 1977: 113)[18]

It was during this time that I met George Jennings, a wonderful man, who played bass and was running a jazz club in a pub in the Isleworth district of London. George was also the bassist in a successful Skiffle group run by Bob Cort. Bearded and energetic, Bob was an advertising executive by day and a skiffler by night … One night George turned up with a pile of Bob Cort records and told me to go home and learn them. Ken [Sykora, the guitarist] was leaving the group to concentrate on his career at the BBC and George had put me up for the now-vacant position. (Flick 2008: 18–19)

And both musicians depended for their livelihoods on the 'fixers' we have already mentioned. To break into film-studio employment, Blades had to audition for Gordon Walker (who fixed for Muir Matheson) at the Gaumont-British studios) and Gerry Williams (principal cellist at the LSO, who fixed for Idris Lewis at Elstree). Vic Flick describes the significance of the 1961 recording of John Barry's *Stringbeat* album, which featured Flick's electric guitar sound. Recorded with an orchestra at EMI Studio 2, Flick knew that 'all the contractors, or fixers, in the recording industry at that time were violin players – and all of them were sitting in a row a few feet in front of me!'. He was, by then, well aware of the power of the big fixers Charlie Katz, Sid Sax, Harry Benson, Sid Margo and Alec Firman over 'the greater majority of the recording, television and radio work that was going on in London and, to a less extent, in the provinces'.[19]

This is also to draw attention to how Flick's career differed from Blades'. Flick's session work was primarily in the recording studio and with the great expansion of the record industry in the 1960s, such session work became in effect a full-time job. If Blades' studio work was always less significant for his profile than his public performances, by the mid-1960s, Flick had become, as a session musician, effectively invisible. It also seems clear that while, for Blades, the classical and commercial musical worlds overlapped in the studio (film music has always been a setting in which classical musicians engaged with commerce), the pop/rock studio practices and technologies that developed in the 1960s established a new kind of occupational distance between classical and popular professionals.[20]

---

[18] Blades' career in cinemas was also certainly assisted by his early meeting with George Black, boss of the GTC circuit.

[19] Flick 2008: 52, 311, 52. Both Blades and Flick take it for granted that the serious pursuit of a musical career meant being based in London, something confirmed by PEP (PEP 1966: 59).

[20] There remained places where players of various different backgrounds did still perform together – in the orchestras for musicals and the remaining variety acts, for example.

Gordon Thompson suggests that during the 1960s there emerged two distinct but overlapping career trajectories for popular musicians: there were musicians who primarily played live and musicians who made their income from studio work:

> In the studio, musicians constituted the raw physical and artistic labour that transformed the ideas of songwriters and music directors into a sonic reality that producers and engineers could capture and process and that corporations could sell. In this context, two groups of musicians encountered each other. One crowd held the studio as their natural environment. Indeed, they spent a significant number of their waking hours each week at EMI, Decca, Olympic, Lansdowne, IBC, and the other London recording studios. The intruders, the touring musicians, arrived at the studio ready for posterity. (Thompson 2008: 252)

As the term 'posterity' suggests here, this distinction was ideological as well as pragmatic. By the end of the 1960s, session musicians' status was being challenged by musicians who wrote their own songs, took charge of their own music making in the studio and constructed a new relationship between live and recorded performance. As promoter Jef Hanlon puts it:

> Rock started writing its own script ... We got to a fork in the road where pop music and rock music became two separate things. And rock music created its new hierarchy of entrepreneurs, of power brokers, of influential people. (Hanlon 2010)

In the recording studio this meant a new kind of power struggle: musicians saw themselves rather than the producers as having the right to make the creative decisions.[21] Different players' different assessments of themselves as musicians also involved financial calculations. Session players like Flick, who stayed in the studio through the 1970s, continued to make a good living (a much better living than most musicians now pursuing rock stardom), but colleagues who, like Jimmy Page and John Paul Jones, left the studio to pursue their own creative muse could, if they were successful, become much wealthier.

Flick touches on his peculiar economic position when he discusses his contribution – the iconic guitar twang – to the James Bond Theme:

> Being directly involved with that piece of music, I was always under the impression that [Monty] Norman's writings were turned into something commercial by John Barry to which I added the guitar sound and the interpretation. Together we made the recordings successful and distinctive. Mr Norman has made many hundreds of thousands of pounds. John Barry has made millions from the spin off. I made about seven pounds ten shillings. (Flick 2008: 124)[22]

---

[21]   See Frith 2012.

[22]   John Barry got paid £250 for arranging Norman's title theme for *Dr No* and, even though the theme was used throughout the film, no extra payment, credit or royalties. His

Blades makes the same point about his equally iconic contribution to the sound of British cinema:

> If I had received a royalty for every stroke heard on my largest Chinese tam-tam (large gong) since 1935 I could have made a bonfire of my instruments years ago. But as I recorded the gong strokes that heralded the Rank Organisation films throughout the world as part of my orchestral duties – and have similarly recorded them on several subsequent occasions – I have been obliged to work for my living and keep my drumheads in good condition. (Blades 1977: 150–1)

Looking back on the 1960s, Flick clearly feels under-rewarded for his contribution to the success of recording artists who became big stars, but, at the time, many of these artists may well have made less money from their records than he did. As Thompson notes:

> recording contracts provided so little money that a band such as Herman's Hermits needed to tour because most of their income came from live performances. In the days before arenas and suitable amplification, touring meant small theatres seating at best several hundred people, rarely more. Record companies needed touring groups to sell records, and musicians needed a steady income, even if it meant sleeping in buses. (Thompson 2008: 13)

In these years popular musicians had to spend disproportionate amounts of time on the road (just as session musicians spent disproportionate amounts of time in studios). Successful acts gradually did increase the amount they received from recordings, but it would be another 20 years before suitable larger venues became available in the UK to enable the more successful touring acts to make a reasonable income without such a heavy performing schedule. And 1960s session musicians were more secure in their earnings than the new touring pop and rock acts for another reason: they were better protected by the Musicians' Union. For musicians dependent for income on the live circuit:

> agents commonly took a percentage off the top of any bookings they arranged (or even bookings they hadn't arranged), often leaving touring musicians to pay for all the expenses they incurred on the road, including housing, wardrobe, cleaning, food and transportation, from the meagre remains of what a local promoter was willing to pay. Musicians could easily have a hit record, return from a successful tour and still struggle to pay the bills. (Thompson 2008: 25)

Even after signing recording contracts, then, groups in the mid-1960s found themselves in the same situation as the semi-professionals described by the Hollies:

---

arrangement had such an impact, though, that he had a highly lucrative career as the scorer for subsequent Bond films (Fiegel 1998: 97–8).

> If you belong to a newly-formed group, you will probably be grateful for any gigs to play, and at this stage you can only expect a nominal fee. It is doubtful whether this amount will even cover your group expenses – hire purchase on instruments and equipment, travelling costs, etc – and you will probably have to subsidise the group with your own earnings. Playing in a beat group is nowadays an expensive business, even if it is only a hobby. (The Hollies 1964: 37)

In the recording studio, by contrast, recording sessions 'were regulated by an agreement between the record companies and the Musicians' Union, which set payment rates for three-hour sessions with extra fees if a musician played more than one instrument' (Thompson 2008: 253). This is not to say that session musicians always felt that their interests were being well represented. In Vic Flick's view, 'I ought to have made considerably more than I did if the Musicians' Union had had their act together back in the 1960s' (Flick 2008: 124). Just what the Musicians' Union was doing in this period will be the subject of the rest of this chapter.

The Musicians' Union

As noted in Chapter 1, the origins of the Musicians' Union lie in the formation of the Amalgamated Musicians' Union (AMU) in 1893 by Joseph Williams, a clarinettist in the band at the Comedy Theatre, Manchester, who persuaded musicians from Birmingham, Dundee, Glasgow and Liverpool to join him in this single organisation, a response to the emerging oligopolistic ownership of the music hall and variety circuit. The AMU was immediately involved in 'a series of bitter recognition disputes' and a sense of perpetual struggle was to characterise future years.[23] In 1921 the AMU, whose power base remained in the North of England, merged with the London Orchestral Union of Professional Musicians to form the Musicians' Union. The London Orchestral Union had also been founded in 1893 (as the London Orchestral Association) by Fred Orcherton, a flautist in the Queen's Hall Orchestra. As Annette Davison points out, the two organisations differed not only in their geographical reach but also in terms of their ideology:

> The AMU was established as a trade union, accepting everyone, including 'second jobbers', female musicians and amateurs; anyone who drew an income from performing music. By contrast the LOA was established as a society for the very best 'professionals' and expressed disgust at the notion of music as a 'trade'. It admitted neither women nor part-time musicians. (Davison 2013)

By 1921, the AMU had four times as many members as the London Orchestral Union and was dominant in the new amalgamated entity, but the ideological difference between the two groups of musicians remained significant as the source

---

[23]   Jempson 1993: 7.

of continuing internal policy disagreements. As an editorial in the *Musicians'
Journal* put it in 1924:

> Musicians occupy a place in society which falls partly on one and partly on the
> other side of the line dividing the proletariat from the liberal professions; and
> they offer an example of the difficulty of drawing a sharp distinction between
> intellectual and manual workers. (Quoted in Davison 2013)

What the two organisations' members did have in common (the reason for the
merger) was the need to protect their market interests. We have already described
some of the problems involved here. On the one hand, the new union had to
develop a collective approach to an occupation in which many musicians worked
as freelancers and had a strong sense of their individual market value; on the
other hand, it had to try to enforce some kind of closed shop (so as to prevent
competition for work driving fees downwards) in a workplace in which all sorts of
part-time performers were available. In its efforts to establish itself as an effective
labour organisation in the 1920s and 1930s, the Musicians' Union developed
two strategies for improving its members' bargaining position that were to have
significant effects on British music culture in the 1950s and 1960s.

First, the Musicians' Union came to understand that collective bargaining is
only practically effective in dealing with what one might call collective employers
– organisations employing large numbers of musicians on a regular basis such that
disruption or withdrawal of labour can have immediate economic effect.[24] From early
on, then, the Musicians' Union sought to negotiate national terms and conditions
with large employers of musical labour – music hall, theatre and cinema chains,
the BBC, orchestras and opera companies. This was only patchily successful in the
1930s and 1940s (the Musicians' Union could do nothing about the single biggest
crisis for its members – their replacement by recorded sound in cinemas) and there
is no doubt that in terms of collective bargaining, the Musicians' Union was most
effective in the consensual, corporatist politics of the immediate post-war era. It did
then establish what were, to all intents and purposes, closed shops in the BBC and in
Arts Council-funded music companies, as well as in the commercial music sector, in
recording and film studios, West End theatres and the dance hall and variety circuits
that were still dominated by a small number of large entertainment corporations. As
Benjamin Wolf notes, the Musicians' Union (and other theatrical unions):

> benefited from the institutional system of post-war Britain. Firstly, competition
> between orchestras for players meant that pay rises extracted from one institution

---

[24] 'The unions have tremendous bargaining power because they can bring a
performance to its knees – orchestra not playing, stage hands not working' (Claude Moser,
who joined the Board of the Royal Opera in 1964). Moser goes on to note that musician
strikes – which closed the Opera House for weeks at a time in the 1970s – are 'devastating
on your finances and devastating on the public image' (quoted in Wolf 2010: 196).

could be exploited to exact similar pay rises elsewhere – a practice that was referred to as 'leapfrogging' ... Secondly, union demands received legal support from industrial tribunals ... Thirdly, the unions benefited from the existence of the Arts Council, for wage increases could only be paid from tax increases. (Wolf 2010: 197)

In the post-war period (really until the 1970s), Musicians' Union arguments for pay rises in terms of 'musical quality, technical skill and social equity' appealed more to the Arts Council (and, it seems, industrial tribunals) than orchestra or opera house managers' arguments that they could not afford them and as, in the end, it was the Arts Council that footed the bill, the Musicians' Union usually found itself in a strong position. As John Tooley, general administrator of the Royal Opera House, complained to the Arts Council in 1971:

Unfortunately, to date, the unions have found that with this and other state-subsidised organisations pressure has always achieved something extra for them, and the talk of closure has never been turned into reality. (Quoted in Wolf 2010: 197)

The Musicians' Union's second strategy for improving is members' market power involved trying to prevent competition for their services. Such competition could take two forms: technology (and, in particular, recordings – we discuss this in more detail below) and other (non-union) musicians. We have already discussed the problem of amateurs (the other bane of professional musicians' lives in the early days of the Musicians' Union, military bands, were less significant in public entertainment after the Second World War). We turn now to the threat of foreign or, in Musicians' Union terms, 'alien' musicians and the so-called Musicians' Union 'ban' on visiting American instrumentalists that we outlined in Chapter 1.

The Musicians' Union's official history records that, from the start, Joe Williams 'sought to reduce competition, particularly from European musicians who had almost unrestricted access to work in Britain'; in 1901 it petitioned King Edward VII to prevent 'the wholescale importation of foreign bands'.[25] The Musicians' Union was never, then, simply concerned about American musicians – even in 1947, there were press reports of Musicians' Union members demonstrating outside Covent Garden in protest at the Vienna Philharmonic Orchestra being employed in place of the usual pit band to accompany the Vienna State Opera.[26] And British musicians' anxiety about foreign competition was never confined simply to members of the Musicians' Union. Simon McVeigh suggests that arguments about national musical culture can be traced back to the 1830s if not earlier (the Society of British Musicians was formed in 1834). On the whole, the ideology of free trade was sufficiently dominant in the nineteenth century that 'musicians from

---

[25]   Jempson 1993: 8.
[26]   Lebrecht 2000: 99.

the continent – and, latterly, from America and the Empire – were both permitted and encouraged to play a full part in London's musical environment'. The city continued 'to be a thriving metropolis of European musical culture throughout the nineteenth century, supplying a musical public hungry for the best, as well as the newest, that Europe could offer' (McVeigh 2007: 7, 10).

By the end of the nineteenth century, British classical musical culture was rooted in an international economy and successful musicians assumed that any cross-border trade in music was good for both their own careers and for the general health of the British musical economy. Such arguments were not completely foreign to the Musicians' Union. In 1945 a delegate conference resolution suggested:

> That this conference, envisaging the tremendous rebirth of musical activity in liberated countries and throughout the world in the post-war period, instructs the EC to establish at every possible opportunity fraternal relations with musical trade unions and associations in different countries; and further supports the reciprocal interchange of orchestras, dance bands, and music of the various countries. (Delegate Conference Resolution, April 1945)

And in 1950 the Executive Committee considered a resolution suggesting that public interest in dance music would be fostered by visits from American bands.[27]

Such internationalism can, though, be contrasted with a kind of musical nationalism that has also been an aspect of British musical life since at least the First World War. In 1914, *Musical News* reported on a meeting of 100 London musicians (presided over by the pianist and composer Sir Frederic Cowen) convened to consider the effects of the outbreak of the war on their employment. The assembly agreed that 'aliens' should cease to be employed in theatres, music halls, touring opera companies or restaurants as instrumentalists, conductors or choristers. The war, the *Musical News* suggested:

> has suddenly brought to a head the long-smouldering resentment against foreign dominance in British musical circles ... [now is] the chance for the native to assert his proper pre-dominance in the land of his birth ... After having their employment prejudicially affected for years past by Germans and Austrians, [orchestral musicians] may be excused if they fail to see how the substitution of French and Belgians is likely to benefit their condition. (Quoted in Fifield 2005: 97)

Such resentment reappeared in the 1930s. Following a call to arms in the *Daily Telegraph* (in an article entitled 'Protection for the British Musician', the paper proclaimed 'the need for drastic action, plain thinking, plain speaking

---

[27]   The EC rejected this proposal, at least in part, because of its irritation that British musicians were still being prevented by the American Federation of Musicians from performing in the USA (Minutes of Executive Committee Meeting, 18–21 July 1950).

and abnormal remedies in these abnormal times'), the Incorporated Society of Musicians published a protectionist manifesto[28] and began a correspondence with the Ministry of Labour (which intensified when an increasing influx of German musicians followed Hitler's rise to power).[29] The Incorporated Society of Musicians continued to campaign for the employment of British musicians throughout the decade – in 1937, for example, John Christie was censured by the Society for not employing enough British musicians at Glyndebourne – and it was equally tireless in lobbying the BBC Music Advisory Committee to put pressure on the BBC to give preference to British composers and performers.[30] Music agent Terry Slasberg describes her task when she went to work for Joan Ingpen in the late 1940s and had to deal with the administrative problems of bringing in foreign artists:

> A labour permit had to be procured – another lengthy operation until we got friendly with the appropriate clerks. The Ministry of Labour, as it was then called, was a stern critic, not allowing just any performer in simply because they were from a foreign opera house. Fortunately they learned that we dealt only in the very best of circles and that, in fact, there were no singers resident in this country capable of the standard required by Covent Garden, especially in the Wagner season. (Slasberg 1993: 7–8)

The Musicians' Union's concern to protect British musicians from foreign competition had its roots, then, in a long history of both well-founded employment anxiety and less well-founded musical nationalism (the least convincing aspect of both the Musicians' Union's and the Incorporated Society of Musicians' arguments about foreign musicians was that British musicians were as good as if not superior to the musicians they were seeking to keep out),[31] but it became significant for the development of popular music in the context of the post-war popularity of American music and musicians.

The Ministry of Labour, while not always convinced by the Union's argument that a UK musician could simply replace the likes of, say, Louis Armstrong or Charlie Parker, was concerned about unfair competition:

---

[28]   Not all its members supported this stance. Myra Hess and Donald Francis Tovey, among others, resigned from the organisation.

[29]   Fifield shows both how Ibbs and Tillett fought such protectionism by gathering evidence from its clients of the benefits of foreign players and how the American Musicians' Guild tried to pursue a similar protectionist policy in the USA. Many members of both the Guild and the Incorporated Society of Musicians found it difficult to reconcile such policies with the realities of international careers (see Fifield 2005: 216–26, 559–60).

[30]   Hughes 1981: 117; Wolf 2010: 74.

[31]   Many jazz historians have pointed out one consequence of this argument: 'denial of the cultural uniqueness of Afro-American music became a central plank of Musicians' Union policy' (Rye 1990: 52).

A Press Communiqué was issued on 29 March 1935, stating that: 'the Minister does not feel able to grant permits freely to American bands to take engagements of the Variety Hall type. He will, however, be glad to revert to his former policy as soon as he can be assured that no less favourable treatment will be accorded to British Bands seeking engagements in the USA'. (Parsonage 2005: 255)

It was at this point that the Musicians' Union secured Ministry agreement that it would be consulted over all permit applications for foreign musicians to work in the UK. In the majority of instances it expressed opposition, but by the end of the 1940s, reciprocity (rather than a straight ban on foreign performers) does seem to have been the issue that most vexed Musicians' Union members and officials. Harry Francis squarely blames the AFM for preventing jazz musicians from performing in Britain (through its refusal to allow British musicians to perform in the USA) and conference reports suggest that delegates shared this view. In 1951, for example, the South West District called for meetings with the *Fédération Internationale des Musiciens* (FIM) and the AFM 'to discuss the possibilities of bringing to an end the present restrictions placed on musicians who require to travel internationally in furtherance of their professional activities'.[32]

By then, reciprocal exchanges with countries other than the USA were, in fact, being negotiated.[33] It was the lack of a reciprocal agreement with the AFM that was the problem. This is customarily described by jazz and blues historians as the Musicians' Union 'ban' on US musicians[34] and there is some confusion about when the ban ended. According to Oliver, the bad publicity following the 1950 prosecutions of the promoters who put on Sidney Bechet caused the Musicians' Union to change its policy and, eventually, in 1956, to lift the ban altogether. Fordham claims the ban ended in 1958; McKay writes that the ban 'finally collapsed in 1955'; Schwartz suggests although that the union's 'protectionist stance' lasted well in to the 1960s, its 'ban against American jazz artists was finally rescinded' in 1957.[35]

Our research suggests that 1955 does indeed see the *de facto* ending of the 'ban', as inter-union agreements were then reached that allowed US/UK reciprocal exchanges to be put into place, with the first taking place in 1956: Stan Kenton played at the Royal Albert Hall on 11 March and the Ted Heath Orchestra played San Antonio Municipal Auditorium on 1 April. The second, in May 1956, had Louis Armstrong's band coming to the UK and Don Rendell's band travelling in the opposite direction. The third involved Sidney Bechet and a French band,

[32] Francis nd.

[33] *Melody Maker* reported such agreements with both France (8 January 1949: 3) and the Netherlands (21 January 1950: 1).

[34] See, for example, Fordham 1995: 20; Godbolt 1984: 28; and Oliver 1990: 14.

[35] Fordham 1995: 83; McKay 2005: 30; Schwartz 2007: 8, 30, 46, 75–6.

which necessitated reciprocal visits to both France (Chris Barber's band) and the USA (Tommy Whittle).[36]

The ending of the 'ban' did not mean an end to all restrictions on the flow of musical labour. What was at issue was exchange rather than a free for all and, for promoters, exchanges were organised around 'man days': the number of performances by UK and US musicians in each other's countries had to be equal over a year; a 'man day' was the unit of measurement (a big band coming to Britain therefore had to be matched by the right number of small combos going to the USA). This system actually lasted into the 1980s and involved agents and promoters in each country effectively trading 'man days' across jurisdictions.[37]

The Musicians' Union's policy on foreign musicians is often described as anti-American or even anti-African-American, but this is misleading.[38] The ban was focused on the USA in part because of the protectionist intransigence of the AFM and in part because of American music's particular mass appeal. This was something that was of concern to other sectors of the British music industry in the 1950s. The Songwriters Guild, for example, campaigned, like the Incorporated Society of Musicians before it, for the BBC to play more British music. As the Communist Party of Great Britain explained in its 1952 tract, *The American Threat to British Culture*:

> The plight of British songwriters is so desperate that the Song Writers Guild of Great Britain have made a formal protest to the BBC against the anti-British attitude of so many performers and dance bands. Out of twenty of the most popular current songs, seventeen are American, one is French and two are British ... British singers repeat the identical US settings parrot-wise. British crooners ape the American in slurred vowels and forced inflexions. Sometimes I wonder if I'm tuned into the BBC at all. (Cited in Lee 2002: 47)

Everything changed following the international success of the Beatles and other British beat groups in the mid-1960s. In 1965, at the height of the 'British Invasion' of the USA, Musicians' Union discussions with the AFM about reciprocal exchanges continued, but it was now UK bands who were in demand in the USA. The Musicians' Union noted with satisfaction that British musicians were receiving better pay deals from American promoters and that 'although exchanges

---

[36]   The promoter involved in these exchanges was Harold Davison. We will discuss his role further in Chapter 7.

[37]   The system was not absolute. In the mid-1960s, both Ronnie Scott's club in London and Manchester's Club 43 were given a limited exemption by the Musicians' Union (and the Ministry of Labour) from the need for reciprocal agreements. They were allowed to employ some foreign nationals without exchanging man days.

[38]   There is some evidence that its account of 'aliens' included racist assumptions (see Cloonan and Brennan 2013), but these were not what drove Musicians' Union policy.

formerly involved jazz musicians, nearly all those groups now visiting the U.S.A. from Britain constitute "beat" or "pop" groups' (EC Report to 1965 Conference: 76). By 1967, it seems that the reciprocal exchange scheme was at last working to the Musicians' Union's satisfaction (though not, perhaps, to the satisfaction of the promoters who had to apply it).

We turn finally to the Musicians' Union's response to the most serious threat to its members' livelihood in the post-war period: recording. The Musicians' Union's first battle with recording technology was decisively lost. Almost overnight, it seemed, cinemas (the biggest employers of musicians in the 1910s and 1920s) replaced their pit bands and organists with sound tracks recorded in film studios (which were to prove an excellent source of income but for a much smaller number of musicians). A parallel struggle was focused on radio and the fear that broadcasters would replace live broadcast studio sessions with record shows.

In this struggle, the Musicians' Union had advantages it had not had in dealing with film exhibitors. Not only was the BBC Britain's only legal broadcaster, but it also had its own commitment to the live (under Lord Reith, the BBC did not regard record based shows as a proper use of radio's unique qualities).[39] Furthermore, Phonographic Performance Ltd (PPL) was not in its early days convinced that radio's continuous use of records as entertainment would boost rather than reduce sales.[40] As Stephen Barnard notes, however, although the BBC/PPL/MU needle-time agreement (in 1935) was:

> forged at a time when records were not of any great importance to British broadcasting, it set a precedent that ensured that any wider usage of records in later years was both expensive and subject to a degree of outside control. (Barnard 1989: 27)

By the late 1950s, the BBC had 21 hours a week needle time for all its radio output, which was increased to 47 hours in 1964.[41] Even as the record industry became dominant in popular music culture, the BBC continued to see its broadcasting role as the provision of live music (most of its pop programmes continued to feature resident studio musicians). This was the context in which American-funded and American-formatted commercial record-playing pirate radio stations offered a

---

[39] See Crissell 2012.

[40] PPL was set up by EMI, Decca and other record companies in 1934 to manage the licence fee income from the performance of records in public places following a court case brought by the record industry against a coffee shop in Bristol: the coffee shop entertained customers by playing records and the industry argued successfully that playing records in public without the permission of the copyright owners (the record companies concerned) was an offence under copyright law (in the same way as performing songs in public without a licence from the PRS).

[41] Chapman 1992: 23; Smith 1968: 773.

completely different (and immediately exciting) account of music radio (an account strongly opposed by the Musicians' Union). Radio 1, established by the BBC in September 1967 to meet the pop radio demand revealed by the now-banned pirate stations, was still subject to needle-time agreements, still mixed records and live performances, but now sought to do this seamlessly – live performances were now supposed to sound exactly like the records.

The influence of the Musicians' Union on the BBC's use of recorded music could be seen too on television. *Top of The Pops* (which was first transmitted on 1 January 1964) was a programme organised around the week's record sales charts. Featured musicians were required to make new recordings for the show (to sound like the original) to which they then mimed their performance (usually only the singer actually performed live). Miming to recordings was not a new phenomenon (lip syncing was used in US music TV programmes like *Your Hit Parade!* and *American Bandstand*); what was odd about the BBC's policy was the requirement that bands make new, programme-specific recordings of their hits, something that became increasingly problematic as record production became more sophisticated. As Jef Hanlon remembers:

> The MU was just a pain in the arse, because they wouldn't let you play, you know they wouldn't let you send a backing track in, you had to re-record your record and it was getting to the point in the recording industry where there was so much overdubbing and multi-tracking and all that where you had a three piece band but there could be 20 different tracks of different instruments, possibly played by people in the 3 piece band but often overdubbed and overdubbed. And to recreate the sound live was very difficult, especially to do live on television. So you wanted backing tracks. (Hanlon 2010)

These changes in recording technology also affected the Musicians' Union's ability to maintain a closed shop in the recording studios themselves. London dominated the UK recording world until well into the 1960s and the comparatively small number of studios (and studio owners) meant that the Musicians' Union's negotiating and monitoring task was relatively straightforward. This changed in the latter half of the 1960s as new, smaller studios appeared. In Thompson's words:

> As independent studios opened and studio time became cheaper and more readily available, the efficient reading and recording skills of a session musician became less valuable to some producers than the spontaneously created accidents of a disposable neophyte. In turn, producers, engineers and directors survived only as long as they could adapt to changes in technology and musical tastes. (Thompson 2008: 16)

In the new technological settings, even unionised musicians began to ignore Musicians' Union stipulations against such things as vocal overdubs.[42]

Conclusion

Most accounts of popular music in Britain are written from a rock perspective, in which it is assumed that the exciting new British sounds that were to emerge in the mid-1960s had been held back from development by a reactionary musical establishment in the 1950s. In these accounts, the BBC and the Musicians' Union are seen as being particularly reactionary and particularly restrictive on musicians' working lives.[43] But this is a rather skewed way of writing history in terms of what might have been instead of what was. The interesting issue is not what British popular music would have sounded like if there had been from 1945 a free international trade in musicians and no needle-time agreements, but how Musicians' Union and BBC policies contributed to the ways in which British pop did develop. Roberts suggests that had the Musicians' Union and the AFM not reached agreement about reciprocity, the 'British invasion' of the USA in the 1960s would not have happened and the history of popular music would have been very different.[44] But it could also be argued that if there had been no restrictions on visiting American musicians in the 1950s, there wouldn't have been a British invasion either – groups like the Beatles simply would not have existed. Gordon Thompson reflects that:

> musically, postwar nationalism worked to London's advantage with British audiences commonly preferring homegrown versions to American originals. The British pop music industry actively sought American disks for indigenous artists to imitate, copying the original arrangements and interpretive tricks. Moreover, British artists could tour the United Kingdom to promote their versions, while the British Musicians' Union successfully blocked visits by many American performers. European promoters found British rockers cheaper to hire, both because they were closer and because they would work for less money than Americans (perhaps one reason that Bruno Koschmider hired the Beatles for his Hamburg club). (Thompson 2008: 5)

From our perspective what is most striking about the uniquely British conditions of popular musical production in the 1950s and 1960s was the emphasis, even as the record industry became ever more influential, on live performance. The non-

---

[42] Records also threatened musicians on the dance floor, but we will postpone discussion of this issue until Chapter 6.

[43] Even the best recent accounts of musicians in this period, Frame (2007) and Thompson (2008), share this tendency.

[44] Roberts 2010.

availability of (American) records on radio and (American) instrumentalists on stage may have restricted consumers' musical choices, but it certainly gave British musicians opportunities not only to play live but also to develop an account of the significance of live performance that was to become essential to the ideology of late 1960s rock music. And if the British musical establishment was neither particularly supportive nor appreciative of the new musical forms coming across the Atlantic after the Second World War, then this was just an added spur to the do-it-yourself music culture that we will discuss in the next chapter.

Chapter 4

Do-it-Yourself!

Very seldom was there any complaint that our folk revival was part of a Communist plot, despite the strong political convictions of many of the prominent singers. We had three years of real excitement and inspiration with skiffle music. And when in due course the craze was superseded, the washboards returned to the cupboard under the sink and the tea-chests to the dump, those of us who had started it at least felt the satisfaction of having changed the face of British popular music. (John Hasted, quoted in McDevitt 1997: 133)

Do you know, skiffle did more than all the Royal Festival Hall classical concerts put together, to get young people interested in music. (Tony Meehan writing in The Shadows 1961: 21)

Introduction

In his 1958 book *Skiffle. The Story of Folk Song with a Jazz Beat*, the Reverend Brian Bird writes:

Today our young people are singing again, and making their own music, with confidence and evident enjoyment. Music which during the gloomy decades of the past century had come to be looked upon as an occupation for hack performers only, or as a 'cissy' extra to be learned at school by a few abnormal individuals, has now become again a national pastime … It is now not thought unworthy that a young man should strum a guitar and sing about the attractions of a girl friend any more than in the days of medieval Italy a Romeo should serenade his Juliet on a balcony. We are rapidly shedding many of our former inhibitions and prejudices about music, and whereas in the past a young man sang only in his bath, he now does it openly on every occasion when he foregathers with his friends – in pubs and clubs, coffee-bars and dance-halls, and over the radio and television network. The Englishman has become a gayer, livelier person thereby. (Bird 1958: 56–7)

As an example of this new generation of young working-class men who took up singing in the 1950s, we will begin this chapter with a brief discussion of the career of Reg Smith. Smith was born in 1939, the son of a professional soldier. He left Chorlton Central Secondary Modern School, aged 15, in 1954, without any qualifications and became a messenger boy for a firm of brokers in Eastcheap.

Smith had taught himself to play the ukulele and now turned to the guitar; after hearing early Elvis Presley records, he and some local friends formed a rock'n'roll band, Reg Smith and the Hound Dogs. The band began to get pub and coffee-bar gigs but kept their day jobs before being approached by a music publisher, Joe Brunnely, who got Reg two weeks as a solo artist (under the name of Reg Patterson, after the boxer Floyd Patterson) in a couple of West End clubs, the Blue Angel and the Condor Club in Soho, for £1 a night and a bowl of spaghetti. He was seen one night by the impresario/manager Larry Parnes. Parnes changed Smith/Patterson's name to Marty Wilde, put together a backing band for him, the Wildcats (led by 17-year-old Big Jim Sullivan on guitar, who recruited Brian Bennett, the 17-year-old resident drummer at the 2i's coffee bar in Soho, 18-year-old Brian 'Licorice' Locking on bass and the slightly older Tony Belcher on rhythm guitar), and negotiated a record deal with Philips and regular slots on the new youth-aimed TV shows *Six-Five Special*, *Oh Boy!* and *Boy Meets Girls*. Wilde became one of the UK's more successful teenage stars, with a series of cover versions of US hits. In 1961 he starred in the first West End production of the musical *Bye Bye Birdie*.[1]

In many respects Wilde's story is typical of late 1950s British pop music: a performer with no musical training or education; his act (including his name and stage persona) put together by commercial operators; studio technology, TV promotion and Wilde's pin-up looks as well as a supply of successful US songs used to cement his emotional identity with his teenage listeners and viewers. For many people at the time, performers like Wilde were seen as essentially a manufactured gimmick. They seemed to have no craft skills of their own and their appeal, like that of rock'n'roll generally, could be dismissed as a transitory teenage fad. This, for example, is Brian Matthew, writing in 1962:

> When the 'experts' announced that rock was dead a lot of us yelled that they were wrong. But in a sense, you know, they were half right. That's to say the immense popularity of the simplest thump and crash form of beat music was on the wane, mammoth package shows with 'star-studded' bills of nonentities with one howling hooligan following another, bawling indecipherable lyrics to indistinguishable tunes, no longer had the mesmeric effect they had had, as more than one 'get-rich-quick' promoter found to his cost ... I sincerely believe that audiences who had grown wild with excitement on the first acquaintance with this music gradually grew immune to its effect. They began to see through the inadequacy of many of the performers who had never really bothered to learn their trade. They began to realize that talent was not after all just an old-fashioned expression for something that wasn't really necessary. (Matthew 1962: 7–8)

Matthew presented the BBC radio shows *Saturday Club* and *Easy Beat*, which from one perspective can be seen as the attempted incorporation of new young

---

[1]   Biographical details from http://www.martywilde.com [accessed 12 September 2012] and Frame 2007: 271–3.

pop performers into the world of professional light entertainment.[2] We can see the same process at work in the (anonymous) sleeve notes for *The Warmth of Wynter*, Mark Wynter's debut album for Decca Records in 1961:

> In the world of entertainment 1960 saw the introduction of a new phase in the tastes of the British record buying public. For too long the tight-jeaned, loose-limbed 'rock idols', with their inarticulate presentation and over-amplified guitars, had dominated the pop scene. So, with the strident strains of rock gradually receding it was evident that the public was eager to welcome a teenage performer capable of interpreting lyrics with style and audibility.[3]

Loose-limbed, tight-jeaned 'rock idols' would, of course, make a comeback and express their own views of performers like Marty Wilde. In Michael Braun's account of the Beatles' 1963 British tour, *Love Me Do*, Paul McCartney reflects on the group's career:

> People keep asking us whether we're going to broaden our scope. I don't know whether we will or not. One of the things about us is that we intrigue people. We seem a little bit different. If you read about Cliff Richard you know the things that he says; you've read about them before. But us ... I remember thinking, about two years ago, 'What have the people who have made it – I mean really made it – got?' It seems it's an awareness of what's going on. I mean, I can imagine Sinatra to be, you know, not thick. I also thought, 'What about the people who made it and then just sort of went?' I mean, look at Marty Wilde. I remember seeing him and being very impressed. Then when he started falling off I wondered what happened? Then we met him; and then we understood. (Braun 1964: 32)

In retrospect, this kind of condescension seems a little premature. Marty Wilde is, at the time of writing, still going strong as part of a successful family music business (run by his wife, Joyce, once a member of the Vernons Girls), fronting a touring band featuring his children, Rikki and Roxy (his older daughter, Kim, having moved on from her own successful pop career to an equally successful career as a gardener).[4] What interests us, however, is not an assessment of what

---

[2] In 1961 Matthew had produced the album *It's All Happening Here* for Oriole Records, featuring the *Saturday Club* and *Easy Beat* resident studio performers (Maureen Evans and Clinton Ford, for example). This album makes no musical reference to what Matthew calls 'rock'.

[3] The sleeve note writer also comments that Wynter 'is one of the few young people in his field who can both read and write music'.

[4] Marty Wilde's touring schedule today takes in many of the same seaside venues that he played 50 years ago. Mark Wynter, meanwhile, is now an actor, specialising in touring productions of Agatha Christie plays.

Marty Wilde had or had not 'got', but the way his career brings into focus the changes in British popular music culture between 1955 and 1965.

There are two questions here. On the one hand, how can we account for the rise of a new sort of do-it-yourself music making in the 1950s? What gave young men like Marty Wilde the ambition and the confidence to become a performing musician in the first place? As Dick Bradley has noted:

> The take-up of rock in Britain established music-making, rather than just music-listening, as an important, respected, even central practice in the lives of huge numbers of (mainly male) youth culture members. Amateurism took root everywhere, among those hitherto most unlikely amateurs of all, working class boys. (Bradley 1992: 75)

On the other hand, given what happened to the first generation of these musicians, exemplified by Tommy Steele, Cliff Richard and Marty Wilde, who found their place easily enough in the established world of entertainment, how can we account for the emergence in the 1960s of a different kind of musical career, a different kind of musical self-consciousness, exemplified by the Beatles?

Do-it-Yourself Ambitions

Amateur musicians, as we discussed in Chapter 3, have long played an important role in Britain's musical economy, but the do-it-yourself music making that emerged first with revivalist jazz and then with rock'n'roll and skiffle in the 1950s was a new kind of amateurism.[5] The Wildcats, for example, had a quite different sense of what it meant to make music for themselves than, say, the members of a brass band or amateur operatic society. John Lowerson quotes a writer in *Amateur Stage*:

> Everything should be done to show teenagers what grand fun a sing-song can be and how much better it is to get around someone's piano and join in the choruses than sit in a darkened room watching TV. (Lowerson 2005: 21)

For the young men who wanted to sing after hearing Elvis Presley or to play guitar after seeing Lonnie Donegan, music making wasn't a hobby, however, and performance wasn't expected to be confined to family gatherings.[6] Nor,

---

[5]   The terms 'do-it-yourself' and 'DIY' do not seem to have been used before the 1950s. They were popularised in Britain by *Barry Bucknell's Do It Yourself*, a BBC TV programme about home improvement that was very successful in the late 1950s. It was, it seems, particularly valued by women, who were unlikely to have been taught the relevant skills at school.

[6]   Bruce Welch: 'We were quite intent on making something with that group [The Railroaders, Welch's school band]. It wasn't just skiffle to us; it was even something more

more significantly, were the new musical dreams shaped by grown-ups. This was most obvious at school. Schools were where many rock'n'roll and skiffle bands were first formed; schools provided the bands' first performing opportunities – in assemblies, school dances and summer fetes. But most school music teachers (even if the curriculum involved a nod to English folk song) wanted nothing to do with these sounds. Jen Wilson, who was at Swansea Secondary Technical School for Girls from 1955 to 1960, remembers:

> I dabbled in acoustic guitar and could perform Lonnie Donegan numbers quite adequately. With Christmas 1959 approaching and my class anxious to participate in the school concert, I suggested a skiffle group ... Surprisingly two or three of the girls said that they had guitars at home (I never knew) but couldn't play them. By the end of the week, three of us were managing to co-ordinate three chords and somebody had made a tea-chest bass. All the class sang 'Rock Island Line' to our accompaniment. Our efforts caused great excitement in the class and the girls would bop or hand jive ... I remember the teachers being exceedingly disapproving and angry as skiffle was not in the academic mission statement of the school. We did not manage the Christmas concert. (Dewe 1998: 54)[7]

And as late as 1967, a textbook for music teachers was warning them that:

> The 'pop' disease is so widespread these days that no child seems to escape it ... To show disgust at the sounds of these records (and they are undeniably disgusting) will achieve little. Better to keep a calm face and insist on your pound of flesh. It is, after all, a music period and not Housewives' Choice ... One good defence is to say to the pupil who asks for pop: 'What has it to do with a music lesson? Do you ask your English teacher for Superman comics? Do you expect to play marbles in P.E. Lessons?' (Terence Dwyer's *Teaching Musical Appreciation*, quoted in Vulliamy and Lee: 1976: 58)

Do-it-yourself music meant, then, DIY ways of music learning. Brian Bennett describes his experience as a Wildcat when the band was employed as Eddie Cochran's backing band on his 1959 British tour:

---

than a hobby. We wanted to prove that we could do things. Maybe make the big time' (The Shadows 1961: 41).

[7]   Dewe has 'Skiffle Reminiscences' scattered through his book. This is the only one by a woman and it seems clear that in this period do-it-yourself music was primarily a male activity. As Jen Wilson notes, in teenage girl music culture 'listening to records on the Dansette, doo-wop a capella, jiving to hand claps and handjiving was the norm. Elvis and [the] Everly Brothers were lovingly practised for public consumption in the toilet block'. Dave Allen notes that one of the few successful female groups in Portsmouth in the late 1950s, the Honeys, began as the Liddell Sisters, miming in costume on stage to current hit records (Allen 2011).

We travelled on British Rail for the majority of the tour 3rd class. During that time we formed the BRSM (British Rail School of Music). As we were not driving the dreaded Dormobile we had time to study music and practice.[8]

These days Brian Bennett is a successful arranger, producer and composer of music for film and television, and, from a historical perspective, what is being described here is not amateur music making but a new way of becoming a professional. In his online memoirs, another Wildcat, Big Jim Sullivan, notes that:

It was the early days of Rock'n'Roll in this country. We were still struggling to learn music, it might be Country, Jazz, Classical, Blues or even Rock'n'Roll. None of us younger musicians wasted too much time doing teenage things.[9]

To become professionals, these musicians had to move on from making music with friends with shared enthusiasm to making music with people they might not know but who had the requisite skill and commitment. In his 1958 autobiography, Cliff Richard describes a moment shared by many subsequent rock bands:

And then came the sad decision. We were getting more professional and my close friend and the group's drummer, Terry Smart, wasn't quite up to it … It was Jet [Harris, bassist] who found young Tony Meehan for us. He called him a cocky little bloke and he was. But Tony had something to be cocky about. He was only sixteen but he'd been playing drums since he was seven. As with all the boys. I asked Norrie [Paramour] to hear him and Norrie said he was terrific and now the Drifters were formed. We'd got the chance and we were building the sound and the act. (Richard 1960: 71)

Cliff was becoming professional under the mentorship of a record company A&R man, whose judgement therefore mattered. George Martin, Paramour's EMI colleague, seems to have played a similar role in the Beatles' decision to replace drummer Pete Best with Ringo Starr as they began to record four years later, but, in general, what was really crucial in this musical world was peer recognition: this generation of musicians came to define themselves as musicians largely by reference to each other (this was the basis of the reputations of both Meehan and Starr). And a further point to make here is that musical peers on the do-it-yourself scene were not necessarily defined by age or musical genre. Local musical networks linked jazz, rock'n'roll, folk and skiffle performers (these terms, as we will discuss in the next section, were not as clear-cut then as they are now) and in the 1950s in particular, National Service meant that many 'young' bands included older members (such as Tony Belcher in the Wildcats and Ian Samwell in Cliff

---

[8]   http://www.brianbennettmusic.co.uk/drummer.php [accessed 12 September 2012].
[9]   http://bigjimsullivan.com/History.html [accessed 12 September 2012].

Richard's Drifters) who had benefited from the musical resources, friendships and playing opportunities that service life could provide.[10]

Older musicians presented another problem along the route to a professional career: commitment. Allan Williams' account of the Beatles' early years reveals both how long the group was prepared to carry the non-musical but committed friend Stuart Sutcliffe and how desperate was their search at various times for a drummer willing to give up a day job. British jazz-band leaders were familiar with this problem. Chris Barber decided his band should be fully professional in 1952:

> I concluded that the way to become a proficient musician was not only to play more but to play as of your life depended on it – and the way to do that was to make your life depend on it. In an amateur band it's immaterial whether the musicians can play well or not, it's just personal fun. It needed to be more than that … it needed to be a professional band.

His musicians thought he was mad: 'None of us believed that it was possible to make a living from playing jazz', says clarinettist Alex Revell. 'We'd had the importance of a secure job drilled into us since we first went to school.' Revell, Barber's best friend, 'opted for a career in engineering' (Frame 2007: 65).

The musicians who opted for a career in music faced two sorts of problem. Immediately there was the basic need to get paid work. By and large, these musicians were not competing with established players (if anything, as the new youth market developed and record sales began to generate pop fads, established players were competing with them, providing cover versions of music they despised for audiences they didn't understand). The Musicians' Union did its best to ensure that anyone performing for the BBC was a Union member and was thus happy to recruit skifflers and rock'n'rollers alike, and there does not seem to have been much local Musicians' Union opposition to, for example, the skiffle contests that toured Britain's variety circuit, though the Plymouth branch did manage to stop the Woodlanders and Steeljack from appearing in the city as part of the 'Stars of *Six-Five Special* Show' in January 1958. *Melody Maker* carried the views of a local union member:

> These skiffle groups, with their meagre musical ability, sprouting everywhere nowadays and playing cheaply, are a menace to the professional musician. (Quoted in Dewe 1998: 135)

Otherwise, like Vic Flick, young musicians developed their professional skills through new music-making opportunities: providing the backing bands of US and

---

[10]   The most brilliant chronicler of the importance of such peer networks in the history of British pop and rock is Pete Frame, initially in his family trees and more recently in his essential book *The Restless Generation* (see http://www.familyofrock.com and Frame 2007).

UK teen pop stars (being the appropriate age was an advantage), providing the rock'n'roll or youth-aimed entertainment at holiday camps, meeting the demand for cheap live dance music from German club owners and, in a small but significant number of cases, becoming specialist studio musicians, drawing, in particular, on their do-it-yourself technological skills, as well as on the sort of self-discipline that had enabled them to make themselves into musicians in the first place. Big Jim Sullivan explains the importance of studio musicians who understood the sort of do-it-yourself music record companies were now releasing:

> Most of the groups couldn't handle the studio, it was a very nerve-wracking experience if you never worked in studio conditions before. You sit there waiting for the RED LIGHT to go on. You could be sitting there for five minutes, waiting while the producer talks to the engineer. Then the light goes on, you know that you mustn't make a mistake for at least 4 minutes. So your concentration must be 100%. If you can't control your nerves you fold and make mistakes. All session people suffer from nerves … I used to get so nervous I took up Yoga to help me calm down …[11]

The second problem these musicians faced was sustaining a career. Humphrey Lyttelton notes that running a full-time band is not like 'painting canvases in a garret'. A band leader has to feed his musicians, and good musicians cost more. Lyttelton realised he had to have a professional band when he found that he could no longer get music of a high enough standard from semi-professionals (who were not developing their skills through constant playing) and he then discovered, like Ted Heath before him, that to pay his wage bills, he had to please a public:

> And there, confronting me, was the sort of inducement to 'commercialism' which, in the jolly amateur days, we used to think belonged only to the wicked world of Tin Pan Alley. (Lyttelton 1958: 82, 115–16)

The argument that commercialism belonged to the wicked world of Tin Pan Alley (or 'the music business') was to become a familiar strand of 1960s rock ideology, but what was involved in the 1950s, as do-it-yourself musicians became professionals, was a tension between two different accounts of musical motivation. If amateurism opened up a space in which they could create something musically new, in order to become successful professionally, DIY musicians needed the energising effect of the market. For band leaders like Lyttelton, the market was the immediately responsive public which paid to see the band live (Lyttelton had his own club and was to some extent self-promoted). For the younger generation of do-it-yourself performers in the 1950s, the public was significantly mediated – by record companies, by broadcasters and by promoters, all of whom were seeking to make sense of the new youth market.

---

[11]   http://bigjimsullivan.com/History.html [accessed 12 September 2012].

We will discuss the making of youth culture further in the next chapter. The point here is that to reach the youth market, musicians needed intermediaries, managers whose job was to sell them to record companies, radio and TV producers, promoters and agents, club owners and so forth, and here it is striking how many of the significant managers also came from outside the established music industry and were also making it up as they went along. Just to give the examples of the best-known names: Larry Parnes and Andrew Loog Oldham came into the music business from the clothing industry. Parnes, who co-managed Tommy Steele and then a series of teen stars, had started out in the rag trade before beginning to invest in the theatre and bar business. Oldham's first job was as a tea boy at Hardy Amies. He then worked for Mary Quant ('he called himself my assistant cum window dresser cum everything else')[12] before entering music PR, working first for Mark Wynter and then Brian Epstein. He became manager of the Rolling Stones in partnership with Eric Easton, an established agent – Oldham was too young to hold his own agent's licence.[13] John Kennedy (Tommy Steele's co-manager) was a photographer who did publicity work for theatre productions. Brian Epstein worked in his father's music store in Liverpool. All of these managers began their music biz careers by 'discovering' their stars.

What discovery meant here, though, was that these managers 'found' their acts playing live; they were excited by the way the acts had *already* established an understanding of what it meant to entertain an audience.

Do-it-Yourself Music

Writing as Francis Newton, the historian Eric Hobsbawm once claimed that:

> Skiffle was unquestionably the most universally popular music of our generation. It broke through all barriers except those of age. Between the ages of eight and eighteen there can have been few inhabitants of Britain, whatever their class, education or intelligence – down to half-wits – who did not, for however short a period, take some active pleasure in it. (Newton 1959: 255)[14]

Or, as Adam Faith put it:

> The skiffle craze hit Britain with all the fury of Asian 'flu. Everyone went down with it. Anyone who could afford to buy a guitar and learn three chords was in

---

[12]   Quant 1967: 104.

[13]   Levy 2003: 97. By 1964, Oldham was contemplating a musical career. He told David Griffiths that he had been doing some sessions 'with a man I've idolised since I was 14 – Marty Wilde' (*Record Mirror*, 15 August 1964).

[14]   Hobsbawm was born in 1917, so the significance of 'our' generation is not altogether clear here.

business as a skiffler ... Skiffle was a bit like mushrooms. It grew in cellars. Nice dark cellars. And it shot up over-night, just like mushrooms do. (Faith 1961: 13–14)

Historians are agreed, then, that skiffle was a remarkable social phenomenon, although, as Mike Dewe observes, none of the various participation statistics provided are reliable. Chas McDevitt suggests that 'at one point in 1957, it was estimated that there were between 30,000 and 50,000 groups in the British Isles', but doesn't say by whom. He does quote a contemporary source on the boom in guitar sales, Ben Davis, managing director of 'one of Britain's biggest wholesale and retail firms':

The demand is so great that no country in the world can hope to keep up with it. Since last September [1956] it has increased more than 10 times. At Christmas people were walking around Charing Cross Road with bunches of notes in their hands looking for guitars. At the moment I have 20,000 on order and wish I could get more. I estimate that this year over 250,000 will be imported into this country, compared with 6,000 in 1950. (Quoted in McDevitt 1997: 8 – no source provided)[15]

McDevitt provides firmer numerical evidence of the skiffle boom in his chapter on skiffle competitions. The London round of the 'National Skiffle Contest', for example (held at the Finsbury Park Empire in December 1957), attracted 78 groups of whom only 50 could be accommodated. The 'First National Skiffle Contest' at Bury St Edmunds (organised by the local Round Table during Easter 1958 and including Paul Oliver among the judges) attracted 44 serious entrants (many more bands put themselves forward) of whom 34 took part. The all-Scotland Skiffle Championship of 1957 had more than 100 entries.[16] But the best evidence of the remarkable effect of skiffle on British musical life in 1956 can be found in local oral histories. In Sheffield, for example, 'most of the young skifflers were still at school':

It was all basically lads who were in your class, 'cos they were handy. It wasn't whether you could play owt. It was just a case of wanting to be in.[17]

---

[15]   As Dave Laing notes, exchange control policy meant that 'it was not possible to import American guitars until the end of the 1950s' (restrictions on the import of Fenders and Gibsons were lifted in 1959). The guitars being sold in 1956 were presumably 'poorly made imports from continental Europe' (Laing 2009: 11).

[16]   Woods 1979: 54.

[17]   Pete Jackson, quoted in Firminger and Lilleker 2001: 15. Hobsbawm is undoubtedly right that skiffle bands crossed class boundaries – they were as likely to be formed at grammar as at secondary modern or indeed (from the personal experience of Simon Frith) independent boarding schools.

With, it seems, every secondary school having its own bands, there were soon plenty good enough to play publicly: 'Cinemas in and around the city would frequently feature skiffle groups just playing through the house PA.' In the words of Frank Peach, lead singer with Ricky and the Rebels:

> I played many of the cinemas around Attercliffe – the Regal, Plaza, Adelphi, Globe, etc. On Sunday nights they used to have groups on. We used to do anything that came along. People would book you for wedding receptions, private functions.[18]

Perhaps because so many skiffle groups were based in schools or youth clubs, competitions were part of local skiffle culture from the start.[19] This was why London promoter Stanley Dale marketed the first national skiffle tour (featuring the Vipers and Jim Dale) as the 'Great National Skiffle Contest'. It reached the Empire Theatre, Sheffield, in the week beginning 23 September 1957. Each night the headliners would be supported by battles between local groups – the Sheffield round featured around 300 performers:

> The winners were nearly always chosen by audience reaction so if a group had a large following success was virtually guaranteed. The promoters would be too intimidated to go against such powerful support even if the group was not up to scratch.[20]

There are similar skiffle memories in all the cities through which the Skiffle Contest passed[21] and the skiffle effect can be traced in many star biographies. There seem to have been few popular musicians born in the early 1940s who did not play, however briefly, in a skiffle band. This is true of the first British teen pop stars (Tommy Steele, Cliff Richard and Adam Faith),[22] the new generation of session musicians (as we have seen), future rock stars (Van Morrison, Jimmy Page, each Beatle) and folk acts (Martin Carthy, Bert Jansch, and the Spinners, who, as the Gin Mill Skiffle Group, were regulars at the Cavern Club).

The remarkable effect skiffle had on British youth culture cannot be doubted. As Paul Oliver has argued, it provided people with opportunities to play and to form small bands, and forming and playing in small bands has been the essence of

---

[18]   Firminger and Lilleker 2001: 15–16.

[19]   These were organised by all sorts of local organisations, from the Rotary Club to the various associations and providers of boys', girls' and mixed clubs as well as by cinema chains (with different groups representing different cinemas).

[20]   Sheffield information from Firminger and Lilleker 2001: 15–16.

[21]   See, for example, Hank Marvin's memories of Newcastle in this period in Phipps, Tobler and Smith 2005: 123–6.

[22]   Though Cliff makes plain that 'if there's one thing I don't dig, it's skiffle' – Richard 1960: 36.

the rock scene ever since.[23] That said, there remains the question of where these opportunities came from in the first place.

'Skiffle' actually describes three different kinds of musical activity that were, for a moment, conflated. The music itself, as has been well documented, emerged from late 1940s revivalist jazz bands (Ken Coyler's and Chris Barber's London-based groups were the first to feature skiffle interludes, but these were soon adopted by numerous provincial New Orleans jazz bands too). In his skiffle history, Chas McDevitt provides biographical sketches of all the skiffle groups that made records. The vast majority were made up of jazz musicians, though sometimes with singers whose repertoire was primarily folk or country. The exceptions were Wally Whyton's Vipers – he was a guitarist who had been playing in coffee bars with, among other people, Tommy Hicks (who became Tommy Steele) and Lionel Bart – and the Worried Men Skiffle Group, which included Terry Nelhams (who became Adam Faith).

Hobsbawm's suggestion that age was the one barrier to skiffle is therefore not quite right. Most of the original skiffle groups were not made up of teenagers and many of the musicians they inspired to make music for themselves were not teenagers either – they were either already making music on an amateur or semi-pro basis or were now more inclined to take it up as a hobby. McDevitt notes the occupations of the Lea Valley Skiffle Group, finalists in the Bury St Edmunds contest: ambulance driver, tailor's cutter, progress chaser, insurance broker and two market porters. The winners of that contest, the 2.19 Skiffle Group from Chatham, included two members of the Band of the Royal Engineers, Jack McCormack on bass (he was to become principal bass for the Royal Philharmonic Orchestra) and Dave Chandler on washboard (he went on to play trombone in the orchestra of the Royal Opera).

Another significant source of older skiffle musicians was the embryonic folk scene. McDevitt describes Alan Lomax and the Ramblers (which included Ewan MacColl, the young Peggy Seeger on banjo, and jazz men Bruce Turner and Jim Bray) as 'a form of pseudo skiffle' from 'the folk purists',[24] but, as MacColl's biographer, Ben Harker, points out, MacColl was used to performing with Colyer and other jazz musicians at political events and the Colyer Skiffle Group's repertoire included numerous songs by Leadbelly and Woody Guthrie, both musicians with whom Alan Lomax had worked. For these political performers, in Harker's words:

> Skiffle managed to combine all the exotic glamour of American culture with a visceral, DIY, anti-commercial ethos and quickly caught on with the nascent folk scene, which had always insisted there were two Americas – one of big business, Hollywood, comic books and cultural imperialism, the other of Joe

[23]   Oliver 2007: 35.
[24]   McDevitt 1997: 93.

Hill, Leadbelly, Woody Guthrie and the cultural resourcefulness of the regular working man. (Harker 2007: 112)

A more British folk take on skiffle was John Hasted's 44 Skiffle and Folk Song Group, which recruited its two female singers, Shirley Collins and Judith Goldbloom, from the London Youth Choir that Hasted had formed to take part in Communist World Youth Festivals (another ex-choir member, Hylda Sims, was in Russell Quaye's skiffle group, the City Ramblers). For these folk ideologues, skiffle provided an ideal type of popular music making and the skiffle club, in particular, was seen as the ideal setting for the performance of political songs. We will discuss this further in the next section.

The second strand of skiffle music making was driven by commerce. McDevitt shows how various commercial interests tried to exploit skiffle's popularity. The Hallelujah Skiffle Group, for example, fronted by Clinton Ford, was set up to be 'the featured Skiffle group for Butlins' TV Commercials'. The Imps were five 12-year-olds signed by EMI, whose one and only record was produced by George Martin.[25] At the same time, even 'authentic' skiffle groups needed to use commercial means to develop their popularity (and income) and had to work with record companies, radio and television broadcasters and variety agents.[26] Take the case of Alan Lomax's Ramblers:

> Lomax envisaged his group as a British equivalent to the Weavers. He hustled up record company interest from Decca but The Ramblers' single and seven-inch EP made no splash in Britain (their only album seems to have been quietly sidelined for German-only release). Aware of the power of television, Lomax also used his Granada connections, negotiating a series to showcase the band's talents. Broadcast over the summer of 1956 the programmes were excruciatingly hokey affairs. The straw-bales in the folksy set created a rheumy allergic reaction in Peggy Seeger; Lomax came across as gushingly earnest, inviting viewers to 'lean back in those easy chairs, grab tight hold of your beer mugs and your teacups, because tonight we're rambling round the world!' Any allusion to the music's political context was excised, including a reference to the Highland clearances. Far from resisting skiffle's American emphasis, the Ramblers now added to it: even MacColl lapsed into fashionable impersonations of American speech. (Harker 2007: 116)

The third strand of skiffle was the teenage band activity we have already described, but about which two further points need to be made. First, for these young musicians, skiffle described not a particular form of music but a way of

---

[25]   McDevitt 1997: 80–2, 87–8.

[26]   One of McDevitt's more intriguing snippets of information is that the Barnstormers Spasm Band (which sometimes featured the jazz discographer Brian Rust on washboard) failed an audition for Hughie Green (McDevitt 1997: 46–9).

approaching all sorts of material; skiffle bands might have had broadly similar line-ups (vocals, guitars, some sort of bass and drums), but their repertoires were quite varied.[27] Bruce Welch reflects that:

> It was sort of jam session music which Hank [Marvin] and I did – we had separate skiffle groups – but at the same time I heard 'Heartbreak Hotel' on *Family Favourites* in January 1956, so there was this amazing change in all of us: we had rock'n'roll coming from America, and Lonnie made us pick up a guitar with the idea that anyone can do it. (Phipps, Tobler and Smith 2005: 203)

McDevitt suggests that skiffle is best thought of as 'party music': it included not just 'blues and jazz standards' and rock'n'roll tunes but also 'folk songs, calypsos and popular hits', while a writer in *Jazz Review*, who had spent an evening at London's Skiffle Club in 1959 watching visiting bands from the suburbs and the provinces, reported that the 'newer skiffle groups do not distinguish between skiffle and rock'n'roll, submerging them all in the same din'.[28]

At the same time, skiffle was not the only thing young musicians did. The individual members of the Shadows, for example, may have been (separately) in skiffle groups before they got together, but their playing experience covered a remarkable range of musical genres. Jet Harris had played in a modern jazz group; Tony Meehan was in a dance band ('waltzes, foxtrots, anything. We even did Irish jigs'); Hank Marvin was in a trad jazz group; Bruce Welch 'got more and more interested in folk numbers. We used to browse through catalogues and old files in the library looking for material'. Such musical eclecticism was equally apparent in the Beatles' early repertoire, as indicated, for example, by the range of material they performed in BBC studios.[29]

In addition, commerce was not a problem for these musicians as it was for the jazz and folk revivalists. It was not just that they were ambitious to have musical careers – to be stars – but that for them, skiffle itself was clearly a kind of pop. As is repeatedly explained in these musicians' memoirs, skiffle inspiration came not from seeing the original skiffle bands, but from hearing a hit record, Lonnie Donegan's 'Rock Island Line'. And for the industry this record symbolised not do-it-yourself music but the importance of the record business and the replacement of big bands by small combos.

---

[27]   There were, for example, Welsh-language skiffle groups. Sarah Hill notes that they were rejected by the Archdruid from playing on the field at the 1957 National Eisteddfod on the grounds that 'skiffle was not music but "rubbish"' (Hill 2007: 58).

[28]   Quoted in MacKinnon 1993: 24; and see McDevitt 1997: 9. In *The Jazz Scene* Francis Newton takes 'rock-and-roll' and 'skiffle' to be the American and British names for the same music (Newton 1959: 254).

[29]   The Shadows 1961: 12, 21, 29, 41. For a comprehensive list of all the songs the Beatles performed for the BBC, see Howlett 1996.

In July 1957, for example, Ivor and Basil Kirchin disbanded their dance band. They, like other band leaders, were aware of the declining popularity of their music, but the Kirchens also criticised their musicians:

> They slouch on to the stand, and the way they sit, so bored with it all. Naturally the skifflers and rock and rollers have dethroned the big bands. The impact of seeing musicians suddenly come alive and throbbing with vitality was enormous. (Quoted in McDevitt 1997: 10)

But the industry attitude to skiffle as a new form of entertainment is best captured in the (anonymous) sleeve notes to Lonnie Donegan's debut album *Showcase*, released on Pye's Nixa label in December 1956:

> Until the opening of his first British variety tour in September 1956, the fabulous success story of Lonnie Donegan was mainly an affair of staggering figures and cold, hard cash, and many a case-hardened critic automatically wrote off any artistic merit in performances which netted such huge disc sales and so high a placing in the best-seller lists.

> But directly he stepped onto a Variety stage, Lonnie confounded the critics and proved that the record-buying public had not been hoodwinked by any overnight shooting star. No meretricious gimmick had boosted those sales: it was personality and talent that had been at work.

> For the successful Variety star cannot rely on that one sure-fire number, on the wizardry of the recording engineer or on the artificial boost achieved by the plugger. He must have a Good Act – an act sufficiently good to impress critics and public on Monday, so that there will be more people coming to pay out their money to see him on Tuesday. And on Wednesday, Thursday, Friday and Saturday. Donegan did more than that. His dynamic rhythmic singing, backed by the compelling beat of his Skiffle Group broke records at Variety theatres and drew in more customers than they had enjoyed for months. At Glasgow, his birthplace, he played to two full houses on the first night of the week – an almost unheard-of thing in modern music-hall.

> No small factor in the success of Lonnie's stage debut has been the fact that cash customers at the box office are presented with the identical line-up and presentation which they find on his records – bearded Micky Ashman on bass fiddle, swinging Nick Nicholls on drums and thick-set Denny Wright, unquestionably one of Britain's leading jazz guitarists, outstanding both in solo work and rhythmic propulsion.

This is interesting for three reasons: the confusion of musical labels (variety, skiffle, music hall, jazz – Donegan is described as 'the first out-and-out jazz singer ever to hit the best-seller lists'); the implicit suggestion that music on record is somehow 'artificial' (and its consumers 'hoodwinked'); and the lack of any reference to the teenage market. In the event, as it turned out, Donegan's subsequent career was indeed as a variety (if not a music hall) act, his living made as a live performer rather than a record seller.[30] But in other respects, explaining his appeal in terms of traditional entertainment suggests an inability to understand that skiffle represented a profound change in the live music market, a change that was only briefly held back by the packaging of new youth stars and trad jazzers on the variety circuit (Acker Bilk, for example, had a career similar to Lonnie Donegan's) and that was defied in vain by the 'death of rock' claims we cited earlier.

For young audiences, in particular, a good night out came to mean dancing to loud music – on stage and on disc – in a club; there was now an alternative way of performing. The Good Act in a variety show or music hall was not the only option. 'It is hard to pin down changes in mood, the sensibility of a time', writes Christopher Logue, 'but towards the end of 1962 I felt the spirit of the fifties had vanished'. 'Music', he adds, 'was everywhere. Music was the heart of the time.'[31] And what he describes is not just a new sound but also a new kind of musical place and a new kind of musical promoter.

Do-it-Yourself Promotion

George Webb was the son of a music hall artiste.[32] He was born in 1917 and after leaving school went to work at a Vickers Armstrong armaments factory. A self-taught jazz pianist, his first venture into music promotion was organising entertainment in his factory canteen. After forming a band with fellow jazz enthusiasts, George Webb's Dixielanders, in 1941 Webb organised for them a regular place to play, the downstairs bar at the Red Barn pub in Barnehurst, which in time became a magnet for other New Orleans jazz enthusiasts. By 1948 there was, in David Boulton's words, a 'boom in amateur jazz-making' and the Red Barn became a model for an increasing number of jazz clubs around the country.[33] Webb joined Humphrey Lyttelton's band, playing now for increasing numbers of young dancers, and in 1951 set up as a full-time jazz promoter, organising, for example, the Sunday night sessions at the Shakespeare Hotel, Woolwich, which were popular throughout the 1950s. From 1955 to 1965 he worked for Jazzshows Promotions, booking acts for the club and concert circuit,

---

[30]   Donegan's last big hit was the self-penned but music hall-styled 'My Old Man's A Dustman' in 1960; his last Top 20 entry was 'Pick A Bale of Cotton' in 1962. Thereafter he worked primarily in cabaret.

[31]   Logue 1999: 300–1.

[32]   Biographical information taken from his obituary in the *Daily Telegraph*, 14 March 2010.

[33]   Boulton 1958: 78–9.

and helping run the Jazz Show Jazz Club, which took over the lease of 100 Oxford Street from the Humphrey Lyttelton Club in 1959. In 1965 he set up his own management and agency company; his clients included R&B acts as well as jazz bands.

Webb was the first of a new kind of promoter – the enthusiast we described in Chapter 1 – creating a new kind of venue, the jazz club. Francis Newton suggests that:

> The 'jazz club' of the 1940s and fifties was not, like the Rhythm Club of the thirties, a place of self-education, where records were heard and dissected, but essentially a place where live jazz by British musicians was encouraged and admired. The revivalist public was therefore less 'learned' than its predecessors, and less 'intellectual'. At all events, the social tone of the movement was set by the amateur and semi-professional musician, and the ordinary inexpert fan, generally of schoolboy or student age. (Newton 1959: 252–3)

But the jazz club also represented a new kind of fluidity between being a jazz fan, a jazz performer and a jazz promoter. Some clubs were thus set up, like Webb's, by musicians needing somewhere to play. The most famous examples are Feldman's Swing Club, established as a Sunday night venue in Mack's Restaurant, 100 Oxford Street, in 1942 (Joseph Feldman was a furrier and amateur clarinettist and the Club was set up to showcase his trio, featuring his child prodigy son, Vic, on drums); the short-lived Club 11 in Great Windmill Street, set up by ten modern jazz musicians in 1948 as the 'first club in Britain to present a solely jazz repertoire, with a policy devised entirely by a co-operative who were also practitioners themselves'; Cy Laurie's all-night club, which took over Club 11's premises in 1950; and, of course, Ronnie Scott's Club, which opened in 1959.[34] And one could add to this list Billy Kaye's Contemporary Jazz Club, Freddy Randall's Club at the Cooks Ferry Inn, Edmonton, which both ran for a while in the late 1940s, and Sandy Brown's self-promoted jazz band balls, which ran in the same period at the Oddfellows Hall, Edinburgh.[35]

Other musicians ran clubs in conjunction with music business partners.[36] Humphrey Lyttelton and his agent/manager, Lyn Dutton, took over the London Jazz Club nights at 100 Oxford Street in 1951, and in 1955 Dutton took over the venue's lease, having already changed the venue's name to the Humphrey

---

[34] The best general history of London clubs is Bacon 1999. The Club 11 quote from Fordham 1986: 43.

[35] One of Brown's jazz fan bouncers, employed following trouble from local gangs, was Tom 'Sean' Connery. See Brown 1979: 44; Robertson 2011: 170; and Turner 1984: 105.

[36] Ronnie Scott and his partner Pete King (who was more of a promoter than a performer by the time Ronnie Scott's opened) were routinely dependent for both expert advice and financial investment on Harold Davison (see Fordham 1986: passim).

Lyttelton Club. The first 'Jazz at the Marquee' gigs were presented by pianist Dill Jones in 1958, but the space was soon taken over by the National Jazz Federation, a promotions company run by Chris Barber and his manager, Harold Pendleton. Dutton and Pendleton were jazz fans (rather than musicians) turned promoters, and such entrepreneurs became increasingly important in the 1950s. Other examples are Jeff Kruger, who as a 21-year-old jazz fan staged his first Jazz at the Mapleton event in a basement room in the Mapleton Hotel in 1952 (where his father organised Jewish dances), changing the name of the club to the Flamingo a few months later; Rik Gunnell, an ex-Smithfield meat market porter and boxer (and, it seems, a fan of jazz club ambience rather than jazz club music), who opened the Two-Way Club on Thursdays at 100 Oxford Street in 1952 (an unsuccessful attempt to feature both modern and traditional groups), the equally short-lived Club Basie and Blue Room and, in 1955, all-night sessions at the Americana and Club Haley before running the Flamingo Club all-nighters from 1959;[37] and Mike Jeffreys, who 'inspired by his love of jazz' dropped out of an economics degree at Newcastle University in the late 1950s to run a pub-based Sunday night Dixieland session, before being financed to open the Marimba Coffee House, which ran jazz sessions every Saturday night from midnight till 3 am.[38] Jeffreys moved these to his own larger club, the Downbeat, in around 1960. The Downbeat was the heart of Newcastle's jazz and blues scene until 1962, when Jeffreys opened 'a more salubrious establishment, the Club A'Go Go' and took on management of the Animals.[39]

George Webb's career also exemplifies the way in which successful enthusiast promoters inevitably became commercial promoters. Bruce Turner describes his club experience:

> The old pre-war rhythm clubs had mainly featured good recorded jazz. They had been run by record collectors who waxed lyrical on such matters as the Iambic Concept in Early Negro Folk Song. The post-was jazz clubs were run by a similar type of enthusiast at first, but very soon they began to do quite well, and were taken over by enterprising business promoters. These sat in little

[37]   Jeff Kruger had moved the Flamingo to Wardour Street in 1957. Gunnell started the All-Nighter Club there in 1959. The two ventures used the same premises (and name) but different promoters. Gunnell's Club was open Friday and Saturday night and Sunday afternoons. Kruger's club was open the other weekday evenings (Bacon 1999: 58).

[38]   Jeffreys' name is variously spelt Jeffrey and Jeffries in pop histories. We are following Ian Carr's spelling here.

[39]   Club details taken from Bacon 1999: 16, 17; Brunning and Smith 2009: 22, 26; Carr 1996: 12, 17; and Robertson 2011: 19–20, 25, 35. There were similar developments in many other British cities. As Jim Godbolt notes, 'from after the war and up to 1963 jazz clubs were formed by the hundreds. Some like the Nottingham, Redcar, Luton, Reading and Wood Green clubs, the Mardi Gras, Liverpool, and the Manchester Sports Guild enjoyed a long life' (Godbolt 1976: 123).

back rooms, away from the incredible din, adding up figures and thinking of the Iambic Concept only rarely. (Turner 1984: 76)

The point, though, is that the enthusiast and the enterprising business promoter could well be the same person.

One aspect of this change of promotional approach was that musical policy was increasingly determined by the market (what audiences wanted to hear) rather than by the promoter's own tastes.[40] Turner describes the dogmatic aspects of the enthusiast club:

> a man has a lot of jazz records, he suddenly notices that some of the music hits him more forcefully than the rest, so he concludes that this must be the *real* jazz. He then sees in a kind of revelation that jazz is authentic only when played by left-handed non-smokers with red hair – or something of that sort. He rushes into print and is soon contacted by other individuals who share his opinion. These start up jazz clubs or promote concerts, making quite sure that only musicians who fit the above description are hired to play. Pretty soon the only available work for jazz musicians is that which is carefully supervised by a few theorists who don't themselves play. (Turner 1984: 106–7)

The two (somewhat contradictory) problems that Turner raises here – commercialism on the one hand and pseudo-authenticity on the other – would become equally familiar, as we shall see, in the 1960s folk clubs. There too, the consequent political arguments were significantly influenced by the Communist Party (Turner himself wrote about jazz for the *Morning Star*). Communists provided a significant strand of revivalist jazz enthusiasm. The Young Communist League's Challenge Jazz Club promoted George Webb's Dixielanders' first Central London concerts in the 1940s (*Challenge* was the Young Communist League's newsletter) and, according to Roger Horton (whose family took over the lease of 100 Oxford Street from Ted Morton in 1964, renaming the venue the 100 Club), Morton himself, Lyn Dutton and other 1950s jazz promoters 'were all in a clique of members of the Communist Party'.[41] Following the formation of Ken Colyer's Omega Brass Band in 1955, revivalist jazz was certainly also heard as the sound of socialist (if not communist) gatherings and, from CND's first Aldermaston March in 1958, public protest.[42]

However, the final points to make about the 1950s jazz club (and its influence on skiffle, folk, blues and rock culture in the late 1950s and through the 1960s) concern not ideology but ambience. Jazz clubs were small performing spaces.

---

[40]   Another effect was the move from the 'jazz club' as a regular night in a hotel, restaurant or pub room to the jazz club as a dedicated venue.

[41]   Brunning and Smith 2009: 37; and see also Godbolt 1976: 29; and Schwartz 2007: 18.

[42]   See McKay 2007: 24–5.

The music sounded loud; listening and dancing were often the same thing; performers and audiences were squashed together. Resources were functional rather than luxurious and while the membership system gave people a sense of being included among a cognoscenti, most clubs until the mid-1960s were cheap enough not to feel exclusive – both commentators then and memoir writers since note the range of people a club might attract and its bohemian role of gathering together various kinds of non-conformist. For Val Wilmer in 1963, the Flamingo:

> had a deep, dark-red feel to it, with a low ceiling the music clung to, and sweat soaking into the crimson walls. There was an innocuous coffee-bar in one corner, the common stimulants being charge and 'blues' (amphetamines), most people just had a drink in the Blue Posts over the road. A liberal racial policy had long made it a favourite for Black American servicemen based in Britain, and its burgeoning Afro-Caribbean clientele now made it feel more soulful than the essentially teenage Marquee. (Wilmer 1989: 112)

Andy Summers, who began playing the Flamingo with the Zoot Money Band around the same time, remembers, too, the sense of danger:

> the Gunnells preside like underworld princes and are reputed to have associations with the Kray twins ... behind [their] sardonic repartee is the perfume of extreme measures. (Summers 2006: 82)

These West End clubs were, after all, part of London's nightlife.

Early jazz clubs were mostly unlicensed – they were, in the words of John Mortimer, 'the temples of New Orleans, warm sex and cold coffee',[43] and many continued that way. John Fordham provides an entertaining account of the bureaucratic process Ronnie Scott and Pete King had to go through to get a licence for their new club in 1959 (they had to begin by forming a 'wine committee') and Roger Horton only managed to get a liquor licence for the 100 Club, in 1965, at the third attempt (his previous applications had been successfully opposed by the Blues Posts, the pub that had been profiting for the previous decade from selling drink to the Club's customers).[44]

As a form of live musical entertainment, skiffle started life in jazz clubs and the early skifflers followed the jazz club model. London's first three skiffle clubs, regular nights at the Roundhouse pub on Brewer Street ('Europe's only Skiffle and Blues club' from September 1955), at 44 Gerrard Street and at the Princess Louise, Holborn (both from April 1956), were each promoted by the resident musicians – the Bob Watson Skiffle Group, John Hasted's Skiffle and Folk Song

---

43 Quoted in Farson 1987: xii.
44 Brunning and Smith 2009: 47; Fordham 1986: 98.

Group, and Russell Quaye's City Ramblers, respectively.[45] But the popularity of skiffle also attracted promoters from different backgrounds. First of all were the coffee bar owners who had already discovered the value of music (on a juke-box) in attracting a primarily young clientele and who now found some of its clients bringing in guitars and playing for themselves. In London the Bread Basket, the Gyre and Gimble and most famously the 2i's became skiffle clubs by default and, in the context of the music industry's developing interest in the teenage market and the increasing importance of record sales, established two ways of working that would have a significant effect on the development of British beat music: first, the evening's entertainment was based on the draw of a resident band and a succession of more or less competent amateur groups; and second, these venues came to be understood as rich picking-grounds for record industry talent scouts and predatory managers and agents. These do-it-yourself venues, in other words, became essential to the new ways of becoming a professional musician we have already described. The 2i's remains iconic in British popular music history not as a place of amateur music making but as a place where a succession of stars were 'spotted'.[46]

The second group of promoters on whom skiffle had a significant effect were folk music ideologues. The promotion of folk music in Britain in the immediate post-war period was primarily ideological and was concerned one way or another with the performance of authenticity. The English Folk Dance and Song Society started a 'Folk Song Club' at Cecil Sharp House in 1949 and the Birmingham Folk Song Club, also under the auspices of English Folk Dance and Song Society, claimed to have been 'running since the end of the war'.[47] Ewan MacColl's Ballads and Blues events emerged from the radio series of that name he made for the BBC in 1953. The Ballads and Blues benefit concert for the *Daily Worker* in the Royal Festival Hall in July 1954, for example, featured music that was 'unadulterated, in the authentic traditional style', performed by MacColl himself, A.L. Lloyd and, among others, Ken Colyer's Skiffle Group. The Good Earth Club, a precursor of John Hasted's 44 Club, was opened by Communist Party members associated with the London Youth Choir and its journal, *Sing*, in 1954. The first folk song club in Glasgow (and, indeed, in Scotland) was started the same year at Allan Glen's secondary school for boys by socialist teacher and songwriter Morris Blythman. The first folk club in Bristol, based at the Communist Club, dates from the same period.[48]

From the perspective of these folk activists, skiffle provided both an opportunity to reach and educate a wider popular audience and a model of how folk promotions could be organised. John Hasted was explicit about this in an article in the 1956–7

[45]   Quaye later opened the Skiffle Cellar on Greek Street. It ran from 1957 to 1960 and was modelled on Cy Laurie's all-night jazz club (McDevitt 1997: 53).

[46]   The best account of this much described process is Frame 2007: 258–91.

[47]   Boyes 1993: 231.

[48]   Brocken 2003: 47; Harker 2007: 111–12; Jones 2009: 8; and Munro 1996: 31.

winter issue of *Sing* magazine, 'How can you start a skiffle and folk song club in your part of the world?'. Georgina Boyes suggests that:

> Hasted's practical and encouraging article demonstrates that much of the organisational format of Skiffle clubs was simply transferred to folk music without alteration. From the choice of pubs as a location to the role of residents and floor singers, folk clubs' debt to Skiffle is clear. Even the aim of trying to 'rebuild a living, urban people's music, and an audience for it', was, in Hasted's view, identical. (Boyes 1993: 232)

The skiffle/folk club links are obvious too in the career of Ewan MacColl. In 1957, in partnership with fellow communist Malcolm Nixon (who as head of the British Youth Festival had ensured that skiffle was included alongside British jazz in the 1957 Moscow World Youth Festival), MacColl began regular Blues and Ballads nights, initially at the Theatre Royal Stratford East and then in the upstairs room of the Princess Louise in Holborn (the Blues and Ballads Club now advertised itself as 'The Hootenanny, A Completely Informal Evening of Folk Music, Ballads, Work Songs and Instrumentation').[49] In Scotland, to give another example, Norman Buchan, a teacher at Rutherglen Academy as well as a member of the political folk act The Reivers, saw skiffle 'as a means of getting Scottish material through to his pupils' (by 1958 Rutherglen Academy had six active skiffle bands) and started a school Ballads Club before, in 1959, launching the first Scottish folk club 'open to the general public'.[50]

Elsewhere, skiffle bands re-formed as folk groups running folk clubs even without such clear political motivation. In 1958, for example, the Ian Campbell Group, the Spinners and the Watersons, all of whom had started out in skiffle, opened their own folk clubs in Birmingham, Liverpool and Hull, respectively. Alternatively, clubs were formed by a political impetus but without the organisational history of either *Sing* or the English Folk Dance and Song Society. The creation of the CND in February 1958 was a catalyst here. As Ben Harker puts it, 'with skiffle still in the air, music-making became prominent in the annual mass marches to Aldermaston ... CND provided both subject matter and ample singing material'.[51] Anti-Polaris activism was particularly significant for the development of folk music culture in Scotland, but many local clubs

---

[49]   Harker 2007: 126–7. Malcolm Nixon set up the Nixon Agency as an aspect of this enterprise and, as the folk scene developed, became increasingly successful as an agent/promoter, representing and organising visiting American acts such as Pete Seeger, the Weavers and Josh White. His partnership with MacColl in Blues and Ballads ended acrimoniously – Nixon was denounced for his commercial opportunism – in 1960 (Harker 2007: 157–8, 302).

[50]   Munro 1984: 34–6. Edinburgh and Glasgow University had both started student Folk Song Societies in 1958.

[51]   Harker 2007: 136.

in the rest of the UK also emerged from the impetus of the CND. MacKinnon gives the example of the Hoy at Anchor folk club in Southend, set up after a CND benefit concert. Founder Myra Abbott was politically active, had been a communist involved in jazz, blues and skiffle clubs, but now wanted to provide:

> A platform for people to perform folk music and for people to listen; we had very little idea of what constituted folk music and its strands. We were very into causes but disillusioned after 1956. The revival of the folk scene took this place. Its main ethos was uncommercial music – we wanted to provide an alternative. (Quoted in MacKinnon 1993: 25)

The spread of folk clubs around Britain from 1958 is certainly striking, indeed almost as remarkable as the earlier emergence of skiffle clubs.[52] *Sing* magazine listed nine clubs in 1959, 36 in 1961 and 78 in 1962; *Melody Maker* estimated that there were 300 in 1965.[53] Folk historians tend to emphasise the arguments and bad feeling that accompanied the folk club 'boom'. On the one hand, there were continuing attempts to determine what was meant by 'authentic' performance, repertoire and audience engagement, whether through Ewan MacColl's explicit 'policy' clubs or through increasingly standardised folk club conventions of appropriate behaviour (folk clubs were soon seen as settings for more serious – quiet – listening than skiffle clubs). On the other hand, in Boyes' words, 'mistrust of all aspects of commercial popular culture was endemic to the [folk] revival, as much an article of faith for Sir Hubert Parry at the foundation of the Folk-Song Society as it latterly was for [Cecil] Sharp and [Ewan] MacColl, Mary Neal and [A.L.] Lloyd'.[54] For many commentators, the result was that folk clubs moved from the centre to the margins of 1960s music culture. In Robin Deneslow's words:

> In the early sixties a folk club was an exciting place to be. The music was varied and so were the characters involved … [but] … gradually, the easy going acceptance of different forms of music broke down. The traditionalists created a ghetto, and a host of excellent musicians were trapped inside. (Deneslow 1975: 143)

However, from our perspective, the folk club had a continuing significance for 1960s music culture for two reasons: first, as a direct effect of the problems that

---

[52] In London the most significant new folk clubs were, interestingly, all based in coffee bars – the Troubador in Earls Court, which was a folk venue from the early 1960s, Bunjies in Lichfield Street, which started folk nights at the end of the 1950s, and Les Cousins, which took over the Skiffle Cellar in Greek Street in 1960 but continued with all-night openings. These clubs, run by commercial rather than enthusiast entrepreneurs, had an open approach to 'folk' performance and became important venues for contemporary singer-songwriters as well as for folk musicians as such.

[53] We have taken these figures from Boyes 1993: 233 and Harker 2007: 156.

[54] Boyes 1993: 239.

beset the folk movement – issues of authenticity and commerce initially posed in jazz clubs and now argued about by folkies became matters of dispute in electric blues clubs too and thus an aspect of the ideology of rock; and second, for many of its audiences in the 1960s, the folk club offered a kind of complementary experience of bohemia to the jazz club of the 1950s, with a more politicised but also a more individualised and artistic sense of non-conformity, organised around music, words and poetry rather than dance. MacKinnon quotes Ian MacCalman of the Scottish folk band the MacCalmans, answering the question of how he became a folk musician:

> I did the thing with the skiffle. A lot of people who got involved in folk music had a basis in jazz-cum-skiffle. It all connected then, and my brothers and me sang together. I got a guitar, met Hamish and Derek in '64 at art college where an awful lot of music came from … the Corries – the Edinburgh School of Art, the same as us. It's not a particularly great answer because it's nothing to do with the tradition. (MacKinnon 1993: 24)

Many folk singers had this sort of background, such as Peter Bellamy ('I was into skiffle, rock'n'roll, American music. At eighteen I went to art school and I performed black American music and then I discovered the English revival') and Roy Bailey ('Skiffle – that's when I began public performances. In 1959 I went to university and met up with Dave Cousins of the Strawbs. He helped teach me the guitar – Leadbelly stuff, Spencer Davis. I formed the Leicester folk song club in 1961').[55] And Mike Heron:

> 'I had been playing in several different bands,' he explains. 'The Saracens were a kind of Hollies imitation while the Abstracts were more Stones/R&B. There was a lot of maracas shaking there. I was also with Rock Bottom and the Deadbeats, which was very art college, and had one of the first electric banjo players.' When not involved with those acts, Mike was a member of a jazz band which played several cafés with a repertoire based on the MJQ. It was in such haunts that he forged a solo career. 'There was a coffee bar called the Stockpot which was run on a New York basis. I played at tables and it was in the middle of all this that I discovered folk music, partly through the first Bob Dylan album'. (Hogg 1993: 92)

When Heron started his performing career in 1960s Edinburgh, 'folk' described a scene that was as much bohemian as Scottish traditional. The influential Howff Club had started in 1961 as one of Jim Haynes' theatrical ventures. The Crown Bar, where Archie Fisher had begun a Tuesday night folk club in 1963, soon also hosted a Thursday night folk club, run by Bert Jansch, Robin Williamson and Clive Palmer. As Tuesdays became more traditional, Thursdays became more

---

'freaky'. In early 1966 Clive Palmer opened the Incredible Folk Club as an all-night venue in Glasgow's Sauciehall Street, and Palmer, Heron and Williamson formed the Incredible String Band, a very different sort of folk group than those once envisioned by Ewan MacColl and John Hasted.

If the skiffle club was the setting in which working-class teenagers boys could start on a professional music career after leaving school, the self-taught musicians in folk clubs had been to art school or university, were more concerned with music as self-expression and had a different sense of what it was to 'entertain' a public. Joe Boyd, who signed the Incredible String Band to Elektra and then took on both the management and production of the band, suggests that by 1965, 'what you're really seeing is the capture of huge swaths of the towering heights of the music business by middle class performers', taking on 'what was originally a working class job'.[56] This was to have a significant effect on both the power relationship between performers, managers, promoters and agents, and on the kinds of venue in which live music was staged. The significance of university folk clubs for the folk economy in the mid-1960s was the first sign of the importance student unions would have in the formation of a live rock-music circuit.

In the end, however, the folk club (like the jazz club)[57] gave way to the blues club as the centre of British musical life not for ideological reasons but for practical ones. As Robin Deneslow argues:

> Being small – and making little effort to expand – the clubs could only afford modest fees for outside artists who appeared. Anything larger than an acoustic duo became uneconomic; amplification was also quite out of the question. The clubs, and those who played them, hadn't the space or money for electric instruments, speakers and roadies – even if amplification of folk had been tolerated in the first place. (Deneslow 1975: 144)

We will discuss the new kind of venue – organised around the electrical amplification of blues, rhythm and blues and rock bands – in Chapter 7. Such venues needed a degree of investment and turnover that completed the transformation of do-it-yourself to commercial promotion.

Conclusion

From 1955 to 1965, 'do-it-yourself' described a way of doing music and a way of doing music business; it involved both ideas of how things should be done and a set of practices – how things could be done. To conclude this chapter, we need to

---

[56]   Boyd 2008.

[57]   Jim Godbolt suggests that following the success of the Beatles and the Rolling Stones, 'jazz clubs and the bands who relied upon them for the best part of their income folded' (Godbolt 1976: 150).

stress, though, that the world of do-it-yourself music was not, as it might seem, somehow set apart from what was happening more generally to music commerce in the 1950s.

The first point to make is that although this chapter has been primarily about live music, all the live music scenes we have described were bound up with recordings. Almost without exception, the musicians who started playing in coffee bars and skiffle clubs in the mid-1950s, for example, cite two hit records, Elvis Presley's 'Heartbreak Hotel' and Lonnie Donegan's 'Rock Island Line', as having given them the initial impetus to perform. Both 'trad' jazz revivalists and 'modern' jazz instrumentalists listened obsessively to records in getting their styles right; British blues musicians almost all began by being record collectors; even the folk revival was inspired by the field recordings played by the BBC from the 1940s, most influentially on the 1950s programme *As I Roved Out*. Record-playing was also established in the 1950s as part of a club's 'live' music appeal, and record-based public musical entertainment was a familiar feature of a night out by the end of the decade. In November 1957, for example, 'The Big Five Night' staged at the Lambeth Town Hall featured 'the Five Greatest Sounding Systems battling for the 1957 Club Championship of Sound and Record' – a useful reminder that in Britain's Caribbean communities 'sounding systems' were already well established.[58]

Second, although it is often asserted that do-it-yourself British music flourished in spite of the best efforts of the BBC to ignore it,[59] the Corporation in fact played a significant role in shaping DIY music cultures. The issue here is not the BBC's musical taste but its national reach and the ethos of public service broadcasting, with its emphasis on live performance and concern for niche audiences rather than the mass market or commerce.

As examples of the BBC's reach, in 1945 the impact of George Webb's Dixielanders 'was suddenly multiplied ten-fold when the BBC Radio Rhythm Club engaged them for a broadcast', while 'Rock Island Line' became a hit not because it was plugged or hard sold by its record company (which certainly didn't expect it to be a big seller) but because three of the BBC's more conservative light music radio presenters, Jack Payne, Chappie D'Amato and Eamonn Andrews, played it on their respective shows and then got increasing numbers of listener requests for it to be played again.[60]

As an indication of its concern for live music and the variety of its music audiences, the BBC began broadcasting a specialist radio skiffle show, *Saturday Skiffle Club* (which later became *Saturday Club*) in June 1957, replacing the theatre organ recital that used to occupy the 10 am slot. The show, initially scheduled for

---

[58]   Patterson 1963: 366–7.

[59]   See, for example, Frame 2007: 290–1.

[60]   Boulton 1958: 75; Frame 2007: 86–7; Leslie 1965: 57. Humphrey Lyttelton claims that by constantly playing 'Rock Around the Clock', 'dear Auntie BBC unwittingly launched the rock'n'roll craze' (Lyttelton 1958: 68).

eight weeks, ran for 61 and featured over 40 skiffle groups and guests.[61] Five years later, the Beatles played their first BBC session in front of an audience at the Playhouse Theatre, Manchester. 'The programme, "Teenagers' Turn", was recorded and broadcast the following day – Tuesday 8 March 1962 on the old BBC Light Programme between 5.00 and 5.30 p.m.'[62] Over the next five years, the Beatles appeared on over 50 BBC radio shows.

In short, the BBC didn't so much ignore new musical movements as fit them into its own account of how music making and music listening should be, an account that was, it is true, not particularly friendly to non-stop hit record shows. However, in its concern for education and live participation, the BBC did contribute significantly to the DIY ethos. Far from being irrelevant to young musicians' interests, BBC programmes helped shape them. This is Andy Summers' description of becoming a guitarist:

> In the first year or so I learn from other kids and the book my uncle gave me, but the great inspiration of the week is a radio programme called *Guitar Club*, which is on at six-thirty every Saturday night. It's hosted with dry English humour by Ken Sykora and features the best British guitar talent – players such as Diz Disley, Ike Isaacs and Dave Goldberg. (Summers 2006: 35)

And this is Bryan Ferry on how he got into jazz and blues:

> The first thing I ever heard on the radio that I really liked was a blues singer called Leadbelly, and I think it was the time of skiffle and that's when all these blues singers were getting played on the radio, in blues programmes, and that was when a lot of people discovered these singers. (Phipps, Tobler and Smith 2005: 57–8)

Third, while this chapter has necessarily focused on the local – on specific clubs and scenes – for the musicians concerned, making a living meant touring. As Dick Heckstall-Smith puts it, 'the Road is the jazz musician's factory bench: the work place', and Ben Harker calculates that in the course of the 1960s, Ewan MacColl and Peggy Seeger 'played to something like 50,000 people in around 500 folk club concerts', driving 40,000 miles a year.[63] Andy Summers describes his career with Zoot Money and the Big Roll Band in similar terms:

> As our reputation grows we begin playing around the country and start an endless round of gigs that have us locked up in a Commer van, crisscrossing

---

[61]   McDevitt 1997: 181–2. For a good overview of the BBC's skiffle policy, see Dewe 1998, Chapter 7: 'Over the points – skiffle takes to the airwaves'.

[62]   Howlett 1996: 10.

[63]   Harker 2007: 179; Heckstall-Smith and Grant 2004: 54.

England on a daily basis ... sometimes managing up to thirteen shows a week.
(Summers 2006: 81, 93)

Such touring musicians had their own effects on local scenes – introducing new numbers, techniques and technology, providing the playing standards to which local performers then aspired – but, more importantly, they also depended on and made necessary a new live music business, a network of grassroots managers, agents and promoters who could link their gigs together and ensure that a tour worked.

A Snapshot of Glasgow in October–November 1962

Glasgow's major state-owned concert venue – St Andrews Hall – was destroyed in a fire on Friday 26 October 1962, following a boxing match staged in the venue.[1] The Scottish National Orchestra (SNO), the organisation most affected by the fire, was forced to cancel two concerts and to move to the unused City Halls, Candleriggs, the refurbishment of which was subsequently funded by the Glasgow Corporation.[2] However, alongside SNO concerts – including programmes featuring Gilbert and Sullivan, Beethoven, Mozart and Rachmaninov (3/6–7/6, or 'six concerts for the price of five' season tickets) – classical concerts were also promoted by the Corporation of Glasgow and smaller groups such as the Milngavie Music Club, Bellahouston Musical Society and the Glasgow Society of Organists. Other venues included the Kelvingrove Art Gallery and Museum, the University of Glasgow and the Royal Scottish Academy of Music, as well as smaller churches, academies and halls. Scotland also benefited from the Arts Council initiative 'Opera for All'. Scottish Opera was established by Sir Alexander Gibson in June 1962, with performances at the King's Theatre.

Both the lack of major promoters[3] and a large state-run venue in the city – an equivalent of Bristol's Colston Hall or Sheffield's City Hall – meant that Glasgow was largely off the pop music touring map[4] and by 1962 had 'nothing you could call a Scottish scene' (George Gallagher, quoted in Hogg 1993: 26). As Brian

---

[1]   The fire was thought to have been started by a smouldering cigarette butt; the venue did not rigidly enforce a no smoking ban: 'it was left to the discretion of the people' ('Origin in main hall', 1962: 12).

[2]   The City Halls are around half the capacity of St Andrews Hall and Glasgow was without a dedicated concert hall until the opening of the Glasgow Royal Concert Hall in 1990.

[3]   In November 1962, a Glasgow businessman, Max Benjamin, made an audacious bid for Elvis Presley to play six nights in the UK for $100,000, to include one night in Glasgow, with all proceeds going to charity; Benjamin had already successfully enticed Real Madrid to the city for £10,000, with £12,000 donated to charity. The plan was for Elvis to perform at Hampden Park to 80,000 people averaging 10s a ticket, but the singer's only visit to the UK remains a stopover at nearby Prestwick Airport in 1960 ('Now Elvis may sing in Glasgow', 1962: 28).

[4]   Bill Haley and the Comets' only Scottish performance was in 1964 at the Barrowland Ballroom, which had suffered a disastrous fire in 1958 and reopened in 1960.

Hogg writes, Scottish music entered the 1960s with a mentality still based on the previous decade whereby ballroom dancing was still in vogue and 'pop bands were just an aside to the main event' (ibid.). As one musician recalled: 'I began to find it just a bit too provincial and wanted to get south' (Bill Patrick, in ibid.: 24) and 'when Alex Harvey left for Germany there was no group left of any real eminence' (Gallagher, in ibid.: 26).

In fact, ballroom wasn't the only form of dancing to be had in Glasgow in 1962. Music for new American fads like the twist and the Madison was also played. The Barrowland Ballroom, for example, held late-night dances at the weekends; Don Lang & the Twisters performed at the Flamingo Ballroom, Cardonald (20 November, 7.30–11 pm, 3/-); Garry Mills appeared at the Olympia Bowl & Ballroom, East Kilbride (16 November, 8 pm–1 am); and the Astoria Ballroom offered a selection of 'Olde-Tyme' dancing, Scottish country and modern dancing Monday to Saturday. The threat of strike action loomed over Glasgow's ballrooms in November 1962, however, as the Musicians' Union called for over 100 musicians to stop work on Saturday 1 December in support of a claim for higher pay[5] at six ballrooms and one club[6] ('Strike of musicians threatened', 1962: 7). Alternative means of keeping the venues open were discussed, including playing gramophone records, employing non-union bands, and hosting bingo ('Alternatives to musicians', 1962: 7), but the strike was called off the night before after an 'amicable agreement' had been reached ('Dance hall strike off', 1962: 28).

Glasgow was still very much a jazz city in 1962, with successes by the locally based George Penman Jazzmen[7] – both as recording artists[8] and on the BBC's *Come Thursday* programme – and the Vernon Jazz Band, which led manager Ron Hutchison to state that: '[We've] never had it so good. We're getting bookings from jazz clubs we never even heard of before' (Buchanan 1962a: 13). British jazz pianist George Shearing performed at Glasgow's Odeon cinema in October 1962 as part of a UK tour, and clubs such as La Cave, off Jamaica Street, and the Musicians' Jazz Club in West Nile Street ran 'after hours' sessions which often began after 11 pm on Fridays and Saturdays, and which featured both traditional and modern jazz.

Folk music has always been widely played in Glasgow, and musicians such as Bert Jansch were active within the folk scene in 1962 in pubs and coffee houses such as the Burns Howff on West Regent Street. Piping and marching bands were also prevalent, and the annual Boys' and Girls' Exhibition in the Kelvin Hall

---

[5]   The dispute between the Scottish Ballroom Association and the Musicians' Union was over an increase of £1 per session to £3 for a four-hour session.

[6]   Venues affected by the possible strike were the Albert, Plaza, Green's Playhouse, Astoria, F. and F. and Flamingo Ballrooms, and the Piccadilly Club.

[7]   The Penman Jazzmen still perform (as of 2011) at King Tut's Wah Wah Hut every Saturday afternoon, even following the death of George Penman in 2009.

[8]   The band recorded a single at London's Abbey Road studios in 1962 for Parlophone ('George Penman, Bandleader', 2009).

featured junior pipers and drummers such as the Junior Jocks from Lanark. Even though audiences for music hall were continuing to fall, 'Mr Music Hall', Alex Frutin, sunk all his money into the opening of the New Metropole in November 1962 following the destruction by fire of the previous Metropole earlier in the year (MacDonald 1962: 8). The continuing popularity of variety acts can also be seen in the success of a charity show at the Empire by Sophie Tucker, accompanied by Royal Variety Performance stars Andy Stewart, Johnny Dankworth, and Mike and Bernie Winters (ibid.).

However, Glasgow had a certain reputation for drunk and disorderly behaviour, with the newspapers featuring reports on a stabbing at a Kirkintilloch dance hall ('Two years for dance-hall stabbing', 1962: 12), under-age drinking ('Teenage drinkers shock a provost', 1962: 10) and even the shooting and subsequent death of Glasgow rock'n'roll singer Thomas McBain on the night express to London on 29 September 1962 ('McBain died in a minute', 1962: 1). Partly in an attempt to control such behaviour and following alleged comments by the Secretary of State for Scotland that 'Scotland was dead after 10pm and we must waken it up' (Leonard Jack, quoted in 'On with the dance – and the drinks', 1962: 10), 1 October 1962 saw the introduction of amendments to the Licensing (Scotland) Act. This allowed public houses to open on weekdays from 11 am to 2.30 pm and 5 pm to 10 pm with 10 minutes 'drinking up' time, and for hotels and restaurants to sell alcohol on Sundays.[9] The changes also affected live music, as dancehalls were also permitted to apply for liquor licences in order to discourage audiences from 'filling themselves up with drink in pubs' before attending the venue. The year 1962 also saw the first licensed jazz spot in Glasgow, and despite forecasts of doom, the inaugural 'B-for-beer' night went quietly with 'a big run on orange juice' (Buchanan 1962b: 10).

References

'Alternatives to musicians'. 1962. *Glasgow Herald*, 23 November.

Buchanan, G. 1962a. 'Jazz bookings'. *Evening Times*, 26 October.

Buchanan, G. 1962b. 'On the town'. *Evening Times*, 19 October.

'Dance hall strike off'. 1962. *Evening Times*, 30 November.

'George Penman, bandleader'. 2009. Obituary. *The Herald*, 27 September. Available at: http://www.heraldscotland.com/comment/obituaries/george-penman-bandleader-1.922589 [accessed 12 September 2012].

MacDonald, I. 1962. 'A new era for "Mr Music Hall"'. *Evening Times*, 8 November.

'McBain died in a minute'. 1962. *Evening Times*, 1 November.

'Now Elvis may sing in Glasgow'. 1962. *Evening Times*, 23 November.

---

[9]   The front pages of both the *Glasgow Herald* and the *Evening Times* one week later announced that hotel bars were 'like a fairground', with drinkers crowding into hotels ('Sunday drinkers go to town', 1962: 1).

'On with the dance – and the drinks'. 1962. *Evening Times*, 19 October.
'Origin in main hall'. 1962. *Glasgow Herald*, 27 October.
'Strike of musicians threatened'. 1962. *Glasgow Herald*, 21 November.
'Sunday drinkers go to town'. 1962. *Glasgow Herald*, 8 October.
'Teenage drinkers shock a provost'. 1962. *Evening Times*, 19 October.
'Two years for dance-hall stabbing'. 1962. *Evening Times*, 25 October.

Chapter 5
Youth

Another café, La Pallette, in a large cellar in Blackett Street became our base … Blackett was a good place for picking up local intelligence. Two young lads from Gosforth, similarly dressed, with whom we'd become pally in La Pallette, told us excitedly about their first visit to the Club A' Go Go the previous evening. We joined them the following Friday. We met them at the Monument and, within five minutes, we were in the A' Go Go entrance in Percy Street. A young man, who looked like a student, sat on a table a few yards inside the door, deeply preoccupied reading a paperback. He lifted his head, smiled at the four of us, took our money, one and sixpence, and gave us directions: up two flights of stairs, passing the busworker's canteen on the way and into the Young Set. We were too young, he informed us, to enter the Jazz Lounge. The initial disappointment was quickly offset. We entered what seemed to me the darkest room I'd ever been in. But before I could adjust my eyes I was transfixed: *I'm Mad Again* by John Lee Hooker blasted out of the speakers and by the time Tony's face came into relief I could see that he was in heaven. (Bill Lancaster remembers being a teenager in Blaydon in 1962–3)[1]

Saturday 5th February: Had bath. Aunty Mary arrived. Pompey 2 Saints 5 – Raining. Went up Birdcage – Herbie Goins (6/-) rubbish, went to Mad House. Zoot Money on 'Jazz Beat'. **Friday 17th June**: English and Art O levels. Went up Lake Road with Pete to buy Animals and Ray Charles LPs. Went to Youth Club in evening. **Wednesday 2nd November**: Went to London. Met Mart at Design Centre (good). National Gallery (had lunch there). Saw Beatniks. Went up Kings Road to Chelsea Antique Market, great furs £2–£5 and army jackets (£4). Went up Wardour Street to Tiles and The Marquee. (From Dave Allen's teenage diary, Portsmouth, 1966)[2]

Introduction

Social historians are generally agreed that, in the words of Harry Hopkins, 'the young were the outstanding financial beneficiaries of the postwar situation'. Hopkins cites figures suggesting that by the late 1950s, teenage real earnings were 50 per cent higher than before the war and he, like other commentators, goes on to

---

[1]   Lancaster 1996: 58–9.
[2]   Allen 1998: 82–3.

argue that the 'Revolt of Youth' that such new affluence made possible (teenagers were estimated to have £900 million annual spending money) was driven by the power of commercial marketing:

> The emergence of the Teenager as a new sub-species of Western Man was a tribute to the multiple skills and infinite ramifications of Admass and the first full-scale demonstration in England of its powers.[3]

At the time, teenage expenditure and teenage marketing were most obvious in the clothing trade and the record business (the public could see and hear the results) and what caused most comment was the fact that young people commanded so much attention, not just from clothes shops and record dealers but from the mass media too, as an increasing number of teen films followed *Rock Around the Clock* round the cinema circuit, as BBC TV launched *Six-Five Special* and ITV *Oh Boy!*, and as the number of magazines aimed at teenage girls (*Marilyn, Valentine, Boyfriend, Honey, Jackie*, etc.) multiplied on newsagents' shelves.[4] Writing in 1965, Peter Leslie concluded that:

> the emergence of adolescent taste as the thing that really mattered ... has proved the biggest shake-up that show business has had within living memory. Today, the teenagers pay the piper – largely because they are the most numerous group with money to spare *on this kind of thing* – and the tunes they call have their elders in a whirl. With astonishment, dismay, curiosity or even fear, the adults find themselves on the outside, looking on at a vast industry with an annual turnover of many millions which is entirely devoted to the satisfaction of caprices and whims expressed by those who, only a few years ago, were expected to be seen and not heard. (Leslie 1965: 14–15, emphasis in original)

In this chapter we will consider the effects of this 'shake-up' from the perspective of the live music business, but before doing so, we should stress that the suggestion that between 1955 and 1965 Britain experienced a 'teenage revolution' needs some qualification.

To begin with, the extent of the change in young people's lives can be exaggerated. On the one hand, teenage 'affluence' as presented in such market research reports as Mark Abrams' influential *The Teenage Consumer* (1959) is overstated; contemporary sociological studies such as Peter Wilmott's *Adolescent Boys of East London* (1966) give a rather different picture of teenage culture. On the other hand, many of the 'new' patterns of teenage expenditure identified by Abrams had had a longer history than he suggests. As David Fowler argues:

---

[3]   Hopkins 1964: 424–5. Peter Lewis makes a similar argument in *The 50s.* He suggests that 1956 is the year that marked 'the explosive discovery of teenage identity – a Youthquake!' (Lewis 1978: 118).

[4]   In 1960 one of the new titles was *Marty*, named after Marty Wilde.

> The interwar period was probably the first time that substantial numbers of teenage wage-earners in Britain found themselves with a significant amount of money to spend on leisure.

Fowler suggests that Abrams overplayed the differences between pre- and post-war teenage life styles and, certainly, one way of describing the changes in youth culture in the 1950s is that the *setting* for well-established youth activities (notably dancing) was transformed, but not the activities themselves.[5]

Second, even this separation of young from grown-up leisure spaces did not happen evenly or at the same pace across the country. In Scotland, for example, dance halls remained important as places where everyone went until well into the 1960s and, in general, certainly in the 1950s, most promoters sought to create teenage spaces or events within existing venues rather than to establish entirely new youth places.

Third, 'teenage' culture was not as uniform across 13–19 year olds as contemporary media reports might suggest. There were class differences in the consumption habits of those who left school at 15 and those who did not; at the very least, working-class teenagers and students looked different.[6] And young people continued to be ambitious to enter music worlds that had nothing to do with Bill Haley or Elvis Presley. The National Youth Orchestra of Great Britain, founded by Ruth Railton in 1948, was well established by the time she retired in 1966 (it performed at the Edinburgh International Festival as early as 1952). Young brass players continued to join brass bands; young would-be jazz or folk performers continued to serve apprenticeships with older players.[7] The continuities in musical life were just as significant as the changes.

This chapter starts, then, with the assumption that terms like 'teenage revolution' or 'youthquake' refer to three rather different processes. First is the construction of a new kind of teenage market in which pop stars were a key component and Larry Parnes the most significant promoter. His approach is well captured in John Kennedy's memoirs of their joint management of Tommy Steele:

> Larry was sitting at the dressing-table working, as usual, at figures, and studying letters he was writing to various manufacturers offering Tommy Steele's name on their products. (Kennedy 1958: 50)

---

[5]   Fowler 1992: 150. One could also argue that young people's equally well-established love of cinema-going also continued, even if cinemas now became places in which to see live music as well as films.

[6]   This, for example, is Bruce Welch's description of Hank Marvin, a fellow pupil at Newcastle's Rutherford Grammar School: 'He looked like what I always thought university lads looked like; he had the blue duffel coat, the college scarf and the banjo, and he was into trad. jazz and all that sort of stuff' (Phipps, Tobler and Smith 2005: 203–4).

[7]   The National Youth Jazz Orchestra was founded by Bill Ashton in 1963.

Second is the reshaping of 'youth' as a social category by state institutions and state regulations. Police officers, head teachers and juvenile-court magistrates became significant media figures, feeding popular press accounts of teenage gangs (beginning with the Teddy Boys), alienation and, in general, what, 50 years later, would be labelled the problem of 'feral' adolescents. Continuing government concern (at both local and national levels) for youth as a problem meant state investment in youth services and a particular kind of youth space, the youth club, and while there was much angst at the time as to whether youth clubs could compete for adolescent attention with the wiles of commerce, they were, without a doubt, significant in the history of live music promotion. This, for example, is how the promoter Stuart Littlewood started his career in the music business:

> My entertainment career started in 1962 at my local youth club in Delph/ Saddleworth. I was helping the then youth club leader Les Mingham, who was a marvellously energetic individual and had great commitment to the youth of the area. We organised various fund raising dances and booked the up and coming pop groups of the day including Ricky and Dane Young and the Hollies, Mike Cadillac and the Playboys and Rev. Black and the Rocking Vicars. At first, they played in the local church hall, later moving into our own youth club building. I helped in distributing the posters and leaflets into the local shops, building the stage and acting as the MC/DJ. As I left school and went to work at the Co-Op as a grocery boy I still continued my work with the youth club and one of the support bands who played, the Exiles, asked me to become their manager/agent.[8]

Third is the construction of youth culture by young people themselves, as a generation seeking to make sense of their distinct post-war experience. 'Youth culture' in this sense was a kind of fantasy, an attempt to enact an ideal through musical resources. This ideal did cross classes. It may have been articulated differently according to young people's various opportunities, but it nevertheless involved a shared commitment to non-conformity with adult norms, whether bourgeois or proletarian. Such youth culture drew collectively on the signs and symbols of romantic dissatisfaction that we discussed in Chapter 4.[9] It is well captured in Brian Jackson's study of Huddersfield's jazz club. This was first formed in 1952 by 'a group of 16-year-old grammar school boys' who began to get together in the evenings with a variety of instruments. The club soon became a regular weekend performing event (with Thursday rehearsals) in a hired room in a café. Its initial membership (early leavers from the grammar school) was

---

[8]   From Stuart Littlewood's memoirs on the Manchesterbeat website: http://www. manchesterbeat.com/agents/stuartlittlewood/stuartlittlewood.php [accessed 12 September 2012].

[9]   The long history of adolescence as an enacted romantic fantasy is discussed in authoritative detail in Jon Savage's *Teenage* (2007).

joined by art and design students, apprentices from the local technical college
and people who had been to secondary modern schools:

> It might have been a grammar school thing at one time, but I think it's broadening
> now. But you can't tell at jazz clubs, can you? You can't tell where they come
> from. They all look the same, and they pretend a bit as well y'know. I know, I've
> done it myself. I bought a tech. scarf and I thought it was marvellous. My sister's
> boy friend has a stripey scarf that looks like some university or other. He works
> in a garage, he's a mechanic – but he's pretending a bit. (Jackson 1968: 121)

The club was still going when Jackson did his field research in the mid-1960s. It
had split and reformed many times; it had met in a variety of pub rooms (at one
point reaching a membership of over 400); it had embraced changing jazz styles,
retaining members into their thirties while continuing to recruit 15 year-olds. What
did not change was members' sense of difference: 'All look down on rock'n'roll,
skiffle, beat, pop, folk or the latest style that sweeps the top twenty'. On the other
hand:

> For most of the group, jazz – even if they like it a lot – is the occasion, the setting,
> for their society, and not its *raison d'être*. 'But I mean, how many people come
> down to hear good jazz. If they want to hear really good jazz, they wouldn't
> come out at all. You'd stop at home and play Morton records, wouldn't you? But
> that's the last thing I go to the Jazz Club for. There I like it as background to all
> that's going on'. (Jackson 1968: 128–9)

For Jackson, the jazz club was a refuge and resource for a 'floating community'
of young people who felt both placed and out of place: working-class grammar
school boys and girls who didn't make it out of Huddersfield to university;
secondary modern leavers who didn't want to reproduce their parents' lives but
were going to anyway. When Simon Frith undertook research in another Yorkshire
town, Keighley, a few years later, he found much the same sort of youth culture
in the local comprehensive school, among working-class fifth formers and early
leavers, focused now on progressive rock rather than jazz, on prog rock pub nights
with particular local deejays, and united in contempt for Marc Bolan's reinvention
of Tyrannosaurus Rex as T. Rex.[10]

Put together these three currents of social change – the teenage consumer, the
youth problem and youth culture – and we have the context for the emergence of
new kinds of music audience, new kinds of music venue and new kinds of musical
entertainment. This can best be illustrated by reference to a third Yorkshire town,
Sheffield, and its Club 60. Club 60 was the brainchild of local musician Terry
Thornton, whose 'original plan', first formulated in the late 1950s, was 'to create
a jazz club, a teenagers' nightclub, a music lovers' club and an arty-type poetry

---

[10] Frith 1978: 39–46.

centre'. This became a do-it-yourself project following a rebuff from Sheffield Council when Thornton tried to promote rock'n'roll at the City Hall. Thornton found suitable premises, an old pub cellar, and refurbished them with the help of volunteers – Sheffield art and design students, local performers and other music enthusiasts. Gatherings of youth, whatever their style (by the early 1960s the provincial media were fascinated by Beatniks), were always seen as problematic. As the local paper reported:

> The sight of a teenage figure walking the city streets in an oversize sweater and faded blue jeans horrifies the average Sheffield citizen. As the rope sandals slap down the road, they hear the snatches of Freud and views on free love so can we blame them for wondering what the youth of today is coming to? Because some of today's teenagers dress that little bit differently with eccentricities in clothing and casual haircuts, parents gain the wrong impression and soon begin to entertain thoughts of delinquency and teenage gang warfare.

Thornton was undaunted and Club 60 opened on 5 October 1960, billing itself as 'the local jazz club with the continental atmosphere'. Its members could enjoy trad jazz on Fridays and modern jazz on Sundays; Saturdays featured 'The Best in local pop, rock, ballads and blues'. Visiting performers (usually billed as 'direct from the London scene') might also appear on other nights. The club was so successful that in 1962 Thornton opened another, bigger venue, the Esquire: 'This will be Sheffield's Greatest Centre of Pop and Trad Music', he claimed. It would also be the place where Sheffield's 1960s youth culture was forged.[11]

The Young Consumer

As Bill Ogersby has documented, social commentators began to draw attention to the increasing financial clout of young British workers almost as soon as the Second World War was over. Ogersby quotes the 1947 Clarke Report on School and Life:

> When juvenile workers are scarce, as they are now, and are likely to continue to be, he [the young worker] quickly realises that he may not be so unimportant as he seemed at first; and after two or three years his income may be larger compared with his needs and with his contribution to maintenance than at any other period of his life. (Ogersby 1998: 24)[12]

---

[11]   Details of Club 60 are from Hale and Thornton 2002: 10–11. For more on the Esquire, see the 'A Snapshot of Sheffield in October–November 1962', pp. 165–7 below.

[12]   This was the first report from the Central Advisory Councils for Education (CACE), which had been established by the 1944 Education Act.

For the next 25 years, teenagers were 'affluent' not so much because they were well paid but because a relatively small proportion of the money they did earn went on their upkeep. As Frith puts it, 'the "affluent teenagers" of the 1950s and 1960s were affluent because their parents were; what was involved was disposable income. One reason for teenagers' good times from 1950 to 1970 was that their parents were fully employed and relatively well off'. And as Cyril Smith observes, youth culture could only emerge when family income was sufficient to allow individual rather than family ownership of radios and record players – hence the teen marketing from the mid-1950s of the transistor radio and portable record players like the Dansette.[13]

Journalists and sociologists now began to observe the dominant role of music in teenagers' lives.[14] Harry Hopkins, for example, claims (without giving a source) that by the end of the decade 'nine out of every ten London teenagers spent some of their leisure listening to records'. 'Every weekend and lunch-hour', he writes, 'the self-service "Browseries" and "Melody Bars" were packed with abstracted teenagers, "winkle-picker" toes tapping, pony-tails swinging.' The 45 rpm single, launched in Britain in 1952, was seen to be a product primarily aimed at and bought by young people – Laurie claims that singles accounted for 80 per cent of UK record sales (by volume) in 1963, and takes this to indicate the dominance of teenage taste in the UK record market.[15] Sociologists, meanwhile, were documenting how record and music listening had become a 'regular pastime'.[16] Ogersby quotes an 18 year old interviewed in Mass Observation's 1949 *Report on Teenage Girls*:

> I go to the jazz club, dancing, tennis, swimming and listening to gramophone records. On Saturday I went to the Bebop Club in the evening ... I packed up my boyfriend because he didn't like me going to Bop clubs ... I don't disagree with my parents except about 'Bop'. That's the only thing, Mother can't stand that, but I like it ... What do I want out of life? Just a nice husband, a baby, a house and 'bop' records. (Ogersby 1998: 58)

And in *The Insecure Offenders*, T.R. Fyvel suggests that 'his love for pop music appears to be the chink in the teddy boy's armour of non-participation'. If Teds were, in general, against hard work and 'getting on':

---

[13]   Frith 1978: 36; Smith 1967.

[14]   Pre-war youth studies usually noted the amount of time young people spent dancing but rarely mentioned any other musical interests or activities.

[15]   Hopkins 1964: 432; Laurie 1965: 72. When EMI launched the 45 rpm single in Britain, all but one of its first batch of 48 releases carried a classical recording. Within a year almost all its new 45 rpm releases featured 'popular' music. When Decca Records followed EMI's lead in 1954, its 45 rpm catalogue included no classical music at all (see Frith 2009).

[16]   See, for example, Venness 1962.

Sweat and toil to learn music is one of the few exceptions. A boy willing to devote every day to practise in a band is not derided for his pains. Even in Ted circles, musical ambition is generally regarded as legitimate. (Fyvel 1963: 240)

When Mark Abrams' teenage consumer report came out in 1959, its quantitative data thus confirmed systematically what had already been documented piecemeal – the emergence of 'distinctive teenage spending for distinctive teenage ends in a distinctive teenage world', in which music occupied the central place. Abrams showed in detail that teenagers spent their money on particular kinds of goods and that teenage spending dominated particular consumer sectors. He calculated, for example, that teenagers accounted for 44 per cent of total spending on records and record players.[17] Put together Abrams' market research with contemporary academic youth studies and what becomes clear is that:

> The young's interest in pop determined the television programmes they watched, the magazines they read, the cafés they went to, the 'necessary tools' – transistor radio, record player, tape recorder, guitar – they sought to own. (Frith 1978: 38)

To put this another way, from the mid-1950s, the media aimed at youth necessarily organised themselves around their 'pop' interests. Within the music magazine market itself, *New Musical Express* increasingly focused on teen pop as it competed for young readers with *Record Mirror* (launched in 1953) and *Disc* (1958), while the increasing number of magazines aimed at teenage girls continued to be packaged as a combination of romance and pop, with the proportion of pop pix and features steadily growing. In Sheffield the local paper, *The Star*, launched its own Teenage Club in March 1959:

> The club held teenage parties in the Green Room above the Gaumont where they could 'meet their favourite pop stars, talk with them, have a cup of tea with them and get their autographs'. Guests at the inaugural party were Marty Wilde and Russ Conway ... It was the success of these parties and the establishing of the Teenage Shows later in the year which led, in 1960, to the Saturday night *Star* including a Teenage Page.[18]

For both the BBC and commercial radio and TV broadcasters, youth programming meant pop music programming, just as for film studios, aware that by the late 1950s teenagers made up half the cinema audience, a youth film meant a film starring a pop star.[19] The significance of such youth magazines, programmes and pictures was not

---

[17]   Abrams 1959: 10; Ogersby 1998: 24.

[18]   Firminger and Lilleker 2001: 24. The Teenage Show became a regular Saturday morning event at the Gaumont. It combined a film showing with a 'jive session' in which local teen bands played live.

[19]   Laurie 1965: 68.

just that they appealed to teenagers but also that they symbolically excluded adults. Ogersby describes a Southern TV programme broadcast for a few months in 1963, *Dad You're a Square*, which 'used a format similar to the BBC's *Juke Box Jury*'. In this case, however, the panel was composed of parents and their teenage children who argued over the relative merits of different discs – the programme crystallising the idea of a popular culture beset by virtually insurmountable generational divisions. And in August 1963, Rediffusion launched *Ready Steady Go*, a programme that 'made few concessions to an adult audience, revelling in a preoccupation with the music, fashions and tastes of the youth scene'.[20]

Three aspects of teenage music consumption were to have particular significance for British music culture. First, the teenage music market was organised around the making and marketing of records. We will discuss the record industry in Chapter 6; the point to make here is that if teenage musical taste was shaped in part by the activities of record companies, record company policies were, in turn, shaped by the activities of teenagers.

Second, selling popular music to teenagers meant packaging a new sort of music star: the pop idol. The origins of pop fandom (what is involved here is primarily, though not exclusively, the attention paid by female fans to male stars) lie in pre-war film star marketing, and in the early 1950s Johnnie Ray's and Dickie Valentine's shows were already being described by startled journalists as involving crowds of noisy young women 'splashing in a crazy pool of adoration'.[21] The novelty of rock'n'roll was that its performers were the fans' own age, came from similar backgrounds and had similar interests. In 1958 John Kennedy described Tommy Steele's fans in just these terms:

> You buy his records. You read every word printed about him. You follow his romance as if it were your own. In a way it is – and there lies the other part of his appeal for you. Doesn't he look just like that young fellow around the corner – the one you're hoping will forget his shyness and date you one moonlight evening? They wear the same kind of clothes. They talk the same kind of way. They come from the same kind of house.[22]

Teen pop stars, more even than film stars, were marketed to be both knowable and accessible. Their 'personalities' were revealed both in the screeds of words about them in young women's magazines and in the posters that could be pulled out and pinned up on bedroom walls and inside desk lids. The new teen TV shows added to the impact of this sort of close-up imagery, and as film actors like Albert Finney and Terence Stamp also started being marketed as simultaneously young,

---

[20]   Ogersby 1998: 39–40.

[21]   This phrase taken from a report by Robert Muller in *Picture Post* (7 August 1954), quoted in Ogersby 1998: 58.

[22]   Kennedy 1958: 160. Kennedy also describes the elaborate measures he took to ensure that Steele's fans did not discover that he had a steady girlfriend.

glamorous and working class, while 'ordinary' young people got to be employed as fashion models or, like Janice Nicholls and Cathy McGowan, to front teen television shows, so the teen idol developed from being an object of audience adulation to being *representative* of youth, standing for youth style in the very act of being consumed.

The first teen pop stars were packaged and sent round the variety circuit as a kind of novelty act. Bruce Welch remembers that when the Shadows started performing:

> It was such early days that there wasn't a music industry. We came into variety, we came into show business, and we were run by much older men, agents, managers, who were 40, 45 years old. The early shows that we would do would have three dancing girls to open, kicking their legs up, then you'd have the guys with the old doves, and that sort of novelty act, plus a couple of comedians. And then we would come on and do a 17-minute slot. (Phipps, Tobler and Smith 2005: 206)

Under Brian Epstein's management, the Beatles too played the variety circuit, featuring in line-ups with comics, dancers and other bands, but, as Shawn Levy points out:

> Few of the bands who surfaced after the Beatles broke through found it appealing – or even necessary – to pander in this way to an older audience or to London impresarios' antique ideas of what made a good show ... [soon] even the stodgiest hands in showbiz recognised that the kids who waited for hours to scream at pop bands didn't want to see dog acts, magicians or singers of novelty tunes as well. (Levy 2003: 149)

Pop stars were now music entrepreneurs' means of access to an increasingly valuable but awkward market, and this meant a decisive shift in the power structure of the live music industry. As Levy notes in the case of the Beatles,

> Only a few months earlier [Epstein] had been sincerely grateful to the likes of West End and variety tycoons Lew Grade and Bernard Delfont for their willingness to make a place for his boys. [Now] he found himself flattered with *their* attentions and requests. (Levy 2003: 149)[23]

The final point to make here is that teenage consumer culture was mediated. It became something collective through the mechanisms of radio, television and magazines, through the retail marketing of clothes and cosmetics, as well as through the process of listening and dancing to the same sounds. Teen pop, as Mary Ingham remembers, bound:

---

[23]   For an entertaining example of the changing power structure see Tito Burns' dealings with Bob Dylan and his manager, Albert Grossman, in the film *Don't Look Back*.

a generation of separate upbringings simply because the same record played everywhere – Boots record booths, the Wimpy's jukebox, Alan Freeman's 'Pick of the Pops' and Radio Luxembourg Top Twenty late on Sunday night under the pillow. Our transistors tuned us in to all the others of our age. The adolescent was no longer the solitary misfit of the family group. (Ingham 1981: 67)

Peter Laurie puts it this way:

Since the mid-fifties there has been a most important change: the teenagers have come into nationwide contact with each other. They have formed a society of their own. It is something very new when, say, a fifteen-year-old girl in a Devon village has more in common with her contemporaries on Tyneside than with her own parents and neighbours. (Laurie 1965: 11)

Laurie is here describing collective consumption, which was fashion driven, 'with London always in the lead', and as teenage culture developed in the 1960s, young stylists had increasing opportunities to enact their sense of community physically in settings specially designed for them. Tom Wolfe famously described one such mod venue in the mid-1960s for readers of the *Daily Telegraph*:

down in the cellar at noon. Two hundred and fifty office boys, office girls, department store clerks, messengers, members of London's vast child work-force of teenagers who leave school at 15, pour down into this cellar, Tiles, in the middle of the day for a break … back into *The Life*. The man on the stage playing the records is Clem Dalton, a disc jockey. Off to one side in the dimness is a soft-drink stand, a beauty parlour called Face Place and an arcade of boutiques, a Ravel shoe store, a record shop, a couple of other places, all known as Tiles Street. There is a sign out there in the Arcade that says Tiles Street W1. The place is set up as an underground city for The Life. (Wolfe 1968: 79)

Teenagers didn't spend all their time consuming, of course, and 'The Life' was only temporary. What teenagers did do all the time was grow up.

Growing Up in Public

In their wide-ranging social study of *English Life and Leisure*, published in 1951, B. Seebohm Rowntree and G.R. Lavers cite statistics showing that three million people in England went ballroom dancing every week in 450 dance halls.[24] The halls were open for dancing to the public six days a week and to club members on a Sunday. From their own observations and interviews, Rowntree and Lavers

---

[24]   The figures were taken from an early piece of research (into 'Britain Off Duty') by Mark Abrams.

concluded that 'a large majority of dancers are young people, mostly between the ages of 16 and 24'. While 'well-to-do' people frequented more exclusive dance venues (in hotels, restaurants and private residences), most public dancers were 'drawn from the working and lower middle class'.[25]

The popularity of public dancing among young people (and particularly among young urban workers) was apparent in Britain from early in the twentieth century. In *The Classic Slum*, Robert Roberts describes how dance halls in working-class districts of Manchester in the 1920s became the focus for both the display of fashion and the enactment of new social rituals among 16–25 year olds, while in January 1920 the Edinburgh *Evening News* reported that:

> Apparently the young people of today are not satisfied with dancing almost every night of the week and therefore the 'Dance tea' has been introduced where they can jazz to their hearts' content all afternoon as well.[26]

Throughout the inter-war period, only cinema-going rivalled dancing in young people's use of their leisure time, and this did not change in the first decade after 1945. In the Yorkshire mining community of Ashton, for example:

> Each Saturday evening throughout the year the Miners' Welfare Institute is used for ballroom dancing. (At each dance there are 400 or 500 people between the ages of 15 and 22, the great majority of them between the ages of 17 and 20.) At Easter, Whitsuntide, August Bank Holiday, and Christmas, more than one dance is held. The number of dances held there at Easter 1953 is typical of such times. There was dancing from 7.30 p.m. until 11.30 p.m. on Saturday night. There was another dance early on Easter Monday morning from 12.15 a.m. until 4 p.m., and a third dance at 8.25 p.m. which lasted until 1 a.m. on Tuesday morning. The popularity of this activity among young people in Ashton can be gauged from the fact that in 1951 the total Ashton population in the age group 15–22 was 716. (Dennis, Henriques and Slaughter 1956: 125–6)

But in the late 1950s, dancing habits did begin to change. The East End adolescent boys studied by Peter Willmott still went dancing, but now in a variety of venues, nearly all of which attracted young people exclusively, whether particular pubs, jazz and youth clubs or 'dance halls like the Lyceum in the Strand, the Royal at Tottenham or Barrie's at Hackney'. Peter Leslie cites figures gathered from a survey of 28 London R&B clubs which suggested that they were by then catering to 10,000 teenage dancers each week: 'three West End clubs alone being visited by *all* of them *at least once per fortnight*'. Between them these clubs had 100,000 members.[27]

[25]   Rowntree and Lavers 1951: 279–80.
[26]   Quoted in Casciani 1994: 45.
[27]   Willmott 1966: 32; Leslie 1965: 184, emphasis in original.

In general it is clear that young people spent as much time dancing in the 1960s as had their parents in the 1930s, but they were dancing in a different way to different music in different sorts of venue – the ballroom had largely been replaced by the club. This change was UK-wide, though outside London it took longer and was on occasion more fraught. In Scotland, for example, dance halls in their 1940s form survived into the mid-1960s, and in many places young dancers had to battle to dance in their own way to their own sort of music. Throughout the 1950s, live music in Scotland was promoted around a circuit of dance halls (in the big cities built as ballrooms, in small towns often just tarted-up town, church or village halls) and a small number of agents were used to 'supply bands for functions and ballrooms all over Scotland'.[28]

Teenage musicians could play in youth clubs, at school or church socials, even in miners' welfare or other working men's clubs, but any band of any sort wanting to cover the costs of touring had to play the dance halls (the cinema circuit was confined to the biggest cities). There were two problems here: dance-hall managers were reluctant to book pop, rock or beat groups (about which they knew little) and they were loath to admit young people who were either improperly dressed or impatient with formal dancing. As late as the mid-1960s, when the Edinburgh Plaza felt obliged to adapt its main ballroom 'to the Rock style':

> The management still clung to the older standards of dress and behaviour. The barring of a prospective customer wearing the latest roll-neck shirt brought newspaper comment. The aggrieved customer complained, 'The management of a public dance hall have no justification for such a restriction in this supposedly enlightened age.' The management responded, 'People should remember it's a dance they're going to, not an après-ski affair'. (Casciani 1994: 119)

The failure of established dance halls to cater for teenage consumers opened up opportunities for a new generation of promoters, but even they could not solve the problem of venues.[29] The immediate solution was to make the teenage dance part of the general evening's entertainment. When Glasgow's rebuilt Barrowland Ballroom was launched on Christmas Eve 1960 (the previous building had burnt down in August 1958),[30] 'the opening night was a Teenage Jamboree and on the following Thursday there was a "Teen Plus Night (for Mammy, Daddy, yes and

---

[28]   Casciani 1994: 74.

[29]   Ronnie Simpson, a young agent at the time (he was to become manager of the Glasgow Apollo), describes these new entrepreneurs as 'a raggle-taggle bunch': 'Johnny Wilson ran a bus company. Albert Bonici ran a café in Elgin, Bert Ewen was an Aberdeenshire baker, Duncan McKinnon was a Border farmer and the Fehilly Brothers, first in Thurso then in Dunfermline, ran venues [though they'd come to Scotland as painters]' (Tobin 2010: 60–1).

[30]   Andrew O'Hagan writes that his mother who 'had stopped going dancing when she got married in 1959 … with a half-joking smirk used to say that she'd never have got married if that [the Barrowlands fire] hadn't happened' (O'Hagan 1995: 49).

Granny!)'", and for Bill Gracie, a dance musician, 'the beginning of the end for big bands started in 1961 ... I clearly remember being told by the management of the Hamilton Salon that a beat group would be playing the second half of one of our nights'.[31]

One problem facing promoters trying to make Scottish dance halls more youth friendly was that many halls were obliged by deals they had done with the Musicians' Union to employ a minimum number of musicians. In Greenock, for example, each dance hall in registering with the local Musicians' Union branch was given its own 'number' rating; any band booked to play a dance had to be at least that big (Thomson 1989: 143).[32] As Ronnie Simpson remembers, at the beginning of the 1960s:

> Ballroom owners in west-central Scotland came to an agreement with the Musicians' Union that a band had to have at least seven members. Most [beat] combos at that time were four or five strong, and maybe the odd six. So we were all out in the cold. But the powers didn't have control over *all* the halls – they ran the 'biggest most popular' ones just because they were the only option for the dancing public. So we started booking community centres and ran Friday night hops against the formal dance nights. (Tobin 2010: 76, emphasis in original)

Even in the mid-1960s, the Strathpeffer Pavilion still operated a rule that all groups had to have at least four members – 'when a trio called 123 played in the Strath they were known as the Four Spots and their manager mimed along on stage'.[33]

By now, though, the 'massive split' between old and new ways of dancing was unbridgeable: 'the young scorned the dances of their parents and their parents were unwilling or unable to do the new dances'. Some ballrooms, like Barrowland, managed to find a way to accommodate both styles (with a Thursday night session for 'over-25s', for example, to which Andrew O'Hagan's granny and her two married daughters went), but 'many refused to allow the new dances and continued to play as before to an aging dancing population'.[34] By the end of the 1960s, most of Scotland's traditional ballrooms had been closed and demolished or were being used for other purposes, such as bingo. Otherwise, dance halls catered exclusively to the young.

There is a paradox here, though, because, as we have already suggested, in many ways they always had done, and the point that we need to stress is that it

---

[31]   Casciani 1994: 116; Tobin 2010: 72.

[32]   Thomson 1989: 143. During the war, venues such as hotels and restaurants 'had been forced to make do with smaller bands. They had discovered that dancers were perfectly happy with this arrangement and managements were therefore reluctant to return to the more expensive bands' (Casciani 1994: 104). After the war, the Musicians' Union in Scotland was determined to protect its members from a similar policy in dance halls.

[33]   Tobin 2010: 100.

[34]   O'Hagan 1995: 50; Casciani 1994: 117–18.

was the long-established youth interest in dancing that drove the development of post-war popular music rather than vice versa. As Humphrey Lyttelton argues, 'it wasn't until some benefactor founded the first jazz-for-dancing club in London that jazz in postwar Britain began to have a chance', and the reason why young people went dancing was not simply because it was an enjoyable way to listen to music. 'Going to the dance', as Raymond Thomson puts it, 'had a procreational as well as a recreational function. The most significant objective was the perennial human motivation – to find a mate'. Or, as Norman Dennis and his colleagues suggest, 'the main function of these weekly dances appears to be that of bringing young people together in a manner which facilitates the approach of the two sexes'.[35]

Dancing, in short, was essential to courtship. An article in *New Society* in 1962 reported research findings that more 16–24-year-old brides met their husbands at a dance than in any other way, a suggestion supported by the anecdotal evidence in Eddie Tobin's *Are Ye Dancin'?*, which he subtitles 'the story of Scotland's dance halls, rock'n'roll, and how yer da met yer maw'. Certainly, as Frith noted in 1978, 'one of the more dramatic leisure statistics is the abruptness with which young women stop going to public dances after marriage'.[36]

Dancing was not simply about youth culture, then, it was also a way of managing the transition from adolescent to adult sexual status, which is one reason why young people dancing have always been seen as a social problem. In 1951 Rowntree and Lavers, having described youth dominance in public dancing, went on to warn that:

> Modern ballroom dancing may easily degenerate into a sensuous form of entertainment, and if self-control is weakened with alcohol it is more than likely that it will do so, which might easily lead to unruly behaviour and not infrequently to sexual immorality.[37]

Their concern that licensing magistrates were 'not nearly alive enough to the dangers inherent in enabling dancers to obtain alcohol' was misplaced, at least in Scotland, where it remained to difficult to drink and dance until well into the 1960s, but the implicit suggestion that young people dancing should somehow be supervised continued to inform 1950s youth club policy. For older dancers, though, the key problem of teenage dancing as it developed in the 1950s was that it lacked the formal order of dance itself. Teenage dancers were, it seemed, no longer regulated by conventional steps, by practised ways of partnering, by the authority of the dance teacher, the band leader or the ballroom maitre d'. The problem was not so much that young dancers *were* drunk or promiscuous but that their music and their dancing suggested that they might be.

---

[35] Dennis, Henriques and Slaughter 1956: 126; Lyttelton 1958: 72; Thomson 1989: 148.
[36] Rowntree 1962; Frith 1978: 66.
[37] Rowntree and Lavers 1951: 282.

Conclusion

In 1949 the staff and students of the Westhill Teacher Training College carried out a study of 80,000 adolescents in Birmingham. One of their findings was that:

> Many young people have a genuine interest in music even though it may only show itself in the popularity of 'jazz concerts' or in the continuous use (or misuse) of the [youth] clubroom piano or gramophone. A leader who knows his job can turn this interest to advantage. One of our own students, who is not herself particularly musical, held the attention of the members of a quite difficult club as she introduced them to a programme of gramophone records on 'Dance Music through the Ages'. The following week, another student, with the aid of some excellent Bureau of Current Affairs posters, took the same group further with a talk on 'Instruments of the orchestra', playing records of instrumental music and pointing to a picture of each instrument as it was heard. (Reed 1950: 119)

In the event, youth workers were less successful than commercial entrepreneurs in turning young people's interest in music to their advantage. The teenage market was ideal for the new fashion-based consumer industries of the 1950s because of its pace of turnover: young people were the obvious targets for continuously 'new' looks and 'new' sounds, and by the end of the 1950s, 'pop' music meant music made and consumed by youth. In the 1960s, though, for at least some young consumers, music became a setting for more subtle choices than simply following the latest teenage trend. In his memoir of growing up in Portsmouth, Dave Allen describes a not uncommon confusion of musical taste and social identity:

> I was way too soft to be a rocker but I loved Little Richard, Gene Vincent and Eddie Cochran and some of my best mates wore chukka boots and quiffs. I used to play snooker with them up in Copnor Road ... At the same time I was going off to folk clubs with Pete and discovering a world of live acoustic music, politics, poetry and beer ... Towering above all of this however was Mod. The challenge then was to sustain a sufficiently credible relationship with other ways of living at the same time. I wanted to be a Mod most of the time while protecting bits for snooker, Gene Vincent, Dylan and Sonny Terry and Brownie McGhee, and, while Mod was the culture of graphics and fashion design, I always preferred fine art – a disastrously snobbish affection in terms of my career and one that seemed to push me away from Mods and towards the intellectual aspects of the folk scene and jazz. (Allen 1998: 76–7)

What interests us about this kind of musical sensibility – each musical choice involving alliances with different youth groups – are its implications for the way live music worked. As he suggests, Portsmouth mods like Allen came to experience an intense emotional identity with the *venues* in which they heard their music. For Allen, this was the Birdcage, which opened in the town in 1965:

> The best way to get a sense of the importance of The Birdcage thirty years on is to get hold of a group of people who grew up in Portsmouth and who will now be between forty-five and fifty-five and ask them about The Birdcage. If they don't know what you're talking about, move on. Most people will either tell you that they never went – probably weren't allowed to go, in which case you can see a sadness in their eyes – or they will begin a succession of stories which may well last for hours if not days. Anyone who fits the criteria of age/place and claims to love popular music has to be able to tell you their Birdcage story. Otherwise they don't really love popular music. (Allen 1998: 63)

Such 'legendary' local venues (Liverpool's Cavern Club, Newcastle's Club A'Gogo and Sheffield's Esquire are others) became a key part of the 1960s live music business and we will discuss this further in Chapter 7. By this time, clubs were also spaces in which other sorts of identity could be explored. In his memoirs of being young in mid-1960s London, Peter Burton suggests that 'the premiere Mod club – the Scene in Ham Yard behind Shaftesbury Avenue – was basically a straight version of Le Duce', a club in a basement in D'Arblay Street (membership 10 shillings a year, admission five shillings per night) 'famous for its jukebox, which houses a massive selection of Motown favourites and soul sounds', an unlicensed club with a coffee machine that 'won't stop hissing and groaning – and breaking down', and:

> predominantly a club for teenagers, it is almost incidental that they are gay or bisexual. *They* come here for the music, to dance, for the speed. Sex is part of their pleasure but a minor part. Something that happens *afterwards*. The older club members are different. The new attitudes confuse them and though they try hard to fit into this unisexual world, they feel a little incongruous. *They* leave early – long before the club closes. (Burton 1985: 30–8, emphasis in original)

Le Duce prefigured the 1970s disco scene to come, but Burton's account also confirms that by 1965, even in Soho, a Saturday night out was essentially a teenage affair.

Chapter 6
The Recording Industry

That hit record changed everything. It was the same group, with the same act, the same material but with an important difference. They were in the Top Ten, the pop metamorphosis. Before 'Too Late Now', £30 an engagement was the norm; after 'Too Late Now', £75; after 'Hippy Hippy Shake' between £250 and £300 a night. (Jim Godbolt, on being agent for the Swinging Blue Jeans in 1963)[1]

Have several numbers ready for your recording session. The A&R man might want to record quite a few songs from your repertoire before it is decided which two will be chosen for your single release ... As you are playing in the studio, the recording manager will be listening to every aspect of your music. When he finally decides how a number should be played he will be able to pinpoint the 'commercial angle'. That is, the way you play and sing which makes you different from anyone else. (The Hollies on 'How to be a Beat Group' in 1964)[2]

Introduction

In 1950 the recorded music sector in Britain was still dominated by shellac 78 rpm records, a format that had been introduced to the mass market at the beginning of the century. Shellac records were fragile, only carried five minutes of music a side and had a high surface noise level when played. The Musicians' Union was at the height of its influence and the protection of jobs in live music performance was its primary objective, to which end it had negotiated deals with the record companies' licensing agency, Phonographic Performance Limited (PPL), to ensure that 'the competition of a musician's recorded work with his live performance' was 'rigidly controlled and compensated',[3] and with the BBC, Britain's only broadcaster, to restrict the playing of records on the radio. This situation was about to be transformed and in this chapter we will describe how the growth of the recording industry in the post-war era changed both the power structure of the British music business and the prevailing ideology of music production and consumption.

Britain's two big record companies, EMI and Decca, emerged from the war as they went into it – as a duopoly, controlling most of the British record market, a market which now grew apace, following the introduction of vinyl records and the

---

[1]   Godbolt 1976: 151.
[2]   The Hollies 1964: 49.
[3]   *Melody Maker*, 17 May 1947: 1.

45 and 33⅓ rpm formats. The boom in record sales from the mid-1950s and the growing use of records in public places brought about a shift in how music was heard: recordings increasingly competed with live performances as the primary or ideal musical experience, and such competition had significant effects on the use of music by radio and television and on their role in music marketing.

The growth of the television industry in Britain, especially following the introduction of commercial TV in 1955, was as striking as the growth in record sales. Initially live music entrepreneurs, rather than trying to compete with the new form of domestic entertainment, reaped huge rewards by using their expertise and power to establish live music shows as mainstream TV programming, while the emergence of a new chart-oriented record culture, the rise of 'disc hops' and the growing media interest in the youth audience all contributed to new business relationships between the live and recorded music sectors. Musical entertainers had previously constructed a national audience gradually by touring. Now records (promoted by radio play and TV appearances) accelerated the speed with which an act could attract a live audience, upsetting the conventional economics of concert promotion.

In some respects the classical world was impervious to these changes. London's orchestras were increasingly reliant on recording session income, and record companies' classical divisions continued to make stars out of their 'exclusively signed' conductors and soloists, but the BBC's classical programming continued to be organised around the broadcast of live concerts, classical concert promoters still paid little attention to record release schedules and record company marketing departments did not yet plan classical sales campaigns around who was performing what and when. John Culshaw, head of Decca's classical division, has described the resulting mess the company made of selling Benjamin Britten's *War Requiem* in 1962:

> Culshaw was convinced of both its musical and its commercial worth – the *Requiem* was being given its first performance as part of the celebrations surrounding the rebuilding of Coventry Cathedral; its launch would be accompanied by a mass of radio, television and press publicity. Unfortunately, Britten was not, historically, a best seller, and Decca's bosses were not convinced that any new classical music sold particularly well – its place in the Decca catalogue was a matter of prestige rather than profit. Culshaw therefore lost the internal argument about how many of the *War Requiem* to press: its run was the same as for previous Britten works. (Frith 1996: 22)

The pressing was far too small. The *War Requiem* sold out in a week and by the time more copies were pressed (Decca's pressing plants were fully booked by pop product), the sales momentum was lost.

On the other hand (as Culshaw's story also suggests), the transformation of the British record industry between 1950 and 1967 involved upsetting its cultural hierarchy. Even though Decca and EMI had always sold more popular than classical records, the classical market had been seen as more significant for the industry's long-term prospects, partly because classical music was seen as being of permanent value (unlike pop's throwaway numbers) – 'record companies saw themselves as analogous to book publishers: their long-term success depended on improving general standards of musical literacy'[4] – and partly because classical record buyers were seen as more likely to invest in technological change, being both more affluent than pop fans and more concerned with the technical qualities of recordings. Classical divisions thus led the way in developing post-war sound technology. When stereo was introduced in 1955, for example, EMI chose senior classical engineer Chris Parker to experiment with the equipment – EMI's first stereo recording was Beethoven's *Fidelio* – and as late as 1964, the trade paper *Retail Business* was warning its readers that stereo records (which by then had about 12 per cent of the market) would continue to be of limited appeal:

> The future of stereo would seem to be limited by the fact that its technical advantages can only be fully realised in the case of classical music … there are important marketing considerations which make it unsuitable for the pops market.[5]

Two years later, *Retail Business* was admitting that the introduction of a cheap stereo pick-up had made nonsense of its prediction, and the unprecedented international album sales in the mid- to late 1960s of British artists like the Beatles, the Rolling Stones and the Who was seen as a triumph for the British recording industry (the Beatles got their MBEs in 1965 for their services to export). But this was a very different British recording industry culturally than it had been when Joseph Lockwood became Chairman of EMI in 1954:

> I found that the whole emphasis was on classical recording so I decided to find out who was responsible for the pop side … and I discovered that they were treated as very low grade people – rather like sergeants in an army whereas Walter Legge [chief classical producer] was a field marshal.

In the early 1960s, at EMI as at Decca, classical sessions began to take second place to pop recordings. Peter Andry, EMI's senior classical producer, remembers that:

> as the shift from Abbey Road being a classically dominated operation took place, we soon realised that, in a commercial environment, it was the pop that was making the bread and we had to accommodate ourselves to that fact.[6]

---

[4]   Frith 1987: 286–7.

[5]   Quoted in Frith 1978: 101; and see Southall 1982: 46–7.

[6]   Quotes from Southall 1982: 48, 111.

However, it was also the commercial success of this new pop-centred business that drew American record labels to the British market, and the impact of American music industry practices on British music culture can also be seen in the diversification of British music radio. The offshore pirate radio stations that flourished from 1964 to 1967, many with the direct investment of US capital and expertise, were followed by the creation of the chart-based BBC Radio 1 in 1967, its jingles made in Dallas, Texas. Popular music culture in Britain in 1967 was very different from how it had been even 10 years earlier, and the recording industry was instrumental in the changes.

Making Records

James Nott has written an excellent account of the early history of the recording business in Britain and notes that one problem in telling the story of the British record industry is that neither of its dominant companies, EMI and Decca, was ever really exclusively 'British'. EMI was the result of a merger in 1931 between the Gramophone Company ('His Master's Voice') and the Columbia Graphophone Company, both of which 'retained close links with the United States' – even as a British-based multinational, EMI had an American managing director, Louis Sterling, and an American-dominated board of directors.[7] The Decca Gramophone Company began as a British musical-instrument manufacturer, switched to gramophone production and was floated as a public company in 1928 by a young stockbroker, Edward Lewis, who then took Decca over and moved it into record production. His biggest coup was to secure Decca the British rights to the American Brunswick label, which at that point had the best popular music catalogue in the USA (it included Guy Lombardo, Bing Crosby, the Boswell Sisters and the Mills Brothers). In October 1934, Lewis launched the US Decca Company, poaching Brunswick's Jack Kapp to be his recording manager. Kapp brought Bing Crosby with him and Crosby's sales made certain Decca's US future.[8]

    The British gramophone industry thus developed during the inter-war period with two distinct characteristics: first, even though EMI and Decca were majority British-owned by 1935, they remained multinational conglomerates which, in Nott's words, 'had either been directly or indirectly influenced by America'; second, both relied on US licensing deals (and the popularity of US acts) to maintain their dominance in the British market. Nott notes that in 1929 there had been almost 50 record and gramophone companies in Britain: 'the industry was large and diverse with firms of all sizes engaged in production'. Eight years later, EMI and Decca had either seen off or acquired their competitors.[9]

[7] Nott 2002: 21.
[8] Frith 1987: 283; and see Barfe 2004: 130.
[9] Nott 2002: 26.

Both EMI and Decca had experience in electronics, and during the Second World War both companies were involved in manufacturing defence equipment as well as a range of electronic and consumer goods. Several of the breakthroughs in defence research were significant for the commercial recording industry. The improved audio fidelity necessary for radar technology, for example, was applied to recorded music, and from 1944 Decca began producing records using its new 'Full Frequency Range Recording' system. Magnetic tape recording technology, developed during the war by the Germans, was worked on after 1945 in both the USA (by Ampex) and Britain (by EMI). The British Tape Recorder 1 (BTR-1) was installed in Abbey Road studios in 1947. From 1952 the BTR-2 became the industry standard, used by the BBC and other studios throughout the country.[10]

For record consumers, the most significant innovation emerging from wartime research was the development of the 45 rpm 7-inch and 33⅓ rpm 12-inch vinyl formats. These were marketed in the USA soon after the war (the former by Columbia from 1948, the latter by RCA from 1949). As *Melody Maker* reported:

> [A] revolution has taken place in the American record business. [The changes] mean that long-playing, slow-spinning plastic discs have been accepted by the public and that the old 78 revs. per minute record is on its way out. The changeover took less than a year to effect ... But there has so far been no move to put [the new discs] on the [British] commercial market. For one thing, the British companies don't intend to make a definite move in one r.p.m. direction until the American 'speed struggle' has resolved itself. For another, they don't believe that the British public can afford to buy the new equipment needed to play the microgroove records. (3 September 1949: 3)

Decca did not introduce LP records into the British market until June 1950 and EMI resisted the new formats until October 1952, by which time their improved durability and longer playing time had won over consumers despite some initial suspicions. *The Record Guide*, an authoritative critical survey of all available classical recordings published in 1951, included an 'Appendix on Long Playing Records'. They are praised for their ability to play long pieces of music without interruption and for their lightness and ease of storage. But the welcome is not unreserved:

> An essential merit of the gramophone has always been the power it gives us to select and discriminate; it will be a sad day when performances of miscellaneous short pieces or songs have to be bought in bulk.

The authors concluded that the LP was a good thing for classical music listeners as long as it did not 'push 78s off the market'.[11]

---

[10]   Southall 1982: 37.
[11]   Sackville-West and Shawe-Taylor 1951: 719.

EMI and Decca remained dominant in the British record market throughout the 1950s, but their US ties had consequences for their relationship with each other in 1952, when the US Justice Department forced the companies to end restrictive trade practices through which they had carved up the global market into 'exclusive' territories and prevented other companies from entering national markets 'by refusing to distribute their products'.[12] One consequence of the ruling was that the US Columbia label (long an EMI partner) signed a new UK distribution deal with the Dutch company Philips.[13] Like Decca and EMI, Philips was a manufacturer of record players, consumer electronics and domestic appliances, and had set up a record label in 1950, primarily focused on classical music and folk. Now the company opened an office in England, releasing its first British recordings in 1953. EMI, meanwhile, compensated for its loss of American repertoire by buying a controlling interest in the US-based company Capitol. The deal had to be cleared by the Bank of England's Foreign Exchange Control Office. EMI made its case partly in terms of its need 'for a stable source of US matrices for distribution in the UK' and partly in terms of its need to access the US record market, which was at this point seven times the size of the UK's:

> The full exploitation of the popular artistes on our own catalogues requires arrangements for the sales of their recordings in the United States market ... This is a question of importance not only to EMI but also to the United Kingdom, because the exploitation of our own popular catalogue in the USA in this manner will create a flow of pressing fees and royalties from the USA to the UK. (Sir Edward de Stein, quoted in Keightley 2007: 7)[14]

Prior to the EMI takeover, Decca had released Capitol recordings in the UK, but it also had its own subsidiary labels that it could use for licensed record releases on both sides of the Atlantic. In the USA, London Records issued UK Decca records; in the UK, the London-American label released recordings from a variety of

---

[12]   Keightley 2007: 6. In the 1930s Decca had given EMI the right to press and distribute Decca records in Asia, Australia and South America in return for Decca's right to press and distribute Parlophone and Odeon records in the USA and Canada (Frith 1987: 282).

[13]   RCA Victor also announced that it would be ending its long-standing distribution deal with EMI, though not until 1957. (Decca took over RCA's UK licence.) Keightley suggests that in 1952 Columbia masters accounted for 25 per cent of EMI's global sales and RCA Victor masters for 50 per cent. In a *Financial Times* special supplement on gramophone records in 1958, EMI's managing director is quoted as saying that 'one [EMI] record in every three was exported' (25 August 1958).

[14]   As Keightley points out, under the terms of the takeover, Capitol retained a high degree of autonomy and was not actually obliged to release EMI's British masters; rather, it had first refusal – which it exercised on the Beatles' initial releases, the reason why these appeared in the USA on the independent labels Vee-Jay and Swan (Keightley 2007: 3).

American independent labels, including Atlantic, Dot, Imperial, Sun, Monument, Hi, Cadence and Speciality (in 1962 EMI set up the equivalent Stateside label for its product from the smaller US indies). The point here is that although music from little US labels had a big impact on young Britons' musical tastes, this only reinforced Decca's and EMI's industry dominance; the companies had between them the rights to most rock'n'roll, teen pop, R&B and early soul records.

Philips needed its Columbia deal to be confident of survival in the British market. Pye/Nixa followed a similar strategy, leasing masters in 1958 from the Chess and King labels ('wresting them from British Decca by sheer determination') and acquiring the UK licence to manufacture and distribute Mercury and Vanguard product. Its R&B franchises were 'aggressively marketed ... available not only in record stores but also at the Boots chain of chemists'.[15] Pye had started out making scientific instruments, radios and televisions, and had moved into the record market by acquiring the Nixa label in 1953 and the Polygon label in 1955.[16] By the end of the 1950s, it, like Philips, had gained enough market share to be grouped alongside EMI and Decca as one of the British majors. In 1959 Pye dropped the Nixa name and allied itself to Lew Grade's television production company, ATV, which acquired a 50 per cent stake.[17]

Of Britain's other significant record labels in this period, only Oriole had ambitions to compete with 'the big four'. The Levy family – retailers of gramophones and gramophone records – first established the Oriole label in 1925, investing in a recording studio and a manufacturing plant. The label folded after a decade, but the recording studio survived. It was, according to John Schroeder, 'the only facility in the country where you could record your own personal message for an occasion such as a birthday'[18] and in 1950 Morris Levy relaunched the Oriole label, making sure now to invest too in his own means of distribution (Oriole won the contract to manufacture and distribute Woolworths' Embassy records). When Schroeder was recruited from EMI to be Oriole's Artists and Repertoire (A&R) manager in December 1961, it was to help Levy become a major record industry player. He did not succeed. In 1964 Oriole (which by now had two pressing plants) was bought by the US company CBS, which wanted UK manufacturing facilities.

Otherwise Britain's small record companies in the 1950s were concerned with niche markets. Topic, the oldest, had been established by the Workers' Music Association as the Topic Record Club in 1939 and was essentially a folk label

---

[15]   Schwartz 2007: 89.

[16]   Nixa, launched in 1950, was the second British company (after Decca) to issue LPs. Its primary purpose seems to have been to handle the catalogue of the Paris-based Compagnie Générale du Disques. Polygon was in part set up to release Petula Clark's records (her father, Leslie, was co-owner), but it also had success with Dorothy Squires and Jimmy Young.

[17]   When John Schroeder went to work for Pye in 1964 it was based in ATV House and in 1966 ATV became 100 per cent owners.

[18]   Schroeder 2009: 71.

(issuing most of Ewan MacColl's work between 1952 and 1966, for example). Topic broke off from the Workers' Music Association in the early 1960s, establishing itself as an independent company in 1963. It remains the UK's oldest independent label.[19] Esquire was set up by Carlo Krahmer (who ran the band at the Feldman Club), his wife Greta and fellow drummer Peter Newmark in 1950:

> As dedicated collectors, they were convinced that a market existed for the new
> British jazz and recordings made by the independent American [jazz] companies
> – neither of which much interested the existing duopoly of Decca and EMI.[20]

Argo was established in 1951 to issue 'British Music played by British Artists', though its first release featured music from Bali. Once the LP market was in place, Argo specialised successfully in spoken-word records (Shakespeare plays, for example). It was taken over by Decca in 1957. Melodisc was launched by Emile E. Shalit, an entrepreneur with eclectic musical tastes, and became important as the British source of Caribbean music – calypso, mento, the Blue Beat label from 1960 – and for recordings of London's expatriate African musicians. Melodisc became distributor for Esquire and Topic as well as for US Savoy and Moe Asch's Disc releases.[21]

Playing Records

The first half of the 1950s marked the most significant changes in British broadcasting since its inception in the 1920s. Live entertainment had always been a key part of television programming – the world's first TV programme, broadcast by the BBC in 1936, was a variety show and consumer demand for television took off with the live broadcast of the Coronation in 1953. By 1955, the number of licence holders had grown to over 4.5 million. Meanwhile, the Television Act passed by Parliament on 30 July 1954 legalised commercial TV broadcasting. Various business groups competed for the new TV franchises, including a consortium put together by three key figures from the theatre and variety world: agent Lew Grade and the two most prominent players in Stoll-Moss Empires, Prince Littler and Val Parnell. This consortium lost their bid to a group led by Norman Collins, the former director of BBC television, but when Collins' group ran short of cash, they combined with Grade, Littler and Parnell to form Associated Television (ATV), which would become the most powerful TV content producer, being franchised as the ITV Channel in London at the weekends and in the Midlands on weekdays.[22]

---

[19]   Harker 2007: 104.

[20]   Fordham 1986: 54.

[21]   Schwartz 2007: 303.

[22]   The other main content producers for ITV at this time were Rediffusion (the channel for London on weekdays), Granada (the Northwest) and ABC (the Midlands at weekends).

ITV began broadcasting on 22 September 1955. Its most successful programme was *Sunday Night at the Palladium*, a direct descendant of the variety era and, in entertainment terms, a complementary programme to the BBC's *Come Dancing*, which had been created by Eric Morley, the director of publicity for the Mecca chain of dance halls, in 1949.[23]

At this point, then, the new medium of television seemed to be reinforcing the power of live music moguls to define popular entertainment. In the mid-1950s, however, there was a change in government legislation that was to have a profound effect on the relative power of the live and recording music industries. The Copyright Act of 1956 immediately began to limit the influence of the Musicians' Union on the use of records for public entertainment.

The early history of the use of records for public performance in the UK is documented in Sarah Thornton's *Club Cultures*. She notes that while records provided background accompaniment to some leisure activities prior to the Second World War, they were not then played in dance halls. In the 1940s, however, improvements in public address systems as well as the depressed British economy led some dance promoters to use records first to supplement and then to replace live dance bands. By 1949, the Musicians' Union was expressing its concern:

> Probably the greatest threat from recorded music to the employment opportunities of our members exists in the field of casual dance engagements. There is abundant evidence that in recent years more and more dance promoters have availed themselves of the services of the public address engineer. In almost every town the man who runs the radio shop, or specialises in the provision of public address equipment, will undertake to supply recorded music for dances or other social events at a small proportion of the fee a good band would charge. (Quoted in Thornton 1995: 38)

In anticipation of this problem, the Musicians' Union had made arrangements with PPL to limit and regulate record entertainment. From 1946, PPL licences were granted with the proviso 'that records not be used in substitution of a band or orchestra or in circumstances where it would be reasonable to claim that a band or orchestra should be employed such as dance halls'. Venues were allowed to play records for periods of not more than 20 minutes when bands took their set breaks – a time limit which proved difficult to enforce in practice.

The Musicians' Union/PPL deal was fraught from the start. In 1950–1 a company called Danceland Records began to produce discs of popular ballroom songs specifically for dance floor use. Because the company had not assigned its performance rights to PPL, it was not subject to the Musicians' Union/PPL agreements. As Danceland's 'recording sessions were held in Mecca ballrooms, the MU suspected that the dancehall chain financed the project'. According to one Union report to its members, 'our agreement with [PPL] enables a considerable

---

[23]   See Barker 2009.

amount of control to be exercised over the public use of records made by the principal recording companies – companies who are members of Phonographic Performance Limited', but with Danceland circumventing this arrangement:

> Just as irresponsible musicians have been known to act as 'scabs' or 'blacklegs' during disputes, there are also musicians with a similar outlook who are prepared to produce what we have learned to regard as 'scab' records. That is to say, records produced almost solely for the purpose of performance where 'live' music could be employed, thus defeating our agreement with [PPL].[24]

In 1955 *Melody Maker* suggested that the Copyright Act then being debated (it became law in 1956) could spell doom for dance orchestras for similar reasons:

> Thousands of musicians may be thrown out of work if a new Copyright Bill becomes law. The Bill passed its second reading in the House of Lords on Tuesday. As it stands at present, the Bill would allow all foreign recordings to be publicly performed without permission of Phonographic Performance Ltd., the company formed by Britain's gramophone record manufacturers to control the public use of their records. This means that anyone running a dance in future could use, say, American jazz records – or any made in foreign countries – without a licence from PPL. (19 November 1955: 1)

As Thornton explains, the Musicians' Union opposed the Act (unsuccessfully) for three reasons:

> First, the record companies maintained exclusive copyright and only volunteered royalties to the MU.[25] Second, although it gave PPL the right to set up musician employment restrictions, it also established a tribunal to which users of copyright material (like broadcasters and dancehall owners) could protest. Third, the new Act permitted the free use of records 'at any premises where persons reside or sleep' as long as no special price was charged for admission and at non-profit clubs and societies whose main objectives were charitable, religious or educational. (Thornton 1995: 40–1)

Disc jockeys did not replace live musicians quite as comprehensively as the Musicians' Union feared, even for public dancing, but the 1956 Copyright Act did mark a new step in the use of records in public spaces. As a Musicians' Union report lamented in 1957, 'records are now used extensively for "Rock 'n' Roll" sessions in many Mecca Ballrooms, in so-called "practice dances" promoted by

---

[24]   *Musician*, October 1951: 8–9; and see Thornton 1995: 39.
[25]   The Musicians' Union had persuaded PPL, when it was set up, to pay a small percentage of its fee income into a Musicians' Union fund in recognition of the musicians whose performances had been recorded.

dancing teachers in large halls, and generally in circumstances where previously their use would not have been permitted by the company'.[26] As the reference here to rock'n'roll suggests, the public use of records was particularly associated with teenage culture and by the late 1950s, this was having an effect on radio and TV entertainment too.

The Impact of Youth

The period between Bill Haley's 'Rock Around the Clock' reaching number one in the British record charts in November 1955 and the first chart entry of the Beatles at the end of 1962 saw significant changes in the recording industry but also significant continuities, and it may therefore be helpful to begin this section by looking briefly at the statistical data on record sales, limited as they are. In their historical study of the British record industry, Gourvish and Tennent document the continuing dominance of EMI/Decca/Pye/Philips: the four labels' share of titles in the charts was above 95 per cent throughout this period. EMI and Decca remained the clear market leaders and until 1961 the British record charts were dominated by American artists. Overall, UK-recorded music production grew from 59.9 million units in 1955 to 77.5 million in 1962 (see Table 6.1).

Table 6.1   UK record production 1955–62 (Gourvish and Tennent 2010: 205)

	78s	45s	LPs
1955	46.3 million	4.6 million	9 million
1962	1.9 million	55.2 million	20.4 million

Gourvish and Tennent note that '45s were popular with the emerging teenage market', as compared to LPs, which were between four and six times as expensive, and, at first glance, the sharp increase in the production of 45s would appear to support the argument that by the early 1960s teenagers were the most significant record market. This may be misleading, however. There are no figures available for the split between teenage and adult consumption of 45s and LPs at this time, but even if the price of an LP in 1962 was only four times that of a single (it was almost certainly higher), then revenue from LPs greatly exceeded that from 45s in 1962, despite the smaller volume of production.[27]

The effects of changes in broadcasting during the 1950s also have to be considered here. The only choices for British radio listeners in this period were

---

[26]   *The Musician*, December 1957: 9.

[27]   Gourvish and Tennent 2010: 197, 205. Keightley (2004) notes a similar situation in the US record market during this time.

the BBC, Radio Luxembourg and, in some areas, the American Forces Network. BBC popular music programming was, as we have seen, partly determined by the long-standing needle-time agreement with PPL, which set out the number of hours per week during which records could be used. Radio Luxembourg had no such restrictions because it was broadcast from outside British jurisdiction. When the station resumed service in 1946, its programming was divided into two categories: record shows and a mix of quiz shows and talent contests such as *Double Your Money* and *Opportunity Knocks*.[28] The dramatic rise in the number of television set owners in the first half of the 1950s and the launch of ITV in 1955 had serious consequences for Radio Luxembourg's programme policy. Many of ITV's most successful shows were modelled directly on Luxembourg formats, and advertisers who had previously sponsored the Luxembourg shows now moved their advertising spend to television, forcing Luxembourg to switch almost entirely to record shows. Many of these were sponsored directly by record companies. Capitol Records had a sponsored show as early as 1951 and 'by 1957 EMI, for one, was sponsoring shows at the rate of one per day, at a total annual cost of £35,000'. Decca, Pye and Philips quickly followed suit, and when Schroeder joined Oriole in 1962, his first act was to make sure that the company was willing to invest in 'our own Luxembourg programme two or three times a week'.[29] The fact that television had stolen much of Luxembourg's family audience also meant that the station's record programmes were increasingly focused on the emerging youth pop music market and by 1964, new youth-oriented labels like Ember and Island were booking Luxembourg's cheaper late-night slots.[30]

The shift towards a record-oriented and age-differentiated music culture in Britain was also reflected in TV programme policy. In 1952 the BBC's *Hit Parade* featured performances of the most popular *songs* of the day, performed not by the recording artists who had made them popular, but by a house band featuring the singers Petula Clark and Denis Lotis. In 1955 a new programme, *Off The Record*, was launched. Hosted by long-time bandleader Jack Payne, this did feature performances by the recording artists who had scored the hit – Tommy Steele, for example, performed 'Rock the Caveman' on a special set, a realistic-looking cave, that had been built in the studio[31] – and in 1957 producer Jack Good created a similar TV programme aimed explicitly at teenagers, *Six-Five Special* (1957–8).

Briggs suggests that this 'became the kind of programme about which older people were uneasy and younger people enthusiastic', marking a new kind of intentional audience polarisation in British broadcasting,[32] but in many respects *Six-Five Special* was the TV equivalent of a youth club, an upbeat opportunity for young people to have fun under the watchful eye of a jolly uncle and aunt

---

[28] Barnard 1989: 32–3.
[29] Schroeder 2009: 78; and see Barnard 1989: 34.
[30] Tennent 2010: 12.
[31] Kennedy 1958: 43.
[32] Briggs 1985: 305.

(Pete Murray and Josephine Douglas) and a salt-of-the-earth ex-boxer (Freddie Mills). The format involved teen stars performing their hits with a backing band of established session musicians looking uneasily facetious and, dissatisfied with the BBC's constrictions on presentation, Good signed a contract with ITV to produce a similar but more focused youth programme, *Oh Boy!* (1958–9), which put a greater emphasis on the emotional relationship between pop idols (filmed in close-up) and their teenage fans. Both *Six-Five Special* and *Oh Boy!* were based on live performances, even if they used artists performing their hit records rather than in-house singers doing cover versions. Other shows, such as ITV's *Cool For Cats* (1957–9) and the BBC's *Juke Box Jury* (1959–67), went a step further: in these programmes, the discs were played directly and then discussed either by a compere (*Cool For Cats*) or by a panel of celebrities (*Juke Box Jury*).

Initially, record stardom didn't really affect the live music business. After the success of Tommy Steele's 'Rock the Caveman', for example, his managers, John Kennedy and Larry Parnes, signed him to Harold Fielding, an agent with a background in jazz and musical theatre, who booked Steele onto the variety circuit. Cliff Richard, meanwhile, after getting his recording deal with EMI, signed a management contract with Tito Burns, a long-time jazz performer, manager and agent who followed the same policy, although Cliff, unusually, travelled with a band, the Shadows, who became recording stars in their own right.[33]

One obvious effect of the late 1950s boom in record sales was felt in record retail. To service the increasing number of retail outlets, in August 1959 Roy Parker launched a new trade paper, *Record Retailer*, which went weekly in March 1960.[34] An early news story (10 March 1960: 2) reported the first ever meeting of the Gramophone Record Retailers Association, and both the meeting and the paper indicate that record retail was becoming a distinct industry sector. Keith Prowse, for example, the biggest theatre ticket agency in Britain, was now a 'very prominent wholesaler and retailer of records', with 30 retail shops; in the early 1960s Prowse had outlets, such as the Squires record mail-order business in London, and Henry Stave, 'one of London's leading classical record shops'.[35]

Record Retailer continued to report the spread of 'Records Only' shops,[36] but an equally significant development was the growth of supermarket interest in record selling, particularly after the abolition of resale price maintenance in 1964. The industry fought unsuccessfully against the legislation's application to records; its immediate effect was to change the big four's distribution policies. As Kevin Tennant has described, they stopped carrying each other's products and exercised

---

[33] Kennedy 1958: 37–48; Lewry and Goodall 1996: 27–8.

[34] The paper changed its name to *Music Week* in March 1972 and continues to this day.

[35] *Record Retailer*, 20 December 1962: 9.

[36] A story on 2 April 1964, for example, features Record Retailers Ltd, 'one of the biggest chains of shops dealing exclusively with records'.

their monopoly power over their own products with various consequences: EMI stopped franchising dealers, expanded its own HMV shop chain and, from 1966, began rack jobbing, giving it some control over which records were stocked in non-specialist stores,[37] independent regional distributors (like Keith Prowse) were driven out of business and:

> From 1965 onwards the number of labels, and hence releases, began to increase rapidly, as new British based independent labels entered the market, encouraged by the spare capacity in the distribution capacity of the Big Four.[38]

From the beginning, *Record Retailer* emphasised the importance of live tours for record sales. An early article, for instance, noted that 'wherever the "Jazz at the Philharmonic" package is seen there is bound to be a large demand for Ella [Fitzgerald]'s records'. In a section entitled 'Tours to Note', the paper reports that Decca had lined up a special promotion campaign to tie in with a tour featuring Bobby Darin, Duane Eddy and Clyde McPhatter. In addition to plugging singles and albums:

> special window display material will be available to dealers in all towns visited by the show, and large display stands advertising Decca discs will be placed in the foyers of the various cinemas and concert halls. Decca who will throw a press reception for the boys are also supplying all national and provincial papers with review copies of the discs being promoted.[39]

Such reports, prosaic as they may be, give an insight into the dynamic between the recording and live industries in the early 1960s, and by the mid-1960s *Record Retailer* was putting equal focus on radio (listing discs that were being supported by Radio Luxembourg) and television (listing who would be appearing on which programmes). A May 1960 *Record Retailer* report captures something of the complex set of relations involved in selling records:

> Impresario Bob Alexander is now discussing a series of London and Provincial ballroom 'big beat nights' which, if successful, could do a great deal to boost popular record sales. Alexander intends to cooperate with local record dealers in the promotion of both his events and the records of the artists he books. 'I will help to arrange for personal appearances in shops for any retailers wherever this

---

[37]   In rack jobbing, a record company makes its products available in racks that it places in retail stores. The record company takes responsibility for stocking and restocking the racks. This became a common way of distributing records in non-specialist outlets like supermarkets.

[38]   Tennent 2010: 13–15, 18. *Record Retailer* reported that 1965 was a boom year, with sales increasing by 25 per cent (2 December 1965).

[39]   *Record Retailer*, 24 October 1960: 26; 17 March 1960: 6.

is possible,' he says. Alexander is holding his first 'Beat Night' at the Majestic Ballroom in Finsbury Park on Monday, May 30th ... The series, both in London and the Provinces, are being organised with the co-operation of the Circuits Management Association who manage the Rank chain of cinemas and ballrooms ... Rank Records are also to cooperate in the promotion of these events and it is certain that many of their artists will be appearing. (26 May 1960: 20)

As record sales became increasingly significant for star making and for the success of live shows, some live music companies experimented with a more direct investment in the recording process. In 1958 the Rank Organisation, important in the British live music sector through its chain of cinemas and dance halls, decided to enter the record business. Its initial idea was to market cut-price discs in its cinemas and ballrooms, but its dependence on Philips for pressing meant that it had to abide by the existing resale price maintenance framework and distribute in the usual way. To this end, Rank took over the record wholesalers Thompson, Diamond and Butcher, and persuaded Dick Rowe to leave Decca and manage the new label. Top Rank's first release, Harry Simeone's 'Little Drummer Boy' (leased from the new 20th Century Fox label) was a big hit and the company also had some success developing British acts such as Craig Douglas and Bert Weedon. Despite heavy use of sponsored shows on Radio Luxemburg and its control of a live music circuit, however, Top Rank lost money. It released too many records with too small a promotional team and in 1960 was handed over to EMI (though Rank retained ownership of Thompson, Butcher and Diamond).[40]

There are other examples of entrepreneurs developing business interests across the live and recording sectors. Jeff Kruger, who had owned and managed the Flamingo since 1952 and diversified into music publishing, now created his own label, Ember Records, which began by doing deals with the Federal and King labels, releasing records by artists, like James Brown, who were popular in his club. In a reverse move, recording engineer and producer Joe Meek used live music to promote his new Triumph label and its artists.[41] His weekly 'Triumph Rock Club' night in London featured a mix of Top 20 discs and Triumph artists performing live, while he also organised a touring package show, with Triumph's discs 'plugged from the stage during each performance'.[42]

---

[40]   Rogan 1989: 33; *Billboard*, 15 August 1960.

[41]   Triumph was funded and its records distributed by the pioneering cut-price label Saga, which primarily issued classical and light music records. Meek's co-director was Saga's classical record manager William Barrington-Coupe, who years later would achieve notoriety for 'faking' the recorded performances of his wife, the pianist Joyce Hatto, who in the 1960s was a Saga artist. Saga saw Triumph as a way of reaching the teenage market, but Meek was dissatisfied with its marketing – which may explain his attempts to do his own live promotion – and quit the label. Saga boss Major Banks then funded Meek's independent production company, RGM Sound (Repsch 1989: 81–96).

[42]   *Record Retailer*, 2 June 1960: 23; quote from 23 June 1960: 2.

Towards a New Industry Model

By 1964, British record companies were releasing around 2,000 singles a year as recorded music production grew from 72.7 million records in 1960 to 90.1 million records in 1967. British artists continued to dominate the charts,[43] a position they maintained between 1961 and 1969, and had begun to make inroads into the US market, beginning with two surprise instrumental number ones in 1962 (Acker Bilk's 'Stranger on the Shore' and the Tornados' 'Telstar') and progressing through the success of the Beatles to the mid-1960s 'British Invasion'.[44]

There were changes now too in the relationship between the 45 and the LP, and their associated markets. The sales of both 45s and LPs grew, but LPs gradually became less identified with the adult market and pop groups began to produce coherent albums rather than simply collections of unconnected songs. This transition culminated with the release of the Beatles' *Sgt. Pepper* in 1967, the last year in which the British recording industry produced more singles than albums.

The 1960s was, in short, a period of unprecedented growth and success – such success, indeed, that US labels started to sever their licensing arrangements with the British majors and to establish their own British label identities. Beginning with Liberty in 1961, American companies sought first to preserve their label names, the first step towards UK independence,[45] and then to set up UK branches. The American Columbia label established its first UK offices under the name CBS in 1962, for example (EMI still held the British rights to the 'Columbia' name) and became the first American major to set up its own wholly owned British subsidiary.

At the same time, a new generation of managers and agents began to create their own labels to cater to the emerging rock market. In August 1965 Andrew Loog Oldham persuaded Philips to press and distribute records on the Immediate label, over which he would have full creative and promotional control, and this became the model for independent rock labels in the second half of the 1960s.[46]

Oldham's persuasive power reflected a more general change in the way in which the British music industry was developing, which can be illustrated by comparing Brian Epstein's recording deal for the Beatles with Oldham's deal for the Rolling Stones. When Brian Epstein agreed to sign the Beatles to EMI's Parlophone label in June 1962, it was a one-year contract with a royalty rate of one penny per double-sided record and a four-year option with annual increments of

---

[43]   Of course, British recording artists were still significantly covering US material. The Songwriters' Guild calculated that of the 94,847 items of popular music broadcast by the BBC in 1963, 39.25 per cent were British and 52 per cent American, the remainder being from other foreign composers/publishers (Leslie 1965: 179).

[44]   Leslie 1965: 178–9; Gourvish and Tennent 2010: 206.

[45]   Which Liberty achieved in 1968 (*Record Retailer*, 1 January 1969: 4).

[46]   With the exception of Island, which opened a London office in 1962 (it had begun in Jamaica in 1959) for the distribution of Jamaican music and moved into rock management from this base. See Tennent 2010: 16.

25 per cent. Epstein had a background in record retailing but had never managed an artist prior to the Beatles, and he has been criticised for accepting what many people (including the Beatles themselves) have considered since to have been an exploitative deal. Johnny Rogan argues that in fact the terms were standard for an unknown group in 1962. Epstein had, after all, already had numerous rejections from other labels.[47]

Andrew Loog Oldham's Decca deal for the Rolling Stones in May 1963 included a better royalty rate of five per cent of the retail price of each record sold, but his real coup was inspired by advice he had received from Phil Spector, who employed him in a PR capacity during a visit to London in 1962:

> All material taped in the studios of a record company remained the company's copyright. By recording the Stones independently, then leasing the record 'masters' back to Decca for manufacture and distribution, Oldham would retain the copyright and, simultaneously, rob Decca of control over what was recorded. Such a deal had not been proposed in the whole history of British recorded music. It was a measure of Decca's desperation to launch the 'new Beatles' that Oldham's conditions were accepted. (Norman 2001: 97)[48]

The unprecedented commercial success of the Beatles and the Stones[49] meant that the power of pop managers continued to grow through the 1960s at the same time as Decca and EMI were facing unprecedented competition from American labels setting up London offices. These two trends were not unrelated: as Joe Boyd argues, 'the Beatles and the Stones … demonstrated that any self respecting major company needed a British A&R presence'.[50]

By the time Pink Floyd were the hot unsigned prospect in 1967, there were many more labels competing for their signatures than had existed when Epstein was looking for a deal for the Beatles only a few years earlier. One competitor was neither American nor a UK independent: Polydor was the pop subsidiary of the German company Deutsche Grammophon, and its British A&R director, Horst Schmolzi, was prepared to make production deals with acts' managers. As Boyd recalls:

> EMI and Decca executives would have had cardiac arrests at the royalty rates and independence of Horst's deals, which is why the wiliest managers went to him.

Smart managers could now play labels off against one another for better deals. Schmolzi lured the Who away from Decca, for instance, 'by giving [managers],

---

[47] Rogan 1989: 158.

[48] And see Rogan 1989: 96.

[49] 'Not one of the previous developments in popular music this century had anything like the shattering impact made by these two groups dramatically rising from obscurity in the early "sixties"' (Godbolt 1976: 150).

[50] Boyd 2006: 137.

[Kit] Lambert and [Chris] Stamp, their own Track Records label'. When he heard
Pink Floyd, he drew up a contract to sign them to Polydor via Boyd's company,
Witchseason Productions. Knowing that the band was in demand, their manager,
Pete Jenner, and booking agent, Bryan Morrison, came up with a plan to give even
greater control to the band and its management:

> Jenner rang the next day to say that Morrison had looked over the Polydor/
> Witchseason contract, found it wanting and proposed a Plan B. His agency
> would put up the money to record the single, then shop it to EMI or Decca as a
> finished master. Based on what he had heard in the studio, he was certain they
> could get a £5,000 advance for it. They wanted me to produce it, but as the
> Floyd's employee, rather than the other way around [...] As Bryan predicted,
> EMI loved the single and offered £5,000 to sign the group.[51]

This kind of wheeling and dealing would have been unheard of for a pop group at
the beginning of the decade, but was now becoming typical of the complexity of
negotiations between artists, managers and record companies, and such changes
in the power dynamics between artist and industry also affected related activities
such as publishing. For decades it had been an accepted practice that one of the
key responsibilities of a label's A&R department was to do as its title suggested
and match artists with appropriate songs. When John Schroeder began working for
Norrie Paramour at EMI in 1957:

> He particularly mentioned music publishers and advised me to treat them with
> respect since their function was to bring new material to our attention, which to
> an extent was our lifeline.

For Alan Warner, who joined EMI four years later:

> These were the heydays of the British cover versions: each week the A&R
> guys received the latest 45s from the States and local music publishers would
> set UK release dates for the songs, allowing British producers to ready their
> versions which, more often than not, were almost duplicate arrangements of the
> originals![52]

By 1964, though, as noted in *Record Retailer*, music publishers were increasingly
promoting their titles through specific recordings:

> I said a few weeks ago that songs without records don't stand much chance in
> Tin Pan Alley. I'd now like to take that statement a bit further – and say that
> even songs with records have only an outsider's chance of getting into the top

---

[51]   Boyd 2006: 137, 139–40.
[52]   Schroeder 2009: 38; Warner 2002.

fifty unless they have a full-scale 'promotional plan' behind them. And it's part of a publisher's job to make sure that the record is 'promoted' in every way – getting the song played on the radio and television, arranging for the artiste to be interviewed by the Press, taking advertising space, and fixing up 'PAs' – personal appearances at shops and stores. (19 March 1964: 18)

This approach was reinforced by the increasing tendency of acts to write their own material. The primary task of publishers was no longer to place a song but to assist in the process by which their client's recording of that song made money.[53]

Concert promotion was equally affected by the growing power of artists as recording stars, especially as the terms set by the biggest acts impacted on smaller acts and changed their expectations of the concert promoter's role. From the mid-1960s, *Melody Maker* began to run stories about strained relationships between promoters and artists. A promoter complained of being 'completely tired of this situation … at the moment any group that enters the top 20 is liable to let you down' (17 September 1966: 25). It was claimed that bands routinely failed to show up for gigs, using any number of excuses such as illness, vans breaking down, arriving with no equipment, disbandment or simple non-fulfilment of a contract due to getting a record in the charts and signing up for better-paying gigs elsewhere (28 January 1967: 8).

Promoters found it increasingly difficult to predict how quickly the popularity of a given act would rise or fall between the booking and the concert. Larry Parnes' teen packages had certainly promoted acts by reference to their records' sales success – the Beatles were billed as 'those "Love Me Do" boys', for example – but one reason for putting several artists together on a bill was to balance out possible shifts in their individual popularity. Now, though, the speed at which a band's appeal could change made it much harder to determine even six months in advance how big an act would be, hence the many disputes over last-minute demands for increased fees. Peter Jenner recalls contracts being written to deal with this problem. 'Charts clauses' were inserted, for example, linking an adjustment to the agreed fee to the chart position of a band's single on the day of the performance. In the end, the issue was resolved by the acts' record companies taking control of their touring schedule, coordinating it with album promotion. In the mid-1960s, however, the rapid growth of the pop concert audience meant that previous ways of calculating live music finance were inadequate and getting a concert right was a process of trial and error. As Jim Godbolt notes, if a group had become less popular since the promoter first booked them, then the promoter would not cover his costs. He could, though, 'disappear into the night and never be seen again. There were many of these fly-by-nights'.[54]

---

[53] Cover versions could, of course, be profitable – all those versions of 'Yesterday' – but became problematic when a song was taken to be uniquely expressive of a 'singer/songwriter', a term that only began to be used in the mid-1960s.

[54] Godbolt 1976: 158; and see Jenner 2008.

TV and radio, meanwhile, were edging ever closer towards record-based programming. There were still popular shows that featured live music, such as *Sunday Night at the Palladium* and *Thank Your Lucky Stars*, but new programmes, most influentially ITV's *Ready, Steady, Go!* (1963–6), had artists mime to their records rather than perform live, and this was also the case with *Top of the Pops* (*TOTP*), the record-chart show that first aired on BBC TV in 1964 (opening with the Rolling Stones). These shows were not only important for breaking new artists, they also helped move records to the centre of British popular musical culture: *TOTP* and (following the appointment of Alan Freeman as its permanent host in 1962) the BBC radio show *Pick of the Pops* put 'the charts' into the public consciousness like never before.

This change did not come without resistance. As we discussed in Chapter 3, the Musicians' Union fought against mimed performance on TV and in July 1966 (after the show moved from Manchester to London) miming on *TOTP* was banned. Live studio performances, however, could not do justice to the records supposedly being celebrated, hence the Musicians' Union compromise we have already described: bands mimed to specially recorded backing tracks (all the musicians on the original track had to be present in the studio). The *TOTP* Orchestra augmented the tracks when necessary; singers could either mime or sing live.[55]

At the beginning of the 1960s, most of the music on BBC radio was performed live and the majority of pop programmes were 'showcases for the various regional dance orchestras, who played big-band arrangements of current hits'.[56] Radio Luxembourg programming did rely on pop records, but many of its shows were the rather unengaging record company slots, showcases for disparate releases many of which were not and never would be hits, and it was not until 1964 that Top 40-style American broadcasting emerged in the UK, courtesy of pirate radio. The first pirate station was Radio Caroline, launched in March by Ronan O'Rahilly, a booking agent who had represented Georgie Fame and knew how difficult it was to get airplay for artists who did not have a major label contract.[57] Caroline was followed by Radio Atlanta (which then merged with Radio Caroline to form two stations, Radio Caroline South and North), Radio Sutch (renamed Radio City), Radio Invicta (renamed King Radio), Radio London, Radio 390, Radio Essex and Radio Scotland.

These stations were funded mainly by American investors, who put in American managerial staff. They all used a Top 40 round-the-clock format and, contrary to swashbuckling mythology, were all conceived as straightforward commercial enterprises – they relied on advertising to survive. They were not much liked by

---

[55]   This policy continued until 1980, when the live orchestra was dropped altogether and only pre-recorded tracks were used.

[56]   Barnard: 1989: 39.

[57]   *Record Retailer* had reported news of a pirate station broadcasting to East Anglia from a lightship moored in Dutch waters in 1961, but it is not clear what kind of programmes it was broadcasting (23 March 1961: 5).

Britain's big four record labels, both because they used discs without any royalty payments and because they took much of their audience from the companies' Luxembourg shows. The pirates did, however, provide valuable promotional opportunities for Britain's new independent labels and this made them popular with the youth music audience then (and an object of nostalgic affection now). In fact, the pirate radio world was not particularly wholesome. Payola as well as copyright theft was routine, as was the manipulation of the pirates' charts, and the backgrounds of several of the stations' financial backers and owners were questionable: public opinion of the stations declined considerably when Radio City owner Reg Calvert was found dead at the home of Radio Atlanta founder Major Oliver Smedley, with Smedley consequently tried for manslaughter.[58]

Pirate radio's influence on the BBC's music policy has been exaggerated. As Barnard notes, the departments servicing the Light Programme were restructured in 1963 *prior* to the advent of pirate radio; the BBC was already concerned to address changes in Britons' popular music habits. A new Popular Music Department was created, which gradually adopted more disc-oriented programming (or the illusion thereof given needle-time restrictions):

> [One] development was the interpolation of pre-recorded musical items into the Light Programme's daytime record programmes (notably the early evening *Roundabout*) to create the impression of a continuous disc format; this was a clear break with the BBC convention of highlighting the performances of individual bands or orchestras in separate showcase programmes. (Barnard 1989: 47)

By 1966, the government had tabled a bill making it illegal to supply offshore radio broadcasters; it reached the statute book in August 1967. BBC Radio 1 was launched six weeks later, the BBC's first record-oriented, youth-oriented, pop-based station, complete with disc-jockey presenters. It immediately became a symbol of how popular music culture in Britain had changed.

Conclusion

This chapter has necessarily been more about institutions than people. It describes how relationships between the different sectors of the British music industry were restructured by post-war developments in the recording business. By 1967, a way of making money out of music was in place that would be dominant for the next 20 years. Record selling was now central to music commerce, and the record industry was taking on its mature shape: a small number of 'majors', multinational companies focused on the Anglo-American market and Anglo-American repertoire, and a larger number of national 'independents', economically unstable and more

---

[58] He was acquitted on the grounds of self-defence: Barnard 1989: 43–6; Tennent 2010: 16.

or less dependent on complex pressing, distribution and production deals with the majors. Record companies' classical divisions were increasingly marginal to record industry profits and policies; jazz and folk occupied even smaller niches. More albums were now produced than singles and the single would soon become more often than not a trailer for the album, a means of access to radio and television. Live music promotion too became tied up with record sales promotion; tours were increasingly funded by record companies and organised around release schedules. The growing market for records (and the increasing use of studio technology to define bands' sound) put further pressure on live promoters to provide bigger and better equipped venues and to focus their attention on the youth music market.

We will discuss this further in Chapter 7. Here we will just make two final comments about the effects of recording on music culture. It is important to understand, first, that the 'boom' in pop record sales from the mid-1950s also meant a way of dealing with market failure. Because so much money could now be made on their hits, record companies could, if they were big enough, more than cover the losses on flops. Furthermore, the majors' obvious inability to predict the new youth public's tastes gave them an impetus to over-invest in talent. Peter Leslie describes the situation by the mid-1960s:

> In any average week about fifty or sixty records are released. The technique with these, unless they are by sure fire hits like the Beatles, is to play them seven times in the first week on Radio Luxembourg, give them three weeks to start selling, and if they don't abandon them.[59] About two of these have any chance of doing well and getting into the charts. The enormous overproduction – in one week after the first of the Beatles' successes, 117 new records were released – shows that it is the teenagers who have something of the upper hand. They contribute the money, but their taste is absolute arbiter. If the record companies had any way of guiding this taste by selection of material, expenditure on advertising, ruthlessness in promotion, so that they could produce to order, they obviously would, and save themselves the £3½ million spent every year on flops. (Leslie 1965: 73)

In the early 1950s, when record companies vied with each other with their own versions of the same song, price competition was still a feasible approach to getting market share (Woolworths thus provided cut-price versions of hit songs on its Embassy label between 1954 and 1965) and this approach continued in the classical world. Between 1958 and 1961, for example, Gala Records (set up by a company called Musical and Plastics Industries) issued cheap records aimed at the classical, light and children's music markets, its costs being held down by its use of new plastics pressing technology.[60] From 1959, Saga (which went through

---

[59]   In 1957 'the policy dictated by EMI called for an Artist to be dropped contractually after three unsuccessful single releases' (Schroeder: 2009: 36).

[60]   Tennent 2010: 8.

various changes of ownership) packaged albums of classical and light music, using refreshed old master recordings or cut-price studio technology and non-star performers, and selling its records at about half the majors' prices. Saga, which was still going strong in 1967, had successfully identified a sector of the classical market that was more interested in price than 'quality' (a sector which the major labels serviced through their record clubs rather than their retail policy).

In the popular music market, record companies were competing not on price but for attention, which meant, in effect, media attention, hence the importance of Radio Luxembourg, the pirates and Radio 1 or, at the beginning of the 1960s, television producer Jack Good:

> The initial response to the release of [Helen Shapiro's] 'Don't Treat Me Like A Child' was a little strange and disappointing, although it did manage to make the charts at twenty eight. The turning point for Helen was her inclusion in the first programme of *Thank Your Lucky Stars* thanks to Jack Good, the producer. After this the sales started to escalate, finally putting the record in the charts at number three. (Schroeder 2009: 62)

The use of music on radio and television, in short, became inextricably linked to record companies' release schedules, as, indeed, did music coverage in newspapers and magazines. For the next 25 years, it would be assumed (not least by academics in the emerging field of popular music studies) that the 'music industry' *was* the record industry.[61]

Our final point is that by the mid-1960s, professional musicians in all genres could expect to spend time in recording sessions. This did not mean that most musicians made a living from their record sales, but it did mean that most musicians did have to think about what it meant to make music in a recording studio and how this related to the way they made music in live performance. This was particularly the case after the introduction of tape recording, which by 1958 Humphrey Lyttelton was calling 'an unmitigated boon':

> If one is looking for realism, it seems to me that the doctored tape, with all the good, fresh stuff intact, stands a better chance than the old method of running the musicians through their paces again and again until a flawless performance is achieved.[62]

Lyttelton's 'Bad Penny Blues', commonly labelled 'the first jazz record to reach the top 20' (in April 1956), was produced by Denis Preston and engineered by

---

[61] See Williamson and Cloonan 2007.

[62] Lyttelton 1958: 46–8. Lyttelton also noted, however, that 'tape surgery, like its medical counterpart, is not without its hazards. I can recall an afternoon spent crawling about an editing room at Abbey Road on my hands and knees with a Parlophone engineer, searching for a missing beat' (ibid.: 47).

Joe Meek. Preston seems to have started his producing career with Melodisc, supervising sessions with Caribbean and African musicians from 1949.[63] At the beginning of the 1950s, he set up his own production company, Record Supervision Ltd, and it can be seen as the first example of the independent producer, making records that were then leased to other companies in various kinds of deals for pressing and distribution. The Jamaican saxophonist, Joe Harriott, who arrived in London in 1951, first recorded for Preston in 1954: he 'was booked to play on a session organised by Preston which produced four "highlife" tracks for the African market', and nearly all Harriott's recording sessions thereafter were organised by Preston, who 'gave Harriott a free hand', whether he was experimenting with free form, engaged with jazz and poetry or working on Indo-Jazz fusion music with John Mayer.[64]

In 1956 Preston established Landsdowne Studios as the basis for his production work and was responsible for a variety of hit recordings, such as Johnny Duncan's 'Last Train to San Fernando' (adapted from a calypso), most of Lonnie Donegan's skiffle output and Chris Barber's 'Petite Fleur'. As Barber remembers:

> Dennis Preston's style of production – 'supervising', as it was then known – was rather more laid back than they [Chris Barber Band] had been used to. 'He did bugger all!' says Barber. 'All he did was drink brandy and leave it to the engineers. He was a producer like a film producer: he couldn't work the studio, but he could see to it that a record got made. If we said we weren't too happy with that take, could we do another? He'd say 'Don't worry, dear boy, you're fussing too much. Just play what's going down well in the clubs – you'll be alright'.[65]

In the actual process of recording, the key figure was Preston's engineer, Joe Meek, who was a crucial part of the Landsdowne set-up. Meek was the sound engineer equivalent of a do-it-yourself musician. Growing up in Newent (on the edge of the Forest of Dean), he had chosen the RAF for his national service so that he could work with radar, and then worked for electrical goods companies such as Currys and the Midland Electricity Board to gain experience of taking

---

[63]   This is by Preston's own account, in an interview in *Melody Maker*, 30 May 1959 (and see Schwartz 2007: 37). In his Diary in the *London Review of Books*, 27 May 2010, Eric Hobsbawm writes that Preston (his cousin) was instrumental in Hobsbawm's access to the British jazz scene from the 1930s. The details of Preston's career remain undocumented. He was, for example, managing Pearl Carr and Teddy Johnson at the time of their 'Sing, Little Birdie' Eurovision Song Contest entry in 1959 (Schroeder 2009: 50) and there is no doubt that a detailed study of Preston's life would reveal much about the British music business in the 1950s and 1960s.

[64]   Robertson 2011: 28–9, 88.

[65]   Frame 2007: 84. Elsewhere, Barber noted that Preston's approach was based on the need to keep production costs to a minimum – Repsch 1989: 321.

apart and remaking all kinds of electrical equipment. When he eventually arrived in London in the mid-1950s, he first found work in the film industry before coming to Preston's attention. He would go on to set up his own studio and to produce 'Telstar', the biggest British global hit before the Beatles.[66]

The careers of people like Preston and Meek are a useful reminder that the rise of the recording industry was not just about the development of big corporations. It also opened up new opportunities for maverick entrepreneurs whose business dealings were often opaque (not least to the musicians with whom they worked), but whose interest in the byways of musical taste, technology and performance was inspirational. Their ability to develop both new ways of making music and new ways of making money out of music would be an important model for independent record producers, studio owners and record company bosses in the rock era to come.

---

[66] Information from Repsch 1989. Meek also engineered Acker Bilk's 'Stranger on the Shore'.

A Snapshot of Sheffield in
October–November 1962

The Sheffield Corporation-owned City Hall in Sheffield was the main concert venue for touring artists in 1962, but was perceived as 'virtually out of bounds' to local musicians (Firminger and Lilleker 2001: 57).[1] Promoter Arthur Howes showcased twice-nightly package tours at the venue, such as Del Shannon, Freddie Cannon and the John Barry Seven (Wednesday 3 October; admission 3/6–8/6), and the Everly Brothers[2] and Frank Ifield (Wednesday 17 October). Promoter Arthur Kimbrell, in association with agent Tito Burns, promoted Bobby Vee and the Crickets (Saturday 3 November) and the Max Bygraves Show (Saturday 17 November), both at the City Hall. Little Richard (with Sam Cooke), promoted by Don Arden, was described as 'electrifying', a 'rootin' tutti-frutti-ing bundle of radioactive rhythm' who performed to 'frenzied' fans.

Promoters were not always so fortunate, however, and, following the box office smashes of Little Richard and Phil Everly, only 80 people turned up for the B. Bumble and the Stingers' package tour's first house at the City Hall, even though the group's 'Nut Rocker' had reached Number 1 in the charts in February 1962 (Tuesday 13 November 1962, promoted by George Cooper). David Luke, manager of the tour for a London agency, complained: 'This is disastrous. We'll lose an awful lot of money. We've come at a time when there's just too much going on in Sheffield. At one time the city had only two or three top groups each year. Now there's so many that people can't afford to see them all'.

As well as popular music, the City Hall also hosted regular classical concerts, often on Friday and Saturday nights, meaning that other styles of music were forced into midweek dates. City of Sheffield Philharmonic Concerts regularly promoted the Halle Orchestra, with Sir John Barbirolli, for example, conducting a 'B-themed' programme that included Berlioz, Brahms and Beethoven (Friday 5 October; 2/-–8/-). Classical music was also promoted by organisations such as the London-based Anglo-Austrian Music Society (the Vienna Boys' Choir, Thursday 15 November; 3/6–12/6), and local groups such as the Sheffield Choral Society and the Sheffield Philharmonic. Students from Sheffield University were

---

[1]   Peter Stringfellow attempted to bring more of a focus on Sheffield bands and organised a showcase for 10 local bands at the City Hall in September 1963 (Firminger and Lilleker 2001: 58).

[2]   Don Everly had to fly home to America due to ill health, and Phil Everly carried on the tour with his backing band.

also active within Sheffield's classical music scene, with the Sheffield University Music Committee[3] presenting 'The Barber of Seville' at Graves Hall (Thursday 8 November). Music hall revivals and variety shows such as 'Gay Time' and 'Show from the Seaside' (direct from a 32-week summer season in Morecambe) were also popular in 1962, performed at Sheffield's Lyceum Theatre. Other important but very different musical worlds were brass band communities, working men's clubs and amateur dramatics societies.

Autumn 1962 saw the craze for 'twisting' hit Sheffield, and the City Hall ballroom became the place for teenage twisters. The Sheffield Corporation presented 'A Special Teenage Nite' with '3½ hours of Non-Stop DANCING' until 11 pm, including twist, rock, Madison and loco-motion and three bands, all for 2/6. Legendary Sheffield-born club owner Peter Stringfellow also took advantage of the new dance craze and began promoting twist nights in August 1962 at his weekly pop and beat night, the Black Cat Club, at St Aidan's Church Hall on City Road.[4] Other twisting nights took place at venues such as the Heeley Church Hall and the Locarno Ballroom.

The date of 7 October 1962 saw the 'grand opening' of the infamous Esquire Club on Leadmill Road – an old flourmill and optical works – which featured the Johnny Dankworth Quintet. This members-only club was owned and managed by Club 60's owner and entrepreneur Terry Thornton and was designed to provide a 'unique platform for a host of new and budding local talent' (Hale and Thornton 2002: 1). The Esquire originally opened four nights a week – two for twist and two for jazz[5] – with dancing, stereo sound, a coffee bar service and quirky decor.[6] Jazz fans at this time could also get their fix at the Shiregreen

---

[3]   The actual student union was closed to non-students at that time.

[4]   Peter Stringfellow became the first promoter to promote the Beatles in Sheffield on Saturday 12 February 1963, paying them £85 (Firminger and Lilleker 2001: 46). The show took place at the Azena Ballroom with Stringfellow selling over 2,000 tickets and with hundreds more turning up on the night (ibid.). Stringfellow later went on to open the Blue Moon Club in May 1963 and the Mojo Club in March 1964, which played host to Howlin' Wolf, Wilson Pickett and Jimi Hendrix, leading Stringfellow in 1965 to claim that the Mojo was one of the top four clubs in Britain (ibid.: 65). Stringfellow also promoted the Rolling Stones a number of times, first at the Gaumont nightclub in October 1963 and later at the City Hall in November 1963, alongside Dave Berry and the Cruisers. Another important venue to open around this time was the Black Swan on Snig Hill in 1963, now the Boardwalk.

[5]   The venue hosted its first all-nighter in late 1964, featuring modern jazz, traditional jazz and rock'n'roll; the all-nighters were held on Saturday nights after the usual show from 7 to 11 pm. The club would reopen from midnight until 8 am (Hale and Thornton 2002: 19).

[6]   The Esquire eventually boasted 27,000 members and artists who performed at the club included the Who, the Yardbirds, the Kinks, Joe Cocker, Alex Harvey, Screaming Lord Sutch and Dave Hawley (Richard Hawley's late father) (Hale and Thornton 2002). Both Club 60 and the Esquire Club closed in 1967 after Terry Thornton became tired of the 'sheer hard slog and increasing and unnecessary bureaucracy', including changes to licensing laws

Hotel, the Wharncliffe Hotel and the Sheffield Jazz Club (members 4/-; non-members 5/-). Among the musicians they would have been able to see were Derek Bailey and Tony Oxley, who in 1963 formed the experimental trio Joseph Holbroke with Sheffield University student Gavin Bryars.

Sheffield at this time had a growing Irish population and many of the pubs catered for folk sessions. The early 1960s also saw the start of many folk clubs, including the Sheffield University Folk Club at the Grapes pub, and later at The Three Cranes on Bank Street, which by 1966 was attracting such well-known names as Ewan McColl, Peggy Seeger, Dominic Behan, Martin Carthy and Paul Simon[7] (Boulding, 2009).

References

Bond, C. 2008. 'Stringfellow on the club that made Sheffield swing in the '60s'. *Yorkshire Post*, 7 November. Available at: www.yorkshirepost.co.uk/nostalgia/Stringfellow-on-the-club-that.4671553.jp [accessed 12 September 2012].

Boulding, T. 2009. Interview with Emma Webster, 29 June.

'Don Everly flies home to America'. 1962. *Sheffield Telegraph*, 16 October: 1.

'Entertainments'. 1962. *The Star, Sheffield*, 1 October: 2.

'Entertainments'. 1962. *The Star, Sheffield*, 5 October: 2.

'Entertainments'. 1962. *The Star, Sheffield*, 19 October: 2.

'Entertainments'. 1962. *The Star, Sheffield*, 30 October: 2.

Firminger, J. and Lilleker, M. 2001. *Not Like a Proper Job: The Story of Popular Music in Sheffield 1955–1975 as Told by Those Who Made it*. Sheffield: Juma.

Hale, D. and Thornton, T. 2002. *Club 60 and Esquire: Sheffield Sounds in the 60's*. Sheffield: ALD Design & Print.

'Rhythmic King Richard rocks the audience'. 1962. *The Star, Sheffield*, 25 October: 2.

'STUNG! That's the box office after Mr. Bumble's visit'. 1962. *The Star, Sheffield*, 14 November: 2.

---

and public entertainment licenses (ibid.: 77). The Esquire Club reopened as the Leadmill in 1980, and Club 60 now operates as a recording studio which occasionally hosts private members' parties and sessions.

[7]   Boulding recalled one particular occasion when 'a little fat dark-haired lad' – Paul Simon – offered to play for 'a couple of quid', but nobody knew him they declined. 'He went on to greater things, including allegedly nicking "Scarborough Fair" off the guy who arranged it in the way he later played it unacknowledged. And that, of course, was Dave Swarbrick's old pal, Martin Carthy. They all went back to a guy called Mike Wild's house on Granville Road afterwards, and this Paul Simon got in with the company and kept saying, "Play us that one; it's really good". Nobody heard of him again for about six years when he topped the charts in America' (Boulding, 2009, emphasis in original).

Chapter 7
Venues, Audiences and Promoters

When The Big Three played Hamburg, they brought with them Adrian Barber, a tall, lanky, good-looking boy, a tremendously able sound technician. He helped to invent the big-box amplifiers that allowed Beat music to blast out to full effect. Before he came on the scene, the amplifiers were tiny affairs with very little power. (Williams 1976: 185)

Manchester's most famous club in the 1960s, the Twisted Wheel, started out as a self-proclaimed 'beatnik type' café called the Left Wing, which, in its advertising material, offered entrance for 'Feminine-type cats' at a reduced rate. (Haslam 1999: 86)

[Lord] Montagu [of Beaulieu] explained to me that he was aiming for 'a British version of the American Newport Jazz Festival, if you like, but I think I saw the festival ideally as the Glyndebourne of Jazz, or hoped it might become that'. (McKay 2004: 104)

Introduction

This chapter is divided into three sections. In the first we describe how established venues – music halls and variety theatres, dance halls and ballrooms, town halls and concert halls – adapted to cultural change in post-war Britain; how the club scene developed as jazz, folk, skiffle, beat and R&B performers and audiences met and mingled in the same spaces; and how new touring opportunities emerged in cinemas, festivals and colleges. In the second section we describe the tensions that arose between venues and audiences, leading to widespread accounts of audience misbehaviour in the form of 'riots' and 'hysteria', and consider how live music technology struggled to keep up as concerts moved from clubs and theatres to arenas and large outdoor spaces, and as audiences came to expect music to be properly amplified. Finally we will examine the careers of some of the key promoters of the period as a way of documenting how the live music business did and did not change between 1950 and 1967.

Venues

In the 1950s, the growth of television viewing was the most obvious threat to live entertainment. Television was routinely blamed for dwindling audiences, an opinion shared by most showbiz historians. Frank Bruce, for example, after describing the 'spate' of Scottish theatre closures – the Leith Gaiety (1956), the Greenock Empire (1957), Dunfermline Opera House and the Falkirk Roxy (1958), the Paisley Theatre (1959), the Edinburgh Empire (1962), the Glasgow Empire (1963) and the Aberdeen Tivoli (1966) – states baldly that 'the main culprit was television'.[1] By 1955, the threat to variety theatre orchestras was serious enough that the Trades Union Congress appealed to Parliament to pass a bill allowing the state to buy ailing theatres to protect musicians' employment. The problem was not just TV; it was also clear that variety was becoming outmoded entertainment. 'I blame managers and agents who are often sadly out of touch with what the public wants', wrote a reporter in *Melody Maker* in 1955. For a brief period, the halls sought to stay open by putting on sex-and-variety shows (mostly produced by Paul Raymond), but, as a theatre writer observed in 1956, this was 'a short-term policy for an industry with a very small expectation of life. I believe the variety houses are doomed'.[2]

There is also plenty of evidence to suggest that variety theatres were willing to follow new musical trends in order to survive. Artists who appealed to youth audiences, such as Johnnie Ray, toured the established variety circuit and, considering that *Blackboard Jungle* only made its UK screen debut in 1956, variety performers and promoters were remarkably quick to embrace the newfound popularity of rock'n'roll. In May that year the London Palladium announced a new show starring Harry Secombe, entitled 'Rocking the Town'; in August *Melody Maker* reported that:

> The new Tony Crombie group – the first full-time rock-and-roll outfit in the country – has already been signed for a No.1 Variety tour. Billy Marsh, of the Bernard Delfont office, in association with the Jeff Kruger agency, is to present the band as star attraction in a complete rock-and-roll show on the Moss Empires circuit.[3]

By 1959, however, it was clear that the variety circuit would not survive the changes in audience tastes. A front-page *Melody Maker* story on 2 May, reporting the closure of three significant variety halls – the Chiswick Empire in London, the Sheffield Empire and the Sunderland Empire[4] – restated the argument that 'two

---

[1]   Bruce 2000: 127.

[2]   Quoted in Robinson 2007: 85 and see *Melody Maker*, 10 September 1955: 1; 2 February 1955: 17.

[3]   *Melody Maker*, 13 May 1956: 1; 11 August 1956: 1. The reviewer for the *Sunderland Echo* was unimpressed by the Crombie group's performance at the Sunderland Empire: 'I enjoy good jazz, and I can tap my feet to a pulsating rhythm as well as most, but I found the renderings of Mr Crombie's Rockets to be nothing more than clangourous, ear-splitting uproar' (Robinson 2007: 85).

[4]   As its historian notes, the Sunderland Empire 'was not to stay dark for long. Within days of the theatre closing Sunderland Corporation was considering a rescue package. In

main factors have brought about the decline in Variety – TV and indifferent bills'. The addition of rock'n'roll to variety shows had not, it seemed, stopped audience decline. Moss Empires' joint Managing Director Leslie MacDonnell admitted that 'variety as we knew it is dead', but went on to claim that 'the theatre is very much alive. What the public wants are "Spectaculars" – the super type of revue. I'm going to see they get them!'. In the event, this was rhetorical bravado rather than the start of a theatrical revival.

The second significant live music circuit in the immediate post-war period was made up of dance halls and ballrooms. In Chapter 5 we described how in the 1950s teenagers began to frequent new dance spaces (coffee bars and youth clubs) and to dance to records, thereby rejecting the 'big band in a ballroom' paradigm that had been dominant since the 1930s. The new dance culture opened the way for new dance promoters. If there was a prohibitive cost to hiring a ballroom and a full dance band, most youth clubs and coffee bars could afford a record player and speakers, and young entrepreneurs began to build on the success of these venues by putting on similar dances in larger spaces, such as village and town halls. By 1959, *Melody Maker* was reporting ballrooms' concerns:

> Bosses of Britain's ballrooms plan to probe the wave of disc hops which are springing up all over the country. These record sessions often run in village halls, teenage clubs and civic centres, have already put some dance proprietors out of business. Now, the powerful Association of Ballrooms – which represents over 140 dance halls throughout Britain – will discuss the threat ... Says [Musicians' Union] assistant secretary Harry Francis: 'We have been fighting them all along. They are unfair to the good ballroom proprietor, bad for musicians – and bad for the teenagers. The teenagers are listening to a lot of rubbish instead of good jazz. If this goes on, where are the future dance band musicians to come from?' (6 June 1959: 1)

Dance hall proprietors' commercial interests turned out to be more powerful than their obligations to their musicians. In May 1962 the Mecca-owned Hammersmith Palais (where in 1919 the Original Dixieland Jazz Band made their first British appearance) dropped its monthly jazz band and replaced it with a disc night. This turned out to be indicative of a larger shift in Mecca policy. The 1963 opening of the new Mecca Empire ballroom in Leicester Square advertised not only Ken Mackintosh and his 17-piece orchestra and the Mick Mortimore Seven as the resident bands, but also that 'Monday afternoons and evenings will feature Golden Disc sessions with Johnny Chapman as resident deejay'.[5] As on the variety circuit, though, trying to integrate the new youth market into established entertainment

---

taking over a variety hall, it was going where no local authority had gone before'. The Sunderland councillors who pushed through the takeover 'maintained they were not entering into a business but providing a service' (Robinson 2007: 88).

[5]   *Melody Maker*, 26 May 1962: 5; 23 March 1963: 3.

did not solve the financial problems, and in 1961 Carl Heimann and Eric Morley at Mecca introduced commercial bingo to the UK for the first time, changing the primary function of many ballrooms for good.

Concert halls and town halls continued to be the most significant venues for classical music in Britain between 1950 and 1967 (with the state funding the creation of new classical venues such as the Royal Festival Hall) and in most British cities classical concert halls, new and old, were the best available spaces – in terms of both size and resources – to stage any music for large audiences. During the 1950s and 1960s, London's Royal Albert Hall, for example, hosted not just the Proms but also the Trapp Family Singers, Frank Sinatra, Liza Minnelli, Duke Ellington, the Beatles and the Rolling Stones – in other words, almost any act that could fill it.

Town halls continued to be multi-functional spaces, hosting a wide variety of events and activities, from amateur choir concerts to council meetings, pop concerts and wrestling bouts. The Colston Hall in Bristol provides a good example of the role a town hall could play in civic musical culture. It was originally built in 1867, with three auditoriums that, from the start, offered a variety of entertainments:

> The large hall was used mainly for musical concerts organized by many different groups, especially Friendly Societies and trade unions. Other entertainments such as the phantascope (magical and mysterious!) were also frequently organized. The smaller Colston halls ... were the venue for minstrel shows ... and musical tableaux vivants. (Meller 1976: 210)

After a fire in 1945 (the third in its history), the Colston Hall was reopened in 1951 to mark the Festival of Britain. Local amateur orchestras and choral societies continued their performances there and it was the venue hired by commercial promoters for large touring acts, part of an informal network of concert and town halls across the country. When Harold Fielding promoted Ella Fitzgerald and Oscar Peterson in 1955, for instance, the tour comprised concerts at the Royal Albert Hall, the Colston Hall, Birmingham Town Hall, the Manchester Belle Vue (King's Hall), Sheffield City Hall, Newcastle-on-Tyne City Hall, the Dundee Caird Hall, the Edinburgh Usher Hall, and the Leicester De Montfort Hall.[6]

The other network of relatively large venues that became essential for promoters in this period was the cinema circuit. As their attendances declined in the 1950s, cinemas were forced to look for alternative sources of revenue. They had, for some time, been presenting concerts on Sundays and now cinema owners became open to concert bookings during the week too, as Allen Eyles explains:

> more and more cinemas returned to live shows, including several of the well-equipped Gaumonts. This was not just a Sunday event but spread to weekdays interrupting the run of the film programme. Artists would even perform on

---

[6]   *Melody Maker*, 22 January 1955: 3.

Saturday nights despite tough resistance by film distributors loath to forfeit their
share of the takings on the best night of the week. (Eyles 1996: 148–9)

Cinemas became especially popular venues for touring rock and pop acts in the
1960s. Jef Hanlon, who was then a tour manager, describes the logistics of the
cinema circuit:

> What the tours were then were the Odeons, the Gaumonts and ABCs, live houses
> that had live shows and it was twice nightly, 6.15 and 8.30 and it was 5 or 6 acts
> and if you were top of the bill you got to play 5 or 6 songs because you'd had 5
> or 6 hits – if you'd had 5 or 6 hits – and if you were bottom of the bill you got
> to play your new single and one song and that was two songs and off. And they
> had a compère holding it all together and everybody got on the coach with a
> crate of beer … The outlook was the cinemas circuits 'cause they had seats, they
> had box offices, they had a stage, they had stage lighting, they had stage lighting
> switchboards – the old grandmasters with the big wheel. So they were equipped
> and that's where they went. (Hanlon 2010)

Sometimes artists would tour cinemas exclusively, as Jerry Lee Lewis was meant to
do on his first British tour in 1958 (the tour was cancelled after three nights following
the discovery by the press that his new bride was only 13), but, as Eyles notes,
'the tours typically mixed Rank Theatres with Granadas, ABCs, independents, live
theatres, and municipal halls'.[7] Although such concerts were, in the main, popular
music events, there are also examples of classical music being performed in cinemas:

> One remarkable development occurred when the Royal Philharmonic Orchestra
> needed a new home after the Royal Festival Hall on London's South Bank
> closed at the end of May 1964 for seven months of renovation. The Odeon Swiss
> Cottage was chosen for a series of nine Sunday night concerts … The concerts
> were so popular that the Royal Philharmonic returned for many more series …
> with Rank continuing to add numerous one-day specials of ballet and opera films
> on the same days between the seasons of live shows. The concerts continued at
> least until the end of 1969. Audiences only faded when the orchestra performed
> too many pieces by less popular composers under pressure from its sources of
> funding. (Eyles 2005: 87)

If variety theatres, ballrooms, concert halls and cinemas all had histories stretching
back long before 1950, the loose network of small clubs which featured live music
in the 1950s and 1960s was a product of its time, of the do-it-yourself and youth
cultures we discussed in Chapters 4 and 5.

In his memoir *Second Chorus*, Humphrey Lyttelton recalls that although
jazz clubs had existed before the 1950s, they were largely ignored by the press

---

[7]   Eyles 2005: 86.

until the trad boom. Once trad became commercially successful, 'overnight, we became socially significant, a postwar phenomenon, something to be studied and psychoanalysed'. The *Daily Worker* described the typical Lyttelton Club audience as 'solid, dependable proletarian types'; a critic from *The Times* saw the audience as 'not "blokes" at all, but [upper-class] "chaps"'. Lyttelton remarks that 'in our innocence we had always regarded our patrons as an oddly assorted, heterogeneous, unpredictable mob, as motley a crew as the Foreign Legion itself, who came to the club because they liked to dance – and listen – to jazz'. He describes, from a club perspective, how social dancing moved out of the large dance halls:

> In Britain, jazz club dancing began about ten years ago. Nobody will pretend that, in those ten years, it has reached a very high standard of grace and beauty. But it started under a severe disadvantage. The music was 'Revivalist' in nature at that time – its style and format were lifted from gramophone records of the twenties. The poor dancers who were cajoled into taking the floor at the Leicester Square or the London Jazz Clubs had no records to turn to for guidance … At first, they set about it in the way some adventurous people learn to swim – by jumping in at the deep end and thrashing about for dear life … [Then] jiving was introduced into British dance halls by the American troops during the war. And it began to infiltrate in the jazz clubs when young people – not necessarily dedicated jazz fans – began to desert the big dance halls for the more informal jazz club atmosphere. (Lyttelton 1958: 17–18, 56)

Roger Horton, manager (and then owner) of the Lyttelton Club as it metamorphosised into the 100 Club, has suggested that the 'informal' atmosphere Lyttelton describes was partly an effect of the 'relaxed' attitude towards capacity regulations:

> The first gig I ever did as boss was a jazz night with a very popular band called Alex Welsh and his Band on a Saturday night in 1964 … It cost three and six to get in and we had 931 customers. That was before the days when you had to have a licence, which restricts the number of people you are admitting … today we are allowed to have 290 people. That is our capacity. In those days, the bars were not built as they are now, so it was bigger, but that many people was still absolutely staggering. (Quoted in Burrows 2009: 19)

There was considerable overlap in the audiences involved in music that was variously labelled trad jazz, modern jazz, skiffle, rock'n'roll, R&B and beat, and clubs became central to the ways in which both musicians and entrepreneurs tried to make sense of and cater for the evolving tastes. As rock gained popularity in Britain, *Melody Maker* reported that 'rock-and-roll clubs are opening throughout the country' and that 'the new craze is also hitting the jazz clubs', with many venues adding special rock-only nights to cater to new audiences (14 July 1956: 2). Some clubs were forced to abandon styles that were no longer popular, as was the case with Studio '51, London's oldest operating modern jazz club. It closed in August 1956, only to reopen in September hosting New Orleans jazz with Ken Colyer five nights a week and a rock'n'roll night once a week (11 August 1956: 16). The first club to label itself as R&B opened in 1960, when musician and writer Alexis Korner joined forces with promoter Ian Crinnan to hold weekly Sunday sessions at the St Mary Hall. As Korner explained, 'we feel that with the current popularity of trad jazz and rock, there is room for rhythm and blues which falls midway between the two' (24 September 1960: 20). The presence of R&B in small clubs grew dramatically over the next several years, to the point where, as Chris Roberts put it, 'you'll have a job drawing the line between rhythm and blues and plain old rock on the London scene today' (5 January 1963: 5). Drummer John Steel makes the same point about Newcastle:

> We would be in the jazz lounge [of the Club A GoGo] backing John Lee Hooker or Sonny Boy Williamson; I'd back people like Tubby Hayes and Tony Coe and as well as playing with Eric [Burdon] before we were called the Animals, I also played with Mike Carr at times, playing straight jazz, so there was a beautiful mix of music – modern jazz, R&B and authentic blues men coming over from America, with the new British music going on in the room next door. It was jumping, a fantastic atmosphere. (Phipps, Tobler and Smith 2005: 162)

In 1963 even Ronnie Scott's club, until then a 'jazz only' venue, introduced R&B sessions, manager Pete King noting that 'for the first time we shall be clearing space for dancing'. *Melody Maker* concluded that 'many trad proprietors seem to regard R&B as the cure-all for dwindling audiences. The modern clubs view it as a chance to lure a wider public through the doors' (30 March 1963: 3, 6). By 1965, the paper was reporting that jazz, once the central musical genre of London's small club scene, had moved to the margins and into small pubs:

> Ousted from London's West End by the forces of pop, folk and R&B, jazz today is moving into a scene once the domain of darts throwers, ha'penny shovers and crisp eaters. Jazz and drink have long proved an excellent combination, and as the music has been forced out of the clubs, it's natural it should take to the pubs. Jazz pubs are glorious London phenomena, and in them can be heard the finest musicians in the country, blowing to enthusiastic crowds, gladly foregoing the lure of darts and shove ha'penny. (17 July 1965: 8)

The very volatility of the club scene reveals its importance in managing the changes in live music entertainment, and one paradoxical outcome of these mutations was the discotheque. Both the term 'discotheque' and the particular kind of venue it describes originated in France. 'Discotheque' translates roughly as 'record library' or 'house of music' and is the term for a dance club in which records are played exclusively. Nightclub entrepreneur Regine Zylberberg (then known simply as Regine) claims that her venue, the Whisky-à-Gogo in Paris, was the first to feature uninterrupted disc-playing beginning in 1953:

I laid down a linoleum dance-floor – like in a kitchen – put in coloured lights, and removed the juke-box. The trouble with the juke-box was that when the music stopped you could hear snogging in the corners. It killed the atmosphere ... Instead I installed two turntables so there was no gap in the music. I was barmaid, doorman, bathroom attendant, hostess – and I also put on the records. It was the first ever discotheque and I was the first ever club disc-jockey.[8]

By the end of the 1950s, this kind of club had made its way to London with the opening of La Discotheque on Wardour Street, the Saddle Room and the Ad Lib. These clubs contravened the Musicians' Union's PPL agreement – they played records for dancing without regard for live musicians – but, as Thornton suggests, it was not worthwhile for the Musicians' Union to prosecute such small ventures; it concentrated on fighting for the survival of bands in the large dance hall chains.[9]

As an example of a discotheque we will take the Place, which opened in Stoke-on-Trent in 1962. The Place was a popular Mod club in the 1960s and one of the first venues of its kind in the Midlands. In his own history of the club, owner Kevin Donovan remembers observing that 'the ballrooms and coffee bars did not serve alcohol, whilst the adjacent pubs were packed to the doors, and I realised that the two must logically and eventually merge':

Thus the layout and policy of The Place was formulated: spacious dance floor; disc jockey unit; licensed bar; coffee bar; non-stop records – a Membership Club for the over 18's. In 1962 this was a completely new line of thinking and the sheer uncertainty of the scheme acted as an uncontrollable adrenalin to all of us. There were other coffee dance clubs on the drawing board ... The Twisted Wheel, Manchester, The Mojo in Sheffield, The Dungeon at Nottingham to name but a few. However, they had not linked the maturity of a licensed bar facility to their plans and would consequently provide a different type of image and operation. (Donovan 1981: 5)

Although Donovan's intention was, from the start, to create a venue that played only records, he quickly discovered that his prospective patrons still wanted to hear live music:

In the first two weeks of Placelessness the good people of Stoke-on-Trent had decided there was no point in paying to hear records which were played on the wireless for nothing ... The format was decided, we would become a Discotheque which also provided live music. (Donovan 1981: 14)

The Place thus provided disc-only nights on Mondays to Fridays and featured live groups at the weekends. The live gigs provided the majority of the venue's

---

[8]   Quoted in Schofield 2005; and see Donovan 1981: 4.
[9]   Thornton 1995: 41.

income between 1963 and1965; only then did the disc-only nights grow in popularity.

The precursor to the modern pop festival also developed in this era. Outdoor public concerts had long been popular in Britain. Pleasure gardens, for example, first opened in London in the late seventeenth century and a version of them could be found in many holiday resorts by the end of the nineteenth century. Meller describes the entertainments on offer in the pleasure garden in the seaside resort of Avonmouth in 1870:

> There were 'vocalists, negro-delineators, comic singers, dancers, comedians, etc, hay making and rustic sports, brass band and string band for dancing, trapeze and rope walking acts, outdoor amusements, swings, whirl-abouts, quoits, croquet, American bowling alleys and a new skittle alley', and admission to the Games only cost 4d. (Meller 1976: 210–11)[10]

The term 'festival', however, was primarily applied to celebrations of classical music. Many British cities had such 'musical festivals' in the nineteenth century. The first Edinburgh Musical Festival, for example, held between 30 October and 5 November 1815, featured seven concerts in two venues with 150 performers. It brought in visitors – 'the concourse of strangers towards Edinburgh was unexampled', as a report of the time put it, adding that 'all the lodgings round the city were occupied' – and for the next decade was a significant social event for the local gentry.[11]

By the end of the nineteenth century, 'music festival' also described a competitive event in which local amateur musicians competed in various instrumental classes. The Association of Competition Festivals for Music, Dance and Speech was formed in 1904; the Edinburgh Competition Festival began in 1920 and has been an annual event ever since. Competitors (mostly children) compete in various categories over a two-week period. Such competitions take place annually all over Britain; being a music festival assessor is a useful source of income for music professionals.

In general we could say that in the classical world 'festival' refers to an event in which a variety of live concerts take place at various venues in a locality over several days (hence the Edinburgh International Festival and the Aldeburgh Festival, both established as annual events in the 1940s) and this usage is now common in other music worlds too (the English Folk Dance and Song Society launched the Sidmouth Folk Dance Festival in 1955, which is now an annual Folk Week; the Cambridge Folk Festival, which started in 1965, was modelled on the Newport Jazz Festival, which we will discuss below). What makes the

---

[10]   This could almost be a description of T in the Park! For the economics of the original eighteenth-century pleasure garden, see Olmsted 2002: 121–3.

[11]   McLarty 2010: 8. There was already, it seems, an association being made between a music festival, the attraction of visitors and the local economy.

contemporary pop festival different from these events is that its single entrance fee covers all performances on a specific site; audiences camp overnight at or near the venue. (At other festivals, each concert is booked separately and audiences vary from event to event.) Inspiration here came from the first major US jazz festival, which took place in Newport, Rhode Island, in 1954.[12] This weekend-long celebration of jazz music inspired the creation of several British events. Some of these were indistinguishable from ordinary multiple-act concerts and perhaps labelled themselves as 'festivals' to associate themselves with Newport's success – examples are the BBC Festival of Dance Music and the 'Floating Festival of Jazz', which was presented on a boat travelling 'from London to Margate and back'.[13] The latter example is also a useful reminder, though, that while Newport certainly gave British promoters a model for festival development, jazz in Britain was already associated with outdoor events and public gatherings that had their own influence on how the British pop festival developed.

Riverboat Shuffles featuring jazz bands had been annual events in London since the late 1940s, with day-long trips from Richmond to Chertsey and back emulating 'in spirit, at least' the riverboats that carried dancers up the Mississippi from New Orleans, and, as George McKay has argued, the sense of carnival such cruises sought to sell became associated with jazz in outdoor political events too, in street gatherings and protest marches. McKay notes that 'the first British festival proper', the third annual Beaulieu Jazz Festival, 'the first to be held over an entire weekend, with extensive professional amplification for the many bands, and crash tents and other formal camping facilities', was staged a few months after CND's first annual Aldermaston March in 1958. Both events featured trad bands playing for youthful campers in rural settings and there is no doubt that elements of the 'protest' that provided CND's youthful dynamic also affected Beaulieu's crowd.[14]

The very first Beaulieu Jazz Festival was held in 1956, as Michael Clarke explains:

> Lord Montagu had started running Jazz Festivals at Beaulieu in 1956 as part of his continuing imaginative solutions for the preservation of the Beaulieu estate. The pattern of successful open-air jazz festivals had been established with the Newport, Rhode Island annual festival … In the first year 600 attended at Beaulieu, a few of them camping in the woods nearby before and afterwards, though they were not, as yet, allowed to camp on the festival site itself. This was followed by the first weekend festival held by Butlins at their holiday camp in Clacton, attended by 800 and with performances by, among others, Ted Heath,

---

[12]   There had, in fact, been a longer American tradition of folk music festivals, such as fiddlers' contests, that do seem to have involved competitors and audiences camping overnight, but these events did not have the impact of Newport, which also directly influenced the evolution of the American Folk Festival – see Cohen 2008.

[13]   See *Melody Maker*, 8 January 1955: 16; 11 May 1957: 2.

[14]   McKay 2004: 97. For the Thames Riverboat Shuffles, see Godbolt 1976: 78.

Johnny Dankworth, and Shirley Bassey. In 1957 the Beaulieu festival was held again and 2,000 people came. In 1958 the numbers doubled again to 4,000 and special new amplification equipment was introduced. For the first time large tents were provided for those who wished to stay overnight. (Clarke 1982: 21)

The festival was an important symbolic event for British jazz: pictures and articles in the press depicting a large assembly of jazz fans in an unusual environment lent a kind of tangible visual evidence to support and expand the notion of a 'jazz community'. On the other hand, the large crowds at Beaulieu were not always easy to manage. Beaulieu continued to run until 1961, but in the last three years the festival was marred by crowd disturbances (the main reason why Lord Montagu abandoned the event).[15] Meanwhile, other jazz festivals had sprung up throughout the UK; by 1961, open-air music festivals were occurring almost every weekend during the summer months. Chris Barber commented, rather sourly, that:

> Festival-mania seems to be sweeping the country – but it is high time the people who are in charge of such promotions were taken to task for the shows they are putting on under the banner of a Jazz Festival. If more thought was given to such giant-sized events, I am quite sure that the riots that are associated with jazz in the open air, and the unwelcome publicity that goes with them, would be quashed.[16]

The leading figure in bringing order as well as sustained commercial viability to the new festival movement was Chris Barber's business partner, Harold Pendleton; we will discuss his career further below.

By the mid-1960s, student unions were also becoming important venues for the touring circuit. The National Union of Students was formed in 1922 and student unions had always played an important role in student life; from the mid-1950s onwards, there is evidence of union-sponsored music societies and, in particular, jazz societies promoting concerts on college campuses. The London Jazz Society, for instance, the students' jazz club at the London School of Economics, was established in 1955 and by the beginning of the 1960s there were enough university jazz societies to make up a touring network. A tour featuring Kenny Ball and his Jazzmen in 1961, for example, included dates at Birmingham University, Bristol University, Nottingham University and Battersea Technical College.[17] In the

---

[15]   See McKay 2005: 69–86.

[16]   Barber 1961: 3. Festivals that summer included the all-trad 'Summer Festival of Jazz' at Fulford Hall, Earlswood (*Melody Maker*, 24 June 1961: 4), the 'Grand Two-Day Mammoth Jazz Festival' at Ringwood in Hampshire (*Melody Maker*, 24 June 1961: 9) and the National Jazz Festival at the Richmond Athletic Ground in Surrey (*Melody Maker*, 24 June 1961: 16).

[17]   *Melody Maker*, 30 January 1965: Supplement page 3; 14 October 1961: 5.

same period, as we described in Chapter 4, university folk clubs became equally significant for touring folk musicians.

It was at this time too that the role of 'social secretary' – the student responsible for booking music and other entertainments at their place of study – became an established sabbatical job and a significant starting point for the next generation of commercial promoters. The use of student unions as venues meant treating college students as a specific audience – most student union events were not open to people who were not members of the union. The student market thus became important for the way in which live music developed after 1967, a story we will cover in the second volume of this history.

Audiences

Venues need audiences and the live music experience is shaped by audience behaviour, which a promoter therefore seeks to control. In Chapter 2 we described how the first British screenings of *Blackboard Jungle* and *Rock Around the Clock* led to press reports of young audiences 'rioting', which in turn led to some venue owners and local authorities (such as Glasgow City Council) banning rock'n'roll shows altogether. The *Melody Maker* report on the Glasgow decision suggests that part of the perceived problem was the kind of dancing involved. John Dunsmore, General Manager of the city's Halls Department, explained:

> we do not think this kind of dancing can do us any good. In any case, there are
> dangers which can result in trouble and damage to property. We have experience
> of what can happen when this rock'n'roll takes place. (10 November 1956: 4)

The seriousness of the 'trouble' caused is difficult to determine because incidents involving rock'n'roll were routinely sensationalised in the press, but we can say that *Melody Maker* reports of audience misbehaviour were not restricted to rock'n'roll. Frank Sinatra, it seems, caused scenes of audience 'hysteria' at his British shows in 1950 (15 July: 1), as did Johnnie Ray in 1955 (29 October: 13), and there were regular reports of disturbances at jazz and dance events. An all-night 'Jazz Jamboree' held by Worthing's New Conception Jazz Club, for example, was stopped by police after 'deck chairs were thrown on a bonfire' (14 July 1956: 2); Whitby Urban Council banned jive dancing because it led to rowdy behaviour (17 November 1956: 2); and crowd trouble was associated with jazz festivals so routinely that the Earlswood Jazz Festival in 1961 made headlines for its *lack* of trouble: 'Wot, no Riots?' (15 July 1961: 1).[18]

---

[18]   The National Jazz Festival (which also presented blues, R&B, rock and pop) was forced to change venues throughout the 1960s following local council complaints about audience behaviour. See *Melody Maker*, 'Richmond bans jazz festival' (18 September

Promoters most commonly had difficulty managing audience behaviour when they put on music that encouraged dancing in venues designed for sitting, but they ran up against another problem when they put music designed (by its performers) for listening to in venues that encouraged dancing. Eric Morley, the Director of Mecca Dancing, notes that:

> One reason why jazz show attendances are falling off is because the public is no longer just interested in [listening to the] the music – they want to dance to it. Ballroom promoters who have for years been banning jive are now allowing rock'n'roll, and young people, finding they can rock'n'roll [dance] to jazz or skiffle, want to go to ballrooms and dance while listening to the music. They cannot do this in the theatres but when we try to get these bands they will not go into the dance halls because they are afraid of jeopardising their position with promoters who book them at theatres three or four times a year.
>
> At first that seems perfectly feasible but as all our ballrooms are now playing some form of rock'n'roll, skiffle or jazz, the public is coming to us and gradually, through lack of support, the jazz concerts may fold up. Then the bands would have no bookings at all, either one side or the other, because we would have made our own attractions by this time. Lyn Dutton, who speaks of a 13 percent drop in business, is one of those who does not want to let the bands go into the dance halls. It is in the interests of all jazz and skiffle bands to make as many ballroom appearances as possible. They will find a new public, eager to listen. They will pick up recruits for jazz clubs, leaving those who want to dance as well as listen in the ballrooms. (Quoted in *Melody Maker*, 22 June 1957: 5)

But, as *Melody Maker* reported, acts were not always happy about being moved from theatres to dance halls. Bobby Darin, for example, complained that 'British audiences were the noisiest I have played to anywhere in the world', making it difficult for him to perform (2 April 1960: 1); Heinz gave up playing ballroom dates altogether because he felt their audiences 'just want a sound' rather than the 'visual' performance he was trying to put across (17 August 1963: 3); The Hollies complained that ballroom audiences were too noisy and thus incompatible with the kind of musical experience the band wanted to create. Group members Graham Nash and Eric Haydock preferred the cabaret scene:

> 'I know that the fans like to see us in ballrooms where they feel that they can get closer to us. But I would like the future of the Hollies to be in the field of cabaret. We recently played a week in cabaret at Mr. Smith's Club in Manchester, and we feel we did very well. It gave us the chance to play things like "Puff The Magic Dragon", "Stewball", "Taste of Honey" – numbers we could never do in

1965: 24), 'National Jazz Festival moves to Windsor' (18 June 1966: 4) and 'No more Windsor' (14 October 1967: 3).

ballrooms.' 'When we work cabaret it's different altogether', said Eric. 'Proper dressing rooms, and lighting – and attentive audiences who have come along to listen, and to applaud what they like'. (7 January 1966: 3)

It is also clear that accounts of misbehaviour vary according to the gender of the audience. Male audiences were 'violent' and caused 'riots'; female audiences were 'hysterical'. There are, in fact, numerous reports of female fans causing injury, whether to performers, to security staff or to one another.[19] By the early 1960s, it was routine for promoters to ensure that there was a police presence at concerts featuring artists known to have a significant female following.[20] 'Beatlemania', as a media concept, was thus rooted in a long history of the reporting of the young female audience:

> It began in England with a report that fans had mobbed the popular but not yet immortal group after a concert at the London Palladium on 13 October, 1963. Whether there was in fact a mob or merely a scuffle involving no more than eight girls is not clear, but the report acted as a call to mayhem. Eleven days later a huge and excited crowd of girls greeted the Beatles (returning from a Swedish tour) at Heathrow Airport. In early November, 400 Carlisle girls fought the police for four hours while trying to get tickets for a Beatles concert; nine people were hospitalised after the crowd surged forward and broke through shop windows. In London and Birmingham the police could not guarantee the Beatles safe escort through the hordes of fans. (Ehrenreich, Hess and Jacobs 1997: 524)

The relations between artist, audience and venue were also negotiated through sound technology. One of the key differences between big bands and skiffle groups, for instance, lay in the volume of sound they could produce. Twenty-piece dance bands of primarily brass instruments could play a large dance hall without amplification; a skiffle band made up of banjo, upright bass, washboard and vocals could not.

This is not to say that jazz and dance bands did not use public address (PA) systems. Singers for dance bands were routinely amplified in dance halls and had been for many years. In the 1950s small jazz groups not only used amplification but drew attention to it. When Oscar Peterson and Ella Fitzgerald played the Albert Hall in 1955, for instance, promoter Harold Fielding went out of his way to tell potential ticket buyers that 'we install special Strand Electric equipment in the Royal Albert Hall for our presentations. Therefore ... we make sure that the audience hears two internationally known artistes at their very best'.[21]

---

[19]   See, for example, *Melody Maker* reports of incidents at shows with Paul Anka (15 March 1958: 5), Brian Hyland (9 February 1963: 2) and the Walker Brothers (9 October 1965: 4).

[20]   See, for example, *Melody Maker*, 27 January 1962: 16; 2 November 1963: 1; 19 September 1964: 4.

[21]   *Melody Maker*, 22 January 1955: 10.

For skiffle bands, though, electronic amplification was necessary if they were to be heard by their audiences at all. Stephen Court suggests that 'since skiffle could be played by anybody who had mastered three chords, the huge guitar and sound equipment boom in the mid-1950s was a direct result of that', and once the drum kit replaced the washboard, the other instrumentalists needed additional amplification to balance the overall sound.[22] Drum kits, electric guitars and Selmer 15-watt amps – as well as the more powerful Vox AC30 – became extremely popular in the mid-1950s in skiffle and rock'n'roll groups, and, as Peter Everett explains:

> Just as technology had made possible the four-man self-contained rock'n'roll group, it now gradually began to change the style of the music. The development of the bass speaker cabinet in particular made the stomach-thumping beat of the bass guitar the dominant sound, above which all the other ingredients had to struggle to be heard. The group therefore needed a high-pitched clanging lead guitar, a leather-throated lead vocal and two or three voices shouting out the choruses. (Everett 1986: 45)

For cinema and dance-hall shows, rock'n'roll bands had plugged directly into in-house PA systems; the beat groups now playing smaller clubs usually brought their own. Dave Percy, lead guitarist with Wirral band the Roadrunners, remembers how impressed he and other local musicians were with the Rolling Stones' 'wonderful crisp and clear sound' when they played the Cavern for the first time in November 1963: 'at that time The Stones had probably the best equipment on the market'.[23] If the amplification of instruments had originally been simply a matter of making them loud enough to be heard, sound quality and volume were now becoming aesthetic issues too, and volume was an ongoing issue for dispute. The 100 Club's Roger Horton remembers that:

> The first days of electric music in the club were very oddball. I remember some of those bands like Sounds Incorporated and Brian Poole and the Tremeloes. A lot of those bands played there. We thought they were incredibly loud, but by later standards they weren't anything of the kind. The volume was like that in your front room. (Brunning and Smith 2009: 52)[24]

And as the size of pop concerts grew, ensuring sufficient amplification became a serious problem for promoters. The first British arena concert took place at

---

[22]   Court 1984: 72.

[23]   Quoted in Thompson 1994: 51; and see Boyd 2008.

[24]   Britta Sweers has an interesting description of the problems the early folk rock bands had in 1966–7 moving back and forth between rock-oriented venues (for which their amplified sound wasn't loud enough), and folk venues (for which it was too loud) (Sweers 2005: 117–18).

Wembley Empire Pool in March 1959. A charity run by Vera Lynn called Stars Organisation for Spastics (SOS) organised a 'Record Star Show' which featured, among others, Shirley Bassey, Petula Clark, Max Bygraves, Lonnie Donegan and Humphrey Lyttelton. The event attracted 9,000 people and was such a success that SOS organised a second event, 'The Starlight Dance', in October the same year.[25] The Record Star Show continued as an annual event throughout the 1960s, and the Empire Pool became an accepted live music venue. The *NME* moved its Pollwinnners Concert to Wembley in 1960.

The limitations of existing equipment for the pop groups now attracting huge audiences was most clearly exposed, however, not in Britain but in the USA. When the Beatles played their first Shea Stadium show in 1965, amplification technology had not progressed quickly enough to cope. Vox designed and specially made 100-watt guitar amps for the group – much more powerful than the Beatles' usual 30-watt amps – but even these were unfit for purpose against the roar of the stadium audience. The Beatles were obliged to use the house PA system, which meant that they couldn't hear much either.

Back in Britain, the most widely cited watershed in innovation for electronic amplification was the Watkins 1000-watt 'slave amp' sound system, first used publicly at the Windsor Jazz and Blues Festival in 1967. Ironically, the Festival is now remembered for its terrible sound, mainly because local residents complained about the huge volume and so promoters were forced to turn it down. Artists like Eric Clapton and Jeff Beck 'had their sound reduced to a near pathetic level'.[26]

Promoters

The most important change in the live music business between 1950 and 1967 can be summarised in terms of genre. Dance bands and musical performers in variety theatre entertainment drove the economy of live music between the Second World War and the rock'n'roll era. After rock'n'roll and into the late 1960s, pop groups were the fastest growing part of the live music economy, and demand for big bands and variety all but disappeared. Some promoters were unable to adjust to these changes, but a remarkable number did adapt: many of the most important figures involved in promoting pop in the mid-1960s were

---

[25]   Tudor 2003: 15. Although it was not until concerts began at the Empire Pool that indoor concerts to audiences of 9,000 became a regular occurrence in Britain, there are earlier examples of comparably large-scale indoor live music events. In 1948 and 1949, for example, two 'Band Cavalcade' concerts took place at the Empress Hall in Earls Court. These concerts featured multiple dance bands on the bill and the concert in 1949 was reported to have had an audience of 7,846 (*Melody Maker*, 1 January 1949: 1).

[26]   The *Melody Maker* review, quoted in Barroso 2011; and see UK Rock Festivals 2011; Watkins 2011.

from pre-pop backgrounds. This could easily have alienated them from their young clients, but the older promoters used their experience to gain an edge in the competition with younger, less well-connected entrepreneurs. To illustrate this, we will focus here on the careers of two men: Harold Davison and Arthur Howes.

Harold Davison was perhaps the most powerful man in the British live music business during the 1960s. He managed the pop and jazz interests of the Grade Organisation, promoting the biggest jazz artists himself while overseeing many of the most significant pop concerts of the era. He pioneered reciprocal band deals between the USA and the UK in the 1950s, and remained the key figure in the 'man hours' trade that made Anglo-American touring possible in the 1960s. It was Davison, for instance, who had the necessary connections to help Brian Epstein negotiate an exchange for the Beatles on their first USA tour, trading it for a Woody Herman big band tour of the UK.[27] By 1967, Davison was making deals at the very top level of the British music industry, convincing Sir Joseph Lockwood of EMI to buy the Grade Organisation and its music interests.[28]

Davison was born in 1922 and showed an early interest in writing and performing jazz.[29] He joined the RAF in 1941 and on his discharge, in 1946, gave up on a career as a musician and instead chose to enter the music business as a promoter. His first venture was a series of three Sunday dance-band concerts. According to Davison, 'the first one [Paul Fenouhlet] was a disaster; I didn't even have enough money to get a taxi home. The second one [the Oscar Rabin Orchestra] wasn't bad, and for the third one I was saved by a band called the Squadronaires, an RAF band, and that sort of helped me get started'. As an enthusiast musician with a good mind for business, Davison quickly made inroads into the British dance-band world, which, he realised, was being overlooked by the then variety-oriented entertainment industry:

---

[27]   Herman was not received as well in Britain as the Beatles had been in the USA. From *Melody Maker*: 'Impresario Harold Davison this week hit out at British jazz fans for "not giving Woody Herman the support he deserved ... As a four-day tour ... the visit was not nearly as successful as one expected and I am surprised and disappointed that British jazz fans cannot support one of the greatest bands ever. I am very disappointed that audiences have not been terribly good. People grumble that we only bring in the same people year after year – but look what happens when we bring over a band that is the talk of America. Admittedly one doesn't expect to draw the same audience that one expects for such as Louis Armstrong and Ray Charles, but I expected a better turnout than this"' (18 July 1964: 5).

[28]   EMI, which controlled Thames Television, was compelled to sell off the Davison talent agency by the Independent Television Authority. Davison bought it back (for rather less than he had originally sold it to the Grades, according to Barrie Dickins) and then did a merger deal with MAM, the agency formed by Gordon Mills, manager of Tom Jones and Engelbert Humperdinck (Dickins 2009).

[29]   Biographical information from an interview with Harold Davison in 2010 unless otherwise noted.

> I think one of the reasons why I was successful, I didn't follow the line of the older agents and managers. [The established variety agents like the Grade and Foster agencies] didn't want to know about bands … So I came along and I didn't want to know about the old English acts playing variety – that was out of my hands, that was controlled by the big agencies. So I concentrated on music.

By focusing on dance bands, Davison was able to carve a niche for himself in the industry, also expanding into management and agency. By the end of the 1940s, he was handling business for several bandleaders, including Vic Lewis, Teddy Foster, Johnny Dankworth and Paul Fenouhlet (with whom he had made a loss on his very first concert promotion).

In the 1950s Davison consolidated his grasp on dance-band commerce by merging his business with smaller companies specialising in small groups and trad jazz. He also built up a mailing list to inform ticket-buyers of his promotions:

> People would join our club, and we would notify them a concert's coming in … I found that we could build up our own group of people who were interested in jazz, and they could buy the tickets from us direct, that was how it started. And it got bigger and bigger, it was quite a large part of our organisation … You'd be notified on what musicians were coming in, what attractions were coming, whether it was Frank Sinatra or a small band … and if you wanted tickets you could buy them through our ticket office.

Davison had expanded his business from early on by searching beyond the borders of the UK for promotion opportunities. A *Melody Maker* article in 1947 details his negotiations with the Irish Federation of Musicians to sanction a tour of Ireland for Vic Lewis (19 July: 5) and he was to become the key promoter in dismantling the barriers on the development of an international touring trade.

His breakthrough into the big time came in 1953, when he organised a European tour for Stan Kenton that included a Dublin concert sponsored by *Melody Maker*. Davison organised boats to take British jazz fans across the sea (Kenton couldn't get a permit to play in the UK): 'People came in ships, boats, God knows, it was one hell of thing. But it was successful'. In 1955, through a mix of persistence and negotiating skills, he managed what no concert promoter had been able to do since 1935: he persuaded both the British and the American Musicians' Unions to agree to a reciprocal exchange tour between the Stan Kenton and the Ted Heath orchestras. The exchange took place in 1956 and was the first of many. Davison developed a good working relationship with British musicians by making sure that 'whatever bands we sent to American in exchange for bands coming in, they were treated well and made more money than they would here'. This was possible because British audiences had been so starved of US name bands that the profit made from American musicians touring the UK were sufficient to offset any loss made by the British bands in the USA. Tours by Louis Armstrong, Count Basie, Ella Fitzgerald and Oscar Peterson followed Kenton's visit, and by 1958 Davison was being described in *Melody Maker* as 'the biggest band-agent in the country'.[30]

Davison's next breakthrough came in 1962 when he was asked by Frank Sinatra to promote a series of charity concerts. The connections he made through his association with Sinatra opened the door for him into other areas of showbusiness such as the West End theatre and the film industry, and in 1964 he cemented his position among the elite of the British entertainment industry by joining forces with the Grade Organisation. *Melody Maker* reported the deal as follows:

> London's Grade Organisation has taken over Harold Davison Ltd and its parent companies, it was announced this week. This makes the Grade-Davison link-up one of the most powerful European show business organisations, representing talent in all fields of entertainment. Davison remains managing director of Harold Davison Ltd and the Davison Agency, and also joins the board of the Grade Organisation as executive director. The Grade Organisation has now become a public company. (25 July 1964: 4)

In Davison's own account, this was not a takeover but a business integration that suited both parties:

> It wasn't so much an acquiring. They were going public [on the stock market], and they needed, what am I going to say, a younger guy looking after the music side. [Davison would have been 42 years old in 1964, Lew and Leslie were 58 and 48 respectively.] So I sold my company to them for shares in their company, which was going public. And I became a director with Lew and Leslie, and then Lew of course went over to ATV, and that was it.

Davison himself was aware that while he was the youngest director of the Grade Organisation, he needed to adapt to the changing tastes of much younger people if he was to stay relevant in the pop world. He had brought Bill Haley to Britain in 1957 and seen the audience reaction; he knew that rock'n'roll was good business. Using his exchange contacts, he now started systematically bringing over American pop and rock'n'roll groups. The first British beat group that Davison signed personally as agent was the Dave Clark Five, and by the mid-1960s, partly by merging with agencies like Tito Burns and partly by hiring younger agents like Barry Dickins (son of *NME* editor Percy Dickins), he had a stable of British pop acts to rival any other in the UK. Since he was by this point busy in his role as a Grade director, he worked primarily as head of the agency rather than as a hands-on pop promoter, delegating the latter role to people like Arthur Howes.[31]

---

[30]   7 June 1958: 20. Davison was also now known among his fellow promoters as 'the king of the exchange' (Dickins 2009).

[31]   See Davies 1981: 158–9.

Howes also first entered the live music business as a dance-band promoter. He was born in 1924 in Peterborough, orphaned and then adopted by parents in Yaxley. At the age of 20 he enlisted in the navy, where, according to his personal assistant Susan Fuller, he met up with several fellow servicemen who had worked in the entertainment industry.[32] After the war, he returned to Peterborough, and by the 1950s was regularly promoting dances in local halls and dance-band concerts in Peterborough's Embassy cinema. He was one of several regional promoters in Britain – others included Arthur Kimbrell in Leicester, John Smith in Surrey and Charles Lockyear in Bristol – who would buy individual dates for touring bands from London-based agents. This arrangement worked well for agent-promoters like Davison, who could spread the financial risk on a tour while ensuring that concerts outside London were handled by people with appropriate local knowledge. As Fuller puts it, 'a promoter would sell off the dates if there was a little bit of a risk ... and keep the plum dates for their company'. This was also good business for the local promoters – they could promote bigger name bands than they could usually access.

Howes began to distinguish himself from the crowd of smaller regional promoters in the second half of the 1950s, as he took on higher-profile, more ambitious and presumably lucrative tours. By 1955, he had expanded his activities beyond Peterborough; now he began to diversify into rock'n'roll and youth pop package tours. Larry Parnes may have been the most famous pop packager of this period – not least because he featured his own name in any promotional material – but Howes was the exclusive promoter of Britain's biggest pop star, Cliff Richard, and, although still based in Peterborough, by the beginning of the 1960s he had become nationally well known (he was now one of the promoters who sold tour dates to local entrepreneurs). He had become close friends with both Harold Davison and Leslie Grade, who offered him first refusal to promote many of the more famous names on their roster. As Susan Fuller recalls:

> when we lived in Peterborough, Arthur would go up to town and meet Leslie and he would come back with all the artists, and Arthur would give Leslie first shot at whatever he had. So they had a really good friendship.

Susan Fuller started working for Howes as his junior secretary in late 1961 and recalls that he promoted several different kinds of touring circuits. In addition to the dance bands and package tours, he organised variety tours (with comedy acts like Morecambe and Wise, Dick Emery and Tommy Cooper) and booked the entertainment for large American military bases such as Lakenheath and Mildenhall:

> We were making a fortune in the bases, it was a licence to print money ... We would book the band into the NCO club, and the base would pay Arthur, and Arthur would pay the band. So it was no big gamble.

---

[32]   All information of Howes' career taken from an interview with Susan Fuller in 2011 unless otherwise noted.

It was this steady income that allowed Howes to take risks in his other concert promotions.

When Brian Epstein was looking to book the Beatles on a national tour in 1962, Howes was, therefore, obviously someone to approach. Howes invited the band to Peterborough to play a test event, a support slot for Frank Ifield at the Embassy on 2 December 1962.[33] The crowd (there for Ifield) did not appreciate the Beatles' performance, but Howes was impressed and offered them a contract giving him first option on all their subsequent British tours. He was, by then, Helen Shapiro's agent (through his company General Artistes) and booked the Beatles to open up a package tour on which she headed the bill. The tour started out in February 1963, coinciding with the Beatles' first ascent up the record charts. With the exception of their first headline tour (which was a co-promotion between Danny Betesh, Tito Burns and Peter Walsh), Howes promoted all of the Beatles' subsequent British tours (they stopped performing in the UK in 1965).

If the Cliff Richard tours had not already done so, the success of the Beatles' tours from 1963 to 1965 confirmed Howes' status as the biggest British pop promoter of his time. In 1963, he relocated his offices to London, first in Greek Street and then in Harold Davison's old headquarters in Eros House on Regent Street (Davison had moved into the Grade Organisation headquarters, also on Regent Street).[34] The geographical proximity between Howes, Davison and the Grades mirrored their tight-knit business relationship.

Davison and Howes were not the only significant pop promoters of this time who had a background in dance bands. Tito Burns, for example, was a successful accordionist and bandleader from the 1940s until 1955, when he told *Melody Maker* that he was giving up performing to become a manager and agent (12 February: 20). He started working with jazz artists such as Tubby Hayes, but despite 'absolutely hating rock 'n' roll', his most famous client in the 1950s was Cliff Richard, whom he managed until 1960. Like many of his contemporaries in the business, Burns combined promoting (he not only co-promoted the Beatles' first headline tour but also handled Bob Dylan's 1965 UK appearances),[35] an agency (Dusty Springfield and European representation for many American pop acts) and management (for the Searchers and the Zombies). In 1965, Burns was asked by Allen Klein to act as agent for the Rolling Stones, ousting Eric Easton from the Stones' business entourage. By 1966, Burns' business had developed sufficiently to attract Harold Davison's attention; he negotiated the merger of the Tito Burns agency with the Grade Organisation.[36]

[33] See Creasy 2010.

[34] Davison also helped Howes find somewhere to live in London, close to Davison's own home in Wimbledon.

[35] As already mentioned, he was immortalised in film in D.A. Pennebaker's documentary of that tour, *Don't Look Back*.

[36] Leigh 2010; Norman 2001: 177–8; *Melody Maker*, 16 April 1966: 4; *Billboard*, 1 April 1967: 52.

Harold Pendleton's career is interesting as an example of an adaptable jazz promoter. Pendleton started out as a jazz-loving accountant who became involved in running the National Jazz Federation (NJF), which was founded by Chris Barber in 1948. The NJF was a non-profit-making body that promoted concerts initially in London and then throughout the country; by 1957, it was promoting 200 concerts a year. In April 1958 Pendleton acquired the lease of the faltering Marquee Jazz Club on Oxford Street (the venue moved to Wardour Street in 1964) and through shrewd management made the club a key venue in the jazz, R&B and then rock scenes. As a promoter and venue owner with a reputation for success, Pendleton was involved in the later Beaulieu Jazz Festivals and in the summer of 1961, when Beaulieu was suffering from the worst crowd disturbances in its short history, he staged the first National Jazz Festival at the Richmond Athletic Ground. Under Pendleton's guidance, this event evolved in line with changing trends, becoming first the National Jazz and Blues Festival, presenting an increasingly mixed bill of jazz, pop, R&B and rock, and then moving to a site in Reading where it survives, as the Reading Festival, to this day.[37]

Larry Parnes' showbiz experience had been in theatre rather than music when, in 1956, he became Tommy Steele's manager jointly with John Kennedy (who had been working as a theatre publicist), and Parnes and Kennedy plotted Steele's career as much in theatrical as in musical terms. Parnes once explained that 'if I had an ambition, it was to try and reach as near the top of the ladder as I could … The ultimate was to reach the West End of London, then Broadway. I didn't want to stay a pop manager or a manager of artistes all my life' and, as Johnny Rogan comments, Parnes' 'desire to transform his protégé into an all-round entertainer was eminently logical. In 1956, British rock 'n' roll could not develop in a vacuum outside the sphere of traditional show business'.[38]

Parnes is sometimes credited with promoting the first package shows in Britain, beginning with his 'Larry Parnes Extravaganza' in 1958, though by then the term was already in use in the jazz world.[39] After 1958, Parnes was increasingly associated with the tours he put together to feature the stars he managed. This was, as Rogan explains, 'a matter of circumstance more than intention. The closure of many traditional music halls and variety theatres had forced Parnes to create his own package tours in order to provide his artistes with both publicity and live experience'.[40] The other two significant pop package tour promoters at this time, Don Arden and Robert Stigwood, also came from

---

[37]   *Melody Maker*, 8 January 1955: 8; 12 January 1957: 16; Barroso 2011; McKay 2005: 77.

[38]   Rogan 1989: 20–2, 25, 383.

[39]   Jazz package shows had been promoted by the National Jazz Federation; see, for example, see *Melody Maker*, 12 January 1957: 16.

[40]   Rogan 1989: 42.

theatrical backgrounds. Arden started as a comedian —he had appeared at the London Palladium; Stigwood first worked as a theatrical agent.[41]

We have so far in this section been describing the careers of promoters who started out working with dance bands or variety acts, in jazz or the theatre. We now turn our attention to a younger generation of promoters who were not yet part of the established entertainment world.

The British live music industry in the 1960s was characterised by a core of central promoters in London working with a network of satellite promoters and agents in the regions. By 1967, Danny Betesh was the most important agent and promoter based in Northern England. He was born in Manchester and started his promoting career as a hobby.[42] As a young man, while studying to become a chartered accountant, he began putting on small gigs with three friends. Their first events were held in a 400-capacity unlicensed venue in Macclesfield. As Betesh recalls, these kinds of spaces were called 'coffee dance clubs' and, as the name suggests, occupied a function and size somewhere between a coffee bar and a dance hall. The gigs featured local groups such as the Skyliners and Freddie and the Dreamers (Betesh soon got involved with the latter as their booking agent), and the events were sufficiently successful to develop into a three-nights-weekly club called El Rio.

Building on his success in Macclesfield, Betesh opened two additional coffee bars in the centre of Manchester: the Three Coins (open seven nights a week with live music three nights a week and a DJ playing records otherwise) and Guys and Dolls (records only). Guys and Dolls was located on Kennedy Street, and Betesh and his business partners therefore christened their agency and promotions companies Kennedy Street Artistes and Kennedy Street Enterprises. Since Manchester was close to Liverpool, Betesh developed a good working relationship with Brian Epstein almost as soon as Epstein began managing the Beatles – the Beatles played El Rio and the Three Coins (for fees of £25) before their chart success. By this time, Betesh had also branched out into booking beat groups for theatre and ballroom dates across the North of England.

Thanks to his early connection with Epstein, Betesh was offered a national Beatles tour in May and June 1963, after the completion of their package shows promoted by Arthur Howes. Betesh accepted and, since this was a bigger tour than he was used to, enlisted Tito Burns and Peter Walsh to help in its production. Epstein was unsure whether the Beatles were ready to headline and asked Betesh to book an American star entertainer to top the bill; Roy Orbison was signed up as the main attraction. By May 1963, however, it was clear that the Beatles had no choice but to headline. Betesh had originally agreed with Epstein to pay the Beatles £100 per night. The tour was so successful that he doubled their fee.

---

[41]   Perrone 2007; Rogan 1989: 183–4.

[42]   Biographical information taken from an interview with Betesh in 2010 unless otherwise noted.

The Beatles tour helped consolidate Betesh's status as the key agent and promoter in the North-West, and over the next several years he worked for such successful northern acts as Wayne Fontana and the Mindbenders, Dave Berry (from Sheffield) and Herman's Hermits. He would sell his artists onto the package tours organised by Arthur Howes, Larry Parnes, Don Arden and Robert Stigwood or, occasionally, would buy northern dates from them. He also worked with Jimmy Savile, who at that time was managing Manchester's Plaza Ballroom.

The dramatic growth of the post-Beatles British pop market presented several challenges to concert promoters. The kinds of concerts that Betesh was now booking were constrained by inadequate technology, security and capacity. Amplifiers were not built to be heard over the noise of a hall full of screaming teenagers, and there was little lighting apart from the basic setup of the cinema or town hall where the groups performed. The lack of exits meant that even getting groups safely in and out of venues could be problematic and, most importantly, the number of tickets that could be sold was limited, especially when compared to the capacity of the US venues now being used by the top British acts. As Ringo Starr recalled of the Beatles' first American tour: 'What happened in the States was just like Britain only ten times bigger ... That first Washington crowd was 20,000. We'd only been used to 2,000 at home.'[43]

This was not just a problem for the Beatles. By the end of the 1960s, all the biggest recording stars struggled to fulfil demand for concert tickets playing the kind of touring circuit that had been established in the 1950s. The Rolling Stones stopped touring Britain at the end of their 1966 tour and would not play in the UK again until their Hyde Park concert on 5 July 1969. Star acts who continued touring faced the increasing challenge of how to make money out of a potentially huge live rock audience given the shortcomings of British venues, while, at the same time, small clubs struggled to cope with the rising fees they demanded. Promoters took flak from both sides: audiences blamed them for ticket prices that were too high, artists blamed them for fees that were too low, and both artists and audiences blamed them for poor sound and facilities.

In 1964 *Melody Maker* reported an attempt to organise a formal association of promoters. A dozen club promoters attended the meeting and issued the following statement:

> It was generally agreed today that the formation of a promoters' association has become necessary. The main reason is the unrealistic fees demanded by agencies and managers of groups, which leads to high admission prices and the resultant exploitation of teenagers who attend the dance halls. (28 November 1964: 5)

---

[43]   Quoted in Davies 1979: 208. Starr is referring to their gig at the Washington Coliseum on 11 February 1964, which took place immediately after the Beatles' first Ed Sullivan show appearance. The 1965 Shea Stadium show had an audience of 55,000.

Over the next couple of years, *Melody Maker* reported growing tensions between promoters and performers. The latter didn't just complain about the inadequate facilities offered by venues, they also drew reporters' attention to a litany of crooked promoting practices: promoters advertising that they had booked an artist when no agreement had been made; promoters promising to pay by cheque and not putting it in the post; bands being asked to 'audition' by performing shows at which the promoter took money at the door, and neither giving the band a percentage nor inviting them to return for a paying gig.[44]

Meanwhile, however, promoters were beginning to emerge who were even younger than the groups on the charts and who had neither the prejudices nor the doubts of their seniors. We will take the case of Harvey Goldsmith, whose entry into the live music industry was markedly different from that of Davison, Howes or even Betesh.

Born in Edgware in 1946 (the Beatles were born between 1940 and 1943), Goldsmith grew up listening to jazz, but the trad boom was already tailing off as he reached adulthood.[45] He enrolled at the Brighton College of Technology to study pharmacy in the autumn of 1965, having chosen Brighton partly because he had heard it was good for social events. He was disappointed when he arrived, but quickly became the student representative for pharmacy and in January 1966 created a new social club (appropriately named Club 66). In his own words:

> I took over the common room and just changed the lighting and the atmosphere there and started looking around for local bands, and then began to develop it out. And it became a rip-roaring success. And then I became Rag chairman, and then did a huge event in the Regent Ballroom, and funnily enough it was John Mayall's Bluesbreakers which had Eric Clapton playing in it.[46]

Following his success as a student rep and Rag chairman, Goldsmith became social secretary for the college as a whole, booking bands and developing contacts with London agencies such as Marquee Artists and Rik and John Gunnell. He also started booking acts outside the college, creating his own Kangaroo Club and using existing Brighton venues like the Metropol. He gained a reputation as a reliable student promoter:

---

[44]   See, for example, 9 October 1965 4; 8 January 1966 3; 9 July 1966: 8–9; 11 February: 1967 20.

[45]   That said, Goldsmith's first ever foray into organising a live music event took place in his sixth-form year at Christ College (a grammar school in North London). His school had a jazz society that he and some friends took over and revamped by bringing in local jazz musicians to play live (previously society members had simply listened to and discussed jazz records).

[46]   Biographical information and subsequent quotes are taken from a 2010 interview with Goldsmith unless otherwise noted.

The whole social thing was exploding down there and I was doing events nearly every week. And then I was asked to programme other colleges who didn't seem to have anybody in particular doing it. And I kinda ended up programming, I think, it was twelve colleges along the south coast.

At the beginning of 1967, Goldsmith flew to San Francisco and met the two key concert promoters in that city, Bill Graham at the Fillmore and Chet Helms, at the Avalon Ballroom. Goldsmith was impressed by the way they ran events and, in particular, by their use of psychedelic posters to market their concerts. He struck a deal with Helms and Graham for the rights to sell their posters in the UK and Europe, and by the time he returned to Britain, the psychedelic rock scene in London was also taking shape. John Hopkins and Joe Boyd had been promoting the UFO Club since 23 December 1966, while Peter Jenner and Andrew King were involved in the London Free School movement and managed a new group called Pink Floyd.[47] Goldsmith formed a business partnership with publisher Peter Ledeboer (who had helped with the printing of *Oz*) and created Big O, which published and sold the Fillmore and Avalon Ballroom posters as well as those now emerging from London-based psychedelic designers like Martin Sharp.[48] In April 1967, Hopkins, Barry Miles and David Howson organised a fundraising concert for the *International Times*. The resulting event, 'The 14 Hour Technicolour Dream', took place at Alexandra Palace on 29 April 1967 and brought the underground psychedelic scene to the attention of the broadsheet press. Goldsmith assisted in its production.

The set of experiences that Goldsmith gained from his time as a social secretary and his involvement in London's psychedelic scene made for a very different training in live music promotion than that followed by previous promoters and indicates that, despite the best efforts of older promoters to adapt to changes in British musical culture, there were now scenes, artists and economies that could not be managed in the conventional ways. In 1967 Harold Davison, by then a veteran promoter, was asked whether he thought the 'Grade-Davison so-called monopoly' was a good thing for the music business:

Well, the obvious reply is that there's no monopoly. And it is fairly obvious there can be no monopoly, otherwise, when the Beatles came on the scene the Grades, or Davison, or whatever you like to call it would have taken them. All these super-attractions that are around – they don't necessarily belong to us.[49]

---

[47]   See Boyd 2006: 143–66.

[48]   The printing press used for the posters as well as *Oz* and *IT* was also used that year by Tony Elliot for the first issues of *Time Out*.

[49]   Quoted in *Melody Maker*, 8 April: 12. In fact, Brian Epstein had considered selling the Beatles to Bernard Delfont, who offered him £150,000. Epstein thought this a good deal but 'John told me to fuck off' (Levy 2002: 296).

Conclusion

One way of describing the development of the British live music business from 1950 to 1967 is in terms of two different kinds of promoter: the first grew up in the era of dance bands, jazz and variety theatre, and was then forced to adapt to a live music economy that was increasingly organised around records and record stars, the youth market and teen beat groups, while the second, younger generation began by doing-it-themselves and became – sometimes unwittingly – catalysts for new forms of musical entertainment to which their elders had to adapt.

However, this account is too neat. The history of live music in post-war Britain is not simply about dance-hall and variety promoters responding to changes imposed on them by pop groups and their fans; in many cases it was the older generation of promoters who drove innovations in promoting practice and shaped what was meant by a 'pop concert' in the first place. The artists who are usually characterised as disrupting Britain's showbiz establishment – the Beatles and Rolling Stones, for example – came to fame, after all, by working within existing entertainment conventions. Even the underground UFO Club used an established agency to book its shows.[50]

That said, there can be no doubting the profound changes in British popular music culture over the span of a generation: teenagers in the late 1960s had a quite different experience of music from that of their parents (who had grown up in the 1940s).[51] Someone falling asleep in 1950 and waking up in 1967 would have been astonished by the ubiquity of television, by the sales pitch of BBC Radio 1, by the way young people took over city centres on Friday and Saturday nights, by the sheer amplified volume of the music in the clubs, by how much people danced to records (and by the apparent disorder of the dancefloor), by the confidence of performers and by the raucous exuberance of their performances. Only if our 1967 Rip Van Winkle had gone to a classical event would he have found a reassuringly familiar concert repertoire, setting and etiquette.

But, as yet, such changes had been absorbed into Britain's live music business rather than transforming it. In this chapter we have described the resulting problems, and it was through their resolution over the next decade, primarily through unprecedented growth – in the size of venues, audiences, record sales and musical income – that the promotional business would be significantly reshaped, that live musical events would become more professionally complex, more politically charged and more theatrically and technologically spectacular. These developments are the concern of volume 2 of this history.

We will end volume 1 with a different point: by 1967, it was already clear that popular music was being taken seriously as a form of musical art as well as a form of musical commerce. That year, the Arts Council gave its first ever grant to a jazz musician, Graham Collier, a decision that at once signalled a shift in Arts

---

[50] See Boyd 2006: 148.

[51] And their own children's musical lives would not provide nearly as big a contrast.

Council music policy and suggested that jazz was ceasing to be 'popular' music or, rather, that some kinds of popular music could now be considered by the art music establishment as culturally worthwhile.[52] Four years earlier, William Mann, chief classical music critic of *The Times*, had written an end-of-year reflection on the Beatles which attracted a remarkable amount of attention less for its critical insights than for its critical language: Mann unself-consciously discussed Beatle songs in formal analytic terms and suggested that their music would *last.*[53] Over the next two decades, 'serious' writing about popular music – rock criticism – would become familiar (and eventually dominant) even on the arts pages of *The Times*.

In part this was because this sort of popular music was now understood to matter economically (no-one in 1950 would have predicted that within 20 years British popular musicians would be in such demand in the USA). But in part it was because pop music now had a different kind of audience with different kinds of expectations. There were class issues here – the metamorphosis of pop into rock involved its appeal to a more middle-class demographic – students and young professionals. Rock was 'youth' music for a particular kind of youth; it was do-it-yourself music made by people who thought of themselves as creative artists for audiences who thought of themselves as discriminating listeners. And this had significant consequences for what kind of people – what kind of enthusiasts – now became dominant in both the live music and the record industries: Harvey Goldsmith was the first of a new breed of entrepreneur. But we will end this volume with Mick Jagger. When the Rolling Stones began touring, Jagger finally withdrew from his degree course at the London School of Economics. As he explained to the LSE registrar: 'I have been offered a really excellent opportunity in the entertainment world.'[54] That entertainment world was about to be transformed – not least by the Rolling Stones.

---

[52]   By contrast, in 1965 Ronnie Scott and Pete King unsuccessfully sought a loan from the Arts Council to enable them to move from Gerrard Street to bigger and better premises in Frith Street. After being kept waiting for some time, they were greeted by 'an earnest young assistant' who asked: 'Now then about this Bonny Scott's Club. How can we help you?' They got the loan instead from Harold Davison (Fordham 1986: 135).

[53]   William Mann: 'What Songs the Beatles Sang', *The Times*, 23 December 1963. Mann began by asserting that 'The outstanding English composers of 1963 must seem to have been John Lennon and Paul McCartney', and went on to suggest that 'the virtue of the Beatles' repertory is that, apparently, they do it themselves'.

[54]   Levy 2002: 192.

The Rolling Stones: Richmond 1963

In early 1963 the up and coming Rolling Stones were playing regularly across London, having been part of Alexis Korner's move to overcome the dominance of traditional jazz in London clubs by finding a space for more R&B-influenced acts.[1] The Stones began their live career by playing a series of London jazz clubs (the Marquee Jazz Club, the Ealing, the Piccadilly and the Flamingo) between July and November 1962 as well as playing the occasional pub (such as the Woodstock Hotel in Cheam and the Red Lion in Sutton).[2] However, it was a series of gigs that took place in Richmond, Surrey, in early 1963 that is often credited with propelling the band towards national and international stardom.

The band's first Richmond show came on 24 February at the Station Hotel. The venue was run by a Mr C.J. Buckle who decided to put on gigs, which were organised by various people including Johnny Dankworth and Giorgio Gomelsky.[3] It was Gomelsky who booked the Stones into the venue under his Crawdaddy Club banner.[4]

Bill Wyman reports that on the Thursday before the first Richmond show, members of the band went round London flyposting and that in due course 'the place was to mean much more to the band's future than money'. He also notes that as at other shows, 'because of Brian [Jones]'s accounting system, the gig never seemed to make money'.[5]

According to George Tremlett, the venue:

> was an old-fashioned Victorian pub with a white-washed exterior badly needing
> a fresh coat of paint – and inside frosted glass partitions dividing the rooms, coal
> fires in the grates, and well-polished brass fittings.[6]

The Stones went on to play a residency there for 15 consecutive Sundays. Soon, according to Keith Richards, the Hotel became '*the* place to be every Sunday night'.[7] From 14 April to 16 June, the gigs under the Crawdaddy heading took

---

[1] Dalton 1975: 15, 86–7; Goodman 1965: 66.

[2] Wyman 1991: 657.

[3] Tremlett 1974: 14.

[4] Gomelsky was also booking other shows for the band at this point (Wyman 1991: 146) and was acting in an informal management capacity.

[5] Wyman 1991: 145, 146.

[6] Tremlett 1974: 15.

[7] Dalton 1975: 87, emphasis in original.

place at the Hotel. This came to an end following concern from the brewers who owned the venue that fire regulations were being breached as, according to the *Daily Mirror*, 500 people packed into the venue to see the band and this was 'well over the club's legal limit'.[8]

So the Crawdaddy club and the Stones' residency moved to the Richmond Athletic Ground, which the band played another nine times as a residency between 30 June and 22 September 1963.[9] They also played the 3rd Richmond Jazz Festival at the Grounds on 11 August. The importance of live music in showcasing emerging talent is illustrated by the fact that Gomelsky convinced a *Record Mirror* journalist, Peter Jones, to come to one of the shows. He was joined by Norman Jopling, who wrote an ecstatic review of the show and hailed R&B as the saviour of promoters who were looking for something to replace 'teen beat'.[10] It was this review that piqued the interest of Andrew Loog Oldham, who went to the Stones' 28 April gig and immediately determined to be involved in their career. He was too young to hold his own agent's licence, so asked an established showbiz agent, Eric Easton, to come with him to the Stones' show the following Sunday. Easton was equally impressed and agreed to Oldham's idea that he should handle the legalities while Oldham became the Stones' '*de facto* agent/manager'.[11]

The band was initially paid £1 per man or 'fifty per cent of the takings' (Goodman 1965: 86).[12] However, when the first show attracted 150 people,[13] this was raised to £7 10s (£7.50) for the band as a whole, which remained the minimum for their time at the Crawdaddy.[14] By the time they moved to the Athletic Ground, the crowd was up to 500 and the band was being paid £50.[15]

At this point the band would often play two gigs a day at the weekends. Thus, for example, on 14 out of 15 consecutive Sundays between 3 March and 16 June, they played first at Studio 51, 10/11 Great Newport Street, London,

---

[8]   Wyman 1991: 168.

[9]   The band's first single, a cover of Chuck Berry's 'Come On', was released on 7 June 1963.

[10]   Dalton 1975: 18. The first review of the band had been in the *Richmond and Twickenham Times* on 13 April 1963 (May 1963).

[11]   Levy 2002: 97.

[12]   Goodman 1965: 86. At this point the line-up was Charlie Watts (drums), Bill Wyman (bass), Keith Richard (lead guitar), Brian Jones (rhythm guitar), Ian Stewart (keyboards) and Mick Jagger (vocals). Stewart ceased to be an official/on-stage member of the band at Oldham's instigation in May 1963.

[13]   Wyman (1991: 145) reports a 'whispering campaign' against the band in jazz clubs at this point and an attendance of only six people for one gig in Ealing. He claims that 100 people attending the Richmond show on 10 March was 'amazing' (ibid.: 147). By April, the Stones were attracting over 320 people and the Club had a membership of over 700 (May 1963).

[14]   Goodman 1965: 86; Tremlett 1974: 62; Wyman 1991: 145.

[15]   Wyman 1991: 169.

at Ken Colyer's Club (which ran between 4 and 6.30 pm) before going on to play either the Station Hotel (up to 7 April) or the Athletic Club (thereafter). On the missing Sunday they only played at the Crawdaddy.[16] Between 30 June and 22 September, they would clock up another nine joint Colyer and Crawdaddy Sundays, as well as playing Colyer and the Richmond Jazz Festival on the same day (11 August). At this point the show appears to have been two sets of around 45 minutes with no support act.[17]

We have been unable to ascertain admission prices, which were not listed in the ads but are likely to have been around five shillings (25p), as this price was being charged for similar shows around the time. Contemporary adverts in *Melody Maker* list prices from 3/6 up to 10/-, with many venues such as the Marquee, the Ken Colyer Jazz Club and Ronnie Scott's charging differential rates for members and non-members.[18] Tickets do not appear to have been on sale in advance as there are various accounts of queues forming on the day.[19] According to Goodman, at some shows (two 45-minute slots), as some fans left to escape the heat, others waiting outside would be let in. He reports Andrew Loog Oldham as saying that on his first visit on 28 April: 'There wasn't room to swing a cat. It was unbearably hot. But the fans didn't care a hoot.'[20] These fans are described as being 'in their teens and early 20s'. They apparently faced limited opposition from the pub's drinkers who resented the loud music emanating from the club-room at the back of the pub.[21]

While not always advertising the Richmond shows, *Melody Maker* was a key source of information about gigs at this time. It did advertise the first show, on 24 February. Under the heading of 'Jazz Clubs – Outside London… Sunday' was a small ad for the Station Hotel and '**RHYTHM 'N' BLUES** with the inimitable, incomparable **ROLLIN' STONES**' (23 February 1963: 16). The show at the Hotel on 12 May was advertised with '**WARNING**: R and B Sound Barrier to be broken by **ROLLIN' STONES**' (11 May 1963). Gomelsky paid for these advertisements which included one hailing 'the craziest R&B sound of the unparalleled Rolling Stones'.[22]

Bill Wyman reports that by mid-1963:

> we continued our round of bread and butter work. Sunday afternoons at the Ken Colyer Club for £25; Sunday evenings at the new Crawdaddy Club for £50; the

---

[16]   Wyman 1991: 659–60.

[17]   Wyman 1991: 148 and 152.

[18]   Ronnie Scott's advertised itself as 'the only Club [sic] presenting top jazz seven nights a week where you can listen, eat and drink until 1 a.m.' (*Melody Maker* 23 February 1963: 16).

[19]   For example, Goodman 1965: 88, Wyman 1991: 182.

[20]   Goodman 1965: 96, 97.

[21]   May 1963; Goodman 1965: 88.

[22]   Wyman 1991: 147.

Ricky Tick for £35; Eel Pie Island for £55; and the Scene Club near Piccadilly Circus where we averaged only £25.[23]

By the time the Stones finished their Crawdaddy residency (to be replaced by the Yardbirds), they had, in Wyman's words, 'outgrown the clubs'.[24] Their first UK tour, with the Everly Brothers and Bo Diddley, began on 29 September 1963, with their first headline tour (with the Ronettes) beginning on 6 January 1964. The Station Hotel is currently a pub called the Bull, while Richmond Athletic Ground continues to host sporting and social events. We shall return to the Rolling Stones in volume 2.

References

Dalton, D. ed. 1975. *The Rolling Stones: The Greatest Rock 'n' Roll Band in the World.* London: W.H. Allen.

Goodman, P. 1965. *Our Own Story by the Rolling Stones*. New York: Bantam.

Levy, S. 2002. *Ready, Steady, Go! Swinging London and the Invention of Cool.* London: Fourth Estate. May, B. 1963. 'Jazz: Nowadays it means the music that goes round and around – or the Rollin' Stones are gathering them in', *Richmond and Twickenham Times*, 13 April: 15.

Tremlett, G. 1974. *The Rolling Stones Story*. London: Futura.

Wyman, B. 1991. *Stone Alone.* London: Penguin.

---

[23] Wyman: 1991: 170.

[24] Wyman 1991: 182.

Bibliography

Abbott, D. 2006. 'UK cinema circuits – Cinematopia: WebPlex's guide to old cinemas', http://cinematopia.co.uk/circuits/circuits_20061008.pdf [accessed 14 September 2012].

Abrams, M. 1959. *The Teenage Consumer*. London: Press Exchange.

Allen, D. 1998. *Almost: Forty Years of Southsea Rock and Pompey Blues*. London: Minerva Press.

Allen, D. 2009. *"Here Come The Sixties": Popular Music in Portsmouth in the 1960s*. Portsmouth: University of Portsmouth.

Allen, D. 2011. *'Pompey Pop' Live: 1945–1969*. Paper presented to the Business of Live Music Conference, University of Edinburgh, 1 April.

Augarde, T. 2004. 'Bright, Gerald Walcan- [Geraldo] (1904–1974)', *Oxford Dictionary of National Biography*. Oxford: Oxford University Press, available online at: http://www.oxforddnb.com/view/article/31792 [accessed 14 September 2012].

Bacon, T. 1999. *London Live*. London: Balafon.

Bailey, P. 1978. *Leisure and Class in Victorian England*, London: Routledge & Kegan Paul.

Bailey, P. 2011, 'Entertainmentality! Liberalising modern pleasure in the Victorian leisure industry', in S. Gunn and J. Vernon (eds), *Peculiarities of Liberal Modernity in Imperial Britain*. Berkeley: University of California Press, 119–33.

Barber, C. 1961. 'The truth about jazz festivals', *Melody Maker*, 29 July: 3.

Barfe, L. 2004. *Where Have All the Good Times Gone? The Rise and Fall of the Record Industry*. London: Atlantic.

Barker, D. 2009. 'Morley, Eric Douglas (1918–2000)', *Oxford Dictionary of National Biography*. Oxford: Oxford University Press, available online at: http://www.oxforddnb.com/view/article/74900 [accessed 14 September 2012].

Barnard, S. 1989. *On The Radio*. Milton Keynes: Open University Press.

Barroso, K. 2011. The Marquee Club website, www.themarqueeclub.net [accessed 14 September 2012].

Beale, R. 2000. 'Paying the piper: The Hallé and the City of Manchester'. *Manchester Sounds*, 1, 71–89.

Becker, H. 1974. 'Art as collective action'. *American Sociological Review*, 39(6), 767–76.

Becker, H. 1984. *Art Worlds*. Berkeley: University of California Press.

Betesh, D. 2010. Interview with Matt Brennan, Manchester, 23 November.

Bird, B. 1958. *Skiffle. The Story of Folk Song with a Jazz Beat*. London: Robert Hale.

Blades, J. 1977. *Drum Roll. A Professional Adventure from the Circus to the Concert Hall,* London: Faber & Faber.

Boulton, D. 1958. *Jazz in Britain.* London: W.H. Allen.

Bowers, J. and Tick, J. eds. 1987. *Women Making Music. The Western Art Tradition.* Chicago: University of Illinois Press.

Boyd, J. 2006. *White Bicycles: Making Music in the 1960s.* London: Serpents Tail.

Boyd, J. 2008. Interview with Matt Brennan, London, 7 November.

Boyes, G. 1993. *The Imagined Village. Culture, Ideology and the English Folk Revival.* Manchester: Manchester University Press.

Bradley, D. 1992. *Understanding Rock'n'Roll. Popular Music in Britain 1955–1964.* Buckingham: Open University Press.

Braun, M. 1964. *Love Me Do.* London: Penguin.

Briggs, A. 1961. *The History of Broadcasting in the United Kingdom: Volume 1 – The Birth of Broadcasting.* Oxford: Oxford University Press.

Briggs, A. 1979. The *History of Broadcasting in the United Kingdom: Volume 4 – Sound and Vision.* Oxford: Oxford University Press

Briggs, A. 1985. *The BBC: The First Fifty Years.* Oxford: Oxford University Press.

Brocken, M. 2003. *The British Folk Revival: 1944–2002.* Aldershot: Ashgate.

Brocken, M. 2010. *Other Voices: Hidden Histories of Liverpool's Popular Music.* Farnham: Ashgate.

Brown, C.G. 1996. 'Popular culture and the continuing struggle for rational recreation', in T. Devine and R.J. Finlay (eds), *Scotland in the Twentieth Century.* Edinburgh: Edinburgh University Press, 210–29.

Brown, S. 1979. *The McJazz Manuscripts.* London: Faber & Faber.

Bruce, F. 2000. *Scottish Showbusiness. Music Hall, Variety and Pantomime.* Edinburgh: National Museums of Scotland.

Brunning, B. and Smith, B. 2009. *The 100 Club. An Oral History.* Burdon, Hants: Northdown.

Burrows, T. 2009. *From CBGB to the Roundhouse: Music Venues Through the Years.* London: Marion Boyars.

Burton, P. 1985. *Parallel Lives.* London: GMP.

Calder, A. 1971. *The People's War. Britain 1939–1945.* London: Panther (first published 1969).

Carr, I. 1996. 'Novocastrian jazz 1950s and early 1960s'. *Northern Review*, 4, 10–18.

Casciani, E. 1994. *Oh, How We Danced! The History of Ballroom Dancing in Scotland.* Edinburgh: The Mercat Press.

Chapman, D. 1968. *Sociology and the Stereotype of the Criminal.* London: Tavistock Press.

Chapman, R. 1992. *Selling the Sixties: The Pirates and Pop Music Radio.* London: Routledge.

Cheshire, D. 1974. *Music Hall in Britain.* Newton Abbott: David and Charles.

Clark, P. 2000. *British Clubs and Societies 1580–1800: The Origins of an Associational World.* Oxford: Clarendon.

Clarke, M. 1982. *The Politics of Pop Festivals*. London: Junction Books.

Clifton, D. and Davies, S. 2004. 'The premises licence', in P. Kolvin (ed.), *Licensed Premises: Law & Practice*. Haywards Heath: Tottel, 156–223.

Cloonan, M. 2003. 'Teaching young pups new tricks? The new deal for musicians'. *Music Education Research*, 5(1), 13–28.

Cloonan, M. 2007. *Popular Music and the State in the UK*. Aldershot: Ashgate.

Cloonan, M. and Brennan, M. 2013. 'Alien invasions: the British Musicians' Union and foreign musicians', *Popular Music*, 3(2).

Cohen, R.D. 2008. *A History of Folk Music Festivals in the United States*. Lanham, MD: Scarecrow Press.

Cohen, S. 1972. *Folk Devils and Moral Panics*. London: MacGibbon and Kee.

Cohen, S. 1991. *Rock Culture in Liverpool*. Oxford: Oxford University Press.

Conley, L. 1950. 'Farewell to the Bottle Party', *Melody Maker*, 11 February: 4–5.

Court, S. 1984. 'Live sound evolution'. *Studio Sound*, 26(6), 72–3.

Cowley, J. 1985. 'Cultural "fusions": aspects of British West Indian music in the USA and Britain 1918–51'. *Popular Music*, 5, 81–96.

Crawford, I. 1997. *Banquo on Thursdays. The Inside Story of 50 Years of the Edinburgh Festival*. Edinburgh: Goblinshead.

Creasy, M. 2010. *Beatlemania! The Real Story of the Beatles UK Tour 1963–1965*. London: Omnibus.

Crissell, A. 2012. *Liveness and Recording in the Media*. Basingstoke: Palgrave Macmillan.

Croft, A. 1995. 'Betrayed spring. The Labour government and British literary culture', in J. Fyrth (ed.), *Labour's Promised Land. Culture and Society in Labour Britain 1945–51*. London: Lawrence & Wishart, 197–223.

Cunningham, H. 1980. *Leisure in the Industrial Revolution*. London: Croom Helm.

Davenport-Hines, R. 2004. 'Rank, (Joseph) Arthur, Baron Rank (1888–1972)', *Oxford Dictionary of National Biography*. Oxford: Oxford University Press, available at: http://www.oxforddnb.com/view/article/31585 [accessed 14 September 2012].

Davies, H. 1979. *The Beatles*. London: Heinemann.

Davies, H. 1981. *The Grades*. London: Weidenfeld & Nicolson.

Davis, T. 1991. 'The moral sense of the majorities: indecency and vigilance in Late-Victorian music halls'. *Popular Music*, 10(1), 39–51.

Davison, A. 2013 'Workers' rights and performing rights: cinema music and musicians prior to synchronized sound', in J. Brown and A. Davison (eds), *The Sounds of the Silents in Britain*. New York: Oxford University Press.

Davison, H. 2010. Phone interview with Matt Brennan, Florida–Glasgow, 21 January.

Deneslow, R. 1975. 'Folk-rock in Britain', in D. Laing (ed.), *The Electric Muse. The Story of Folk into Rock*. London: Methuen, 137–76.

Dennis, N, Henriques, F. and Slaughter, C. 1956. *Coal is Our Life. An Analysis of a Yorkshire Mining Community*. London: Eyre and Spottiswoode.

Dewe, M. 1998. *The Skiffle Craze*. Aberystwyth: Planet.

Dickins, B. 2009. Interview with Matt Brennan, London, 9 June.

Doncaster, P. ed. 1956. *Discland*. London: Daily Mirror.

Donovan, K. 1981. *The Place*. Stoke-on-Trent: Self-published.

Ehrlich, C. 1985. *The Music Profession in Britain Since the Eighteenth Century*. Oxford: Clarendon.

Ehrenreich, B., Hess, E. and Jacobs, G. 1997. 'Beatlemania: a sexually defiant consumer culture?', in K. Gelder and S. Thornton (eds), *The Subcultures Reader*. London: Routledge, 523–36.

Elkin, R. ed. 1950. *A Career in Music*, London: William Earl.

Ennis, P. 1992. *The Seventh Stream: The Emergence of Rocknroll in American Popular Music*. Middletown: Wesleyan.

Everett, P. 1986. *You'll Never Be 16 Again. An Illustrated History of the British Teenager*. London: BBC Publications.

Eyles, A. 1996. *British Gaumont Cinemas*. London: BFI/Cinema Theatre Association.

Eyles, A. 2005. *Odeon Cinemas: From J. Arthur Rank to the Multiplex*. London: British Film Institute.

Faith, A. 1961. *Poor Me*. London: Four Square.

Farson, D. 1987. *Soho in the Fifties*. London: Michael Joseph.

Fiegel, E. 1998. *John Barry. A Sixties Theme*. London: Constable.

Fields, R. 2009. *Minstrels, Poets and Vagabonds. A History of Rock Music in Glasgow*. Glasgow: Macdonald Media.

Fifield, C. 2005. *Ibbs and Tillett: The Rise and Fall of a Music Empire*. Aldershot: Ashgate.

Finnegan, R. 1989. *The Hidden Musicians: Music-Making in an English Town*. Cambridge: Cambridge University Press.

Firminger, J. and Lilleker, M. 2001. *Not Like a Proper Job. The Story of Popular Music in Sheffield 1955–1975 as Told by Those Who Made It*. Sheffield: Juma.

Flick, V. 2008. *Guitarman. From James Bond to the Beatles and Beyond*. Albany, GA: BearManor Media.

Fordham, J. 1986. *Let's Join Hands and Contact the Living. Ronnie Scott and his Club*. London: Elm Tree.

Fordham, J. 1995. *Jazzman: The Amazing Story of Ronnie Scott and his Club*. London: Kyle Cathie.

Forsyth, M. 1985. *Buildings for Music: The Architect, the Musician, and the Listener from the Seventeenth Century to the Present Day*. Cambridge: Cambridge University Press.

Fowler, D. 1992. 'Teenage consumers? Young wage-earners and leisure in Manchester, 1919–1939', in A. Davies and S. Fielding (eds), *Workers' Worlds. Cultures and Communities in Manchester and Salford, 1800–1939*. Manchester: Manchester University Press, 133–55.

Frame, P. 2007. *The Restless Generation. How Rock Music Changed the Face of 1950s Britain*. London: Rogan Books.

Francis, H. no date. 'This thing called jazz', www.jazzprofessional.com/Francis/ Francis [accessed 9 February 2011].

Frith, S. 1978. *The Sociology of Rock.* London: Constable.

Frith, S. 1987. 'The making of the British record industry 1920–64', in J. Curran, A. Smith and P. Wingate (eds), *Impacts and Influences: Essays on Media Power in the Twentieth Century.* London: Methuen, 278–90.

Frith, S. 1996. *Performing Rites: On the Value of Popular Music.* Cambridge, MA: Harvard University Press.

Frith, S. 2009. 'Going critical: writing about recordings', in N. Cook, E. Clarke, D. Leech-Wilkinson and J. Rink (eds), *The Cambridge Companion to Recording.* Cambridge: Cambridge University Press, 267–82.

Frith, S. 2012. 'Creativity as a social fact', in D.J. Hargreaves, D.E. Miell and R.A.R. MacDonald (eds), *Musical Imaginations. Multidisciplinary Perspectives on Creativity, Performance, and Perception.* Oxford: Oxford University Press, 62–72.

Frith, S. and Horne, H. 1987. *Art into Pop.* London: Methuen.

Fuller, S. 2011. Interview with Matt Brennan, Edinburgh, 27 April.

Fyvel, T.R. 1963. *The Insecure Offenders: Rebellious Youth in the Welfare State.* Harmondsworth: Pelican.

Garofalo, R. *Rockin' Out: Popular Music in the USA.* Upper Saddle River: Pearson/Prentice Hall.

Godbolt, J. 1976. *All This and 10%.* London: Robert Hale.

Godbolt, J. 1984. *A History of Jazz in Britain: 1919–1950.* London: Quartet.

Goehr, L. 1992. *The Imaginary Museum of Musical Works.* Oxford: Clarendon.

Goldsmith, H. 2010. Interview with Matt Brennan, London, 10 November.

Gould, G. 1966. 'The prospects of recording'. *High Fidelity*, 16(4), 46–63.

Gourvish, T. 2009. 'The British popular music industry, 1950–75: archival challenges and solutions'. *Business Archives*, 99, 25–39.

Gourvish, T. and Tennent, K. 2010. 'Peterson and Berger revisited: changing market dominance in the British popular music industry, c.1950–80'. *Business History*, 52(2), 187–206.

Grade, Michael. 2009. Interview, http://www.bl.uk/projects/theatrearchive/grade.html [accessed 14 September 2012].

Green, B. 1976. *Swingtime in Tottenham.* London: Lemon Tree Press.

Griffin, C. 1999. 'Not just a case of baths, canteens and rehabilitation centres: the Second World War and the recreational provision of the Miners' Welfare Commission in coalmining communities', in N. Hayes and J. Hill (eds), *'Millions like Us'? British Culture in the Second World War.* Liverpool: Liverpool University Press, 261–94.

Gunn, S. 2000. *The Public Culture of the Victorian Middle Class.* Manchester: Manchester University Press.

Hadfield, P. 2006. *Bar Wars*, Oxford: Oxford University Press.

Hale, D. and Thornton, T. 2002. *Club 60 and Esquire: Sheffield Sounds in the 60s.* Sheffield: ALD Design and Print.

Hanlon, J. 2010. Interview with Martin Cloonan, London, 4 May.

Harker, B. 2007. *Class Act. The Cultural and Political Life of Ewan MacColl.* London: Pluto Press.

Harker, D. 1980. *One for the Money.* London: Hutchinson.

Harker, D. 1985. *Fakesong: The Manufacture of British 'Folksong' 1700 to the Present Day.* Milton Keynes: Open University Press.

Haslam, D. 1999. *Manchester England. The Story of the Pop Cult City.* London: Fourth Estate.

Hayes, N. 1999. 'More than "music-while-you-eat"? Factory and hostel concerts, "good culture" and the workers', in N. Hayes and J. Hill (eds), *'Millions Like Us'? Britsh Culture in the Second World War.* Liverpool: Liverpool University Press, 209–35.

Heath, T. 1957. *Listen to My Music. An Autobiography.* London: Frederick Muller.

Hebdige, D. 1983. 'Posing ... threats, striking ... poses. Youth surveillance and display'. *SubStance*, 11/12, 66–88.

Heckstall-Smith, D. and Grant, P. 2004. *Blowing the Blues. Fifty Years of Playing the British Blues.* Bath: Clear Books.

Henley, D. and McKernan, V. 2009. *The Original Liverpool Sound: The Royal Liverpool Philharmonic Story.* Liverpool: Liverpool University Press.

Hewison, R. 1986. *Too Much: Art and Society in The Sixties 1960–75.* London: Methuen.

Hewison, R. 1995. *Culture and Consensus.* London: Methuen.

Hill, S. 2007. *'Blerwytirhwng?' The Place of Welsh Pop Music.* Farnham: Ashgate.

Hogg, B. 1993. *The History of Scottish Rock and Pop.* London: Guinness Publishing.

Hollies, The (with Anne Nightingale). 1964. *How to Run a Beat Group.* London: Daily Mirror.

Hopkins, H. 1964. *The New Look. A Social History of the Forties and Fifties.* London: Readers Union/Secker and Warburg.

Horn, A. 2009. *Juke Box Britain: Americanisation and Youth Culture, 1945–60.* Manchester: Manchester University Press.

Houghton, M. 1980. 'British beat', in J. Collis (ed.), *The Rock Primer.* Harmondsworth: Penguin, 149–78.

Howlett, K. 1996. *The Beatles at the BBC. The Record Years 1962–1970.* London: BBC Books.

Hughes, S. 1981. *Glyndebourne. A History of the Festival Opera*, 2nd edn. Newton Abbot: David and Charles.

Hustwitt, M 1983. '"Caught in a whirlpool of arching sound": the production of dance music in Britain in the 1920s'. *Popular Music*, 3(1), 7–32.

Hutchins, C. 2000. 'Maurice Kinn obituary', *The Guardian*, 10 August, http://www.guardian.co.uk/news/2000/aug/10/guardianobituaries [accessed 14 September 2012].

Hutchison, R. 1982. *The Politics of the Arts Council.* London: Sinclair and Browne.

Hutchison, R. and Feist, A. 1991. *Amateur Arts in the UK*. London: Policy Studies Institute.

Ingham, M. 1981. *Now We Are Thirty. Women of the Breakthrough Generation*. London: Eyre Methuen.

Jackson, B. 1968. *Working Class Community*. London: Routledge & Kegan Paul.

Jackson, L.A. 2008. '"The Coffee Club Menace". Policing youth. Leisure and sexuality in post-war Manchester'. *Cultural and Social History* 5(3), 289–308.

Jempson, M. 1993. *The Musicians' Union 1893–1993: A Centenary Celebration*. London: Musicians' Union.

Jenner, P. 2008. Interview with Matt Brennan, London, 11 November.

Jones, M. 2009. *Bristol Folk*. Bristol: Bristol Folk Publications.

Jones, R. 2009. *The Art and Sound of the Bristol Underground*. Bristol: Tangent Books.

Keightley, K. 2002. 'Reconsidering rock', in S. Frith, W. Straw and J. Street (eds), *Cambridge Companion to Pop and Rock*. Cambridge: Cambridge University Press, 109–42.

Keightley, K. 2004. 'Long play: adult-oriented popular music and the temporal logics of the post-war sound recording industry in the USA'. *Media, Culture and Society*, 26, 375–91.

Keightley, K. 2007. 'Globalization Blues: Why Capitol Rejected the Beatles' EMI/ Parlophone Masters in 1963'. Paper given to the IASPM-USA Conference, Boston, April.

Kennedy, J. 1958. *Tommy Steele*. London: Souvenir Press.

Kinn, M. 1949. 'No agent wants to handle publicity', *Melody Maker*, 18 June: 3.

Kolvin, P. ed. 2004. *Licensed Premises: Law & Practice*. Haywards Heath: Tottel.

Lancaster, B. 1996. 'After coffee at Sapparetti's'. *Northern Review*, 4, 47–63.

Laing, D. 1985. *One Chord Wonders*. Milton Keynes: Open University Press.

Laing, D. 2003. 'Promoter', in J. Shepherd et al. (eds), *Continuum Encyclopedia of Popular Music of the World*. London: Continuum.

Laing, D. 2007. 'Nine lives in the music business: Reg Dwight and Elton John in the 1960s'. *Popular Music History*, 2(3), 237–61.

Laing, D. 2009. 'Six boys, six Beatles: the formative years, 1950–1962', in K. Womack (ed.), *The Cambridge Companion to the Beatles.* Cambridge: Cambridge University Press, 9–32.

Laurie, P. 1965. *Teenage Revolution*. London: Anthony Blond.

Lebrecht, N. 2000. *Covent Garden. The Untold Story*. London: Simon & Schuster.

Lee, C.P. 2002. *Shake, Rattle and Rain: Popular Music Making in Manchester 1955–1995*. Ottery St. Mary: Hardinge Simpole.

Leigh, S. 2010. 'Tito Burns obituary', *The Independent*, 13 September, http:// www.independent.co.uk/news/obituaries/tito-burns-2077448.html [accessed 14 September 2012].

Leslie, P. 1965. *Fab. The Anatomy of a Phenomenon*. London: MacGibbon and Kee.

Levy, S. 2002. *Ready, Steady, Go! Swinging London and the Invention of Cool.* London: Fourth Estate.

Lewis, P. 1978. *The 50s.* London: Heinemann.

Lewry, P. and Goodall, N. 1996. *The Ultimate Cliff.* London: Simon & Schuster.

Logue, C. 1999. *Prince Charming. A Memoir.* London: Faber & Faber.

Lowerson, J. 2005. *Amateur Operatics. A Social and Cultural History.* Manchester: Manchester University Press.

Lyttelton, H. 1958. *Second Chorus,* London: MacGibbon and Kee.

MacKinnon, N. 1993. *The British Folk Scene.* Buckingham: Open University Press.

Macnab, G. 1993. *J. Arthur Rank and the British Film Industry.* London: Routledge.

Marwick, A. 1991. *Culture in Britain Since 1945.* Oxford: Blackwell.

Mass Observation. 1943. *The Pub and the People.* London: Victor Gollancz.

Martin, L. and Segrave, K. 1993. *Anti Rock: The Opposition to Rock 'n'roll.* New York: De Capo Press.

Matthew, B. 1962. *Trad Mad.* London: Souvenir Press.

McCarthy, A. ed. 1946. *The PL Yearbook of Jazz 1946.* London: Editions Poetry.

McDevitt, C. 1997. *Skiffle. The Definitive Inside Story.* London: Robson Books.

McKay, G. 2004. '"Unsafe things like youth and jazz": Beaulieu Jazz Festivals (1956–61), and the origins of pop festival culture in Britain', in A. Bennett (ed.), *Remembering Woodstock.* Aldershot: Ashgate, 90–110.

McKay, G. 2005. *Circular Breathing.* London: Duke University Press.

McKay, G. 2007. '"A soundtrack to the insurrection": street music, marching bands and popular protest'. *Parallax,* 42, 20–31.

McKibbin, R. 1998. *Classes and Cultures. England 1918–1951.* Oxford: Oxford University Press.

McLarty, I. 2010 'A signal triumph over strong national prejudices: the Edinburgh Musical Festivals of the early Nineteenth Century', MMus Dissertation, University of Edinburgh.

McVeigh, S. 2007. 'A free trade in music: London during the long nineteenth century in a European perspective'. *Journal of Modern European History,* 5(1), 67–94.

Meller, H.E. 1976. *Leisure and the Changing City, 1870–1914.* London: Routledge & Kegan Paul.

Milestone, R. 2007. '"That monstrosity of bricks and mortar": the town hall as a music venue in nineteenth-century Stalybridge', in R. Cowgill and P. Holman (eds), *Music in The British Provinces 1690–1914.* Aldershot: Ashgate, 295–324.

Moore, J. 2006. 'The sensitive matter of work permits', *The British Dance Band Encyclopaedia,* http://www.mgthomas.co.uk/dancebands/American%20Visitors/Pages/Work%20Permits.htm [accessed 14 September 2012].

Morrison, R. 2004. *Orchestra. The LSO. A Century of Triumph and Turbulence.* London: Faber & Faber.

Munro, A. 1996. *The Democratic Muse. Folk Revival in Scotland.* Aberdeen: Scottish Cultural Press (first published in 1984).

Murphy, R. 2004. 'Parnell, Valentine Charles (1892–1972)'. *Oxford Dictionary of National Biography*. Oxford: Oxford University Press, available at: http://www.oxforddnb.com/view/article/56615 [accessed 14 September 2012].

Murphy, R. 2004a. 'Black, George (1890–1945)'. *Oxford Dictionary of National Biography*. Oxford: Oxford University Press, available at: http://www.oxforddnb.com/view/article/56528 [accessed 14 September 2012].

Newton, F. 1959. *The Jazz Scene*. London: MacGibbon and Kee.

Nicholls, J. 2009. *The Politics of Alcohol: A History of the Drink Question in England*. Manchester: Manchester University Press.

Norman, P. 2001. *The Stones*. London: Sidgwick & Jackson.

Norman, P. 2004. *Shout! The True Story of the Beatles*. London: Pan.

Nott, J.J. 2002. *Music for the People: Popular Music and Dance in Interwar Britain*. Oxford: Oxford University Press.

Nott. J.J. 2004. 'Heimann, Carl Louis Bertram Reinhold (1896–1968)'. *Oxford Dictionary of National Biography*. Oxford: Oxford University Press, available at: http://www.oxforddnb.com/view/article/72390 [accessed 14 September 2012].

Ogersby, B. 1998. *Youth in Britain Since 1945*. Oxford: Blackwell.

O'Hagan, A. 1995. *The Missing*. London: Faber & Faber.

Olmsted, A.A. 2002. 'The capitalization of musical production: the conceptual and spatial development of London's public concerts, 1660–1750', in R. Qureshi (ed.), *Music and Marx: Ideas, Practices, Politics*. London: Routledge, 106–36.

Oliver, P. ed. 1990. *Black Music in Britain: Essays on the Afro-Asian Contribution to Popular Music*. Buckingham: Open University Press.

Oliver, P. 2007. 'Taking the measure of the blues', in N.A. Wynn (ed.), *Cross the Water Blues. African American Music in Europe*. Jackson, MS: University of Mississippi Press, 23–38.

Parsonage, C. 2005. *The Evolution of Jazz in Britain, 1880–1935*. Aldershot: Ashgate.

Parsonage, C. and Dyson, K. 2007. 'The history of women in jazz in Britain', in P. Adkins Chiti (ed.), *Women in Jazz/Donne in Jazz*. Rome: Editore Columbo, 129–40.

Passman, D. 2004. *All You Need to Know of the Music Business*. London: Penguin.

Patterson, S. 1963. *Dark Strangers. A Sociological Study of West Indians in London*. London: Tavistock.

Pearsall, R. 1973. *Victorian Popular Music*. Newton Abbot: David and Charles.

PEP (Political and Economic Planning). 1949. *Music. A Report on Musical Life in England*. London: PEP.

PEP. 1966. *Sponsorship of Music: The Role of Local Authorities*, London: PEP.

Perrone, P. 2007. 'Don Arden obituary', *The Independent*, 25 July, http://www.independent.co.uk/news/obituaries/don-arden-458579.html [accessed 14 September 2012].

Phipps, C., Tobler, J. and Smith, S. 2005. *Northstars*. Newcastle-upon-Tyne: Zymurgy Publishing.

Quant, M. 1967. *Quant by Quant*. London: Pan.

Ratcliffe, H. 1947. 'We must beat the record!', *Melody Maker*, 15 November: 4

Ratcliffe, H. 1949. 'Paris-London Band Exchange', *Melody Maker*, 8 January: 3.

Reed, B.H. 1950. *Eighty Thousand Adolescents*. London: George Allen & Unwin.

Reid, D.A. 2004. 'Butlin, Sir William Heygate Edmund Colborne [Billy] (1899–1980)'. *Oxford Dictionary of National Biography*. Oxford: Oxford University Press, available at: http://www.oxforddnb.com/view/article/30887 [accessed 14 September 2012].

Repsch, John, 1989. *The Legendary Joe Meek*. London: Woodford House.

Richard, C. 1960. *It's Great to be Young*. London: Souvenir Press.

Roberts, M. 2010. 'A working-class hero is something to be: the American Musicians' Union's attempts to ban the Beatles, 1964', *Popular Music*, 29(1), 1–16.

Roberts, R. 1971. *The Classic Slum. Salford Life in the First Quarter of the Century*. Manchester: Manchester University Press.

Robertson, A. 2011. *Joe Harriott. Fire in his Soul*. London: Northway.

Robinson, A. 2007. *Sunderland Empire. A Centenary History*. Stroud: Tempus.

Rogan, J. 1989. *Starmakers and Svengalis*. London: Futura.

Rogers, D. 1982. *Rock'n'Roll*. London: Routledge & Kegan Paul.

Rowntree, B.S. and Lavers, G.R. 1951. *English Life and Leisure. A Social Study*. London: Longmans, Green and Co.

Rowntree, G. 1962. 'New facts on teenage marriage', *New Society*, 4 October: 12–21.

Russell, D. 1997. *Popular Music in England*, 2nd edn. Manchester: Manchester University Press.

Russell, D. 2004. 'Stoll, Sir Oswald (1866–1942)'. *Oxford Dictionary of National Biography*. Oxford: Oxford University Press, available at: http://www.oxforddnb.com/view/article/36316 [accessed 14 September 2012].

Russell, T. 1950. 'The Orchestral Player' in R. Elkin (ed.), *A Career in Music*, London: William Earl, 139–58.

Rye, H. 1990. 'Fearsome means of dischord: early encounters with jazz', in P. Oliver (ed.), *Black Music in Britain: Essays on the Afro-Asian Contribution to Popular Music*. Buckingham: Open University Press, 45–57.

Sackville-West, E. and Shawe-Taylor, D. 1951. *The Record Guide*. London: Collins.

Savage, J. 2007. *Teenage. The Creation of Youth 1875–1945*. London: Chatto & Windus.

Savile, J. 1974. *As It Happens*. London: Barrie & Jenkins.

Schofield, H. 2005. 'No holding back French disco diva', http://news.bbc.co.uk/1/hi/world/europe/4372150.stm [accessed 14 September 2012].

Schroeder, J. 2009. *Sex and Violins. My Affair with Life, Love and Music*. Brighton: Pen Press.

Schwartz, R.F. 2007. *How Britain Got the Blues: The Transmission and Reception of American Blues Style in the United Kingdom*. Aldershot: Ashgate.

Shadows, The 1961. *The Shadows by Themselves*. London: Souvenir Press.

Shank, B. 1994. *Dissonant Identities: The Rock'n'Roll Scene in Austin, Texas*. Hanover, NE: Wesleyan University Press.

Sinclair, A. 1993. *Arts and Cultures: The History of the 50 Years of the Arts Council of Great Britain*. London: Sinclair-Stevenson.

Sinfield, A. 1995. 'The government, the people and the Festival of Britain', in J. Fyrth (ed.), *Labour's Promised Land. Culture and Society in Britain 1945–51*. London: Lawrence & Wishart, 181–96.

Slasberg, T. 1993. *The Pleasure Was Mine ... 40 Years a Concert Agent*. London: Thames Publishing.

Smith, C.S. 1967. *Young People at Leisure*. Manchester: Manchester University Press.

Smith, D. 1968. 'Pirate broadcasting'. *Southern California Law Review*, 41, 769–815.

Smith, M. 1999. 'The UK number ones: 1950s sheet music sales', http://www.onlineweb.com/theones/1950_sheet.htm [accessed 14 September 2012].

Smith, T. 2010. Interview with Matt Brennan, London, 15 November.

Southall, B. 1982. *Abbey Road*. Cambridge: Patrick Stephens.

Stapleton, C. 1990. 'African connections: London's hidden music scene', in P. Oliver (ed.), *Black Music in Britain: Essays on the Afro-Asian Contribution to Popular Music*. Buckingham: Open University Press, 87–101.

Summers, A. 2006. *One Train Later*. London: Portrait.

Sweers, B. 2005. *Electric Folk. The Changing Face of English Traditional Music*. Oxford: Oxford University Press.

Taylor, J. 1972. *From Self-Help to Glamour*. Oxford: History Workshop.

Tennent, K. 2010. 'A Distribution Revolution: Changes in Music Distribution in the UK 1950–80'. Paper presented to the Annual European Business History Conference, Glasgow, August.

Thompson, G. 2008. *Please Please Me: Sixties British Pop, Inside Out*. Oxford: Oxford University Press.

Thompson, P. 1994. *The Best of Cellars. The Story of the Cavern Club*. Stroud: Tempus.

Thomson, R.A. 1989. 'Dance bands and dance halls in Greenock, 1945–55'. *Popular Music*, 8(2), 143–55.

Thornton, S. 1995. *Club Cultures*. Cambridge: Polity.

Till, N. 2004. '"First-Class Evening Entertainments": spectacle and social control in a mid-Victorian music hall'. *New Theatre Quarterly*, 10(1): 3–18.

Tobin, E. 2010. *Are Ye Dancin'?* Glasgow: Waverley Books.

Tudor, P. 2003. *Wembley Arena 1934–2004: The First Seventy Years*. Middlesex: Wembley London Ltd.

Turner, B. 1984. *Hot Air, Cool Music*. London Quartet Books.

UK Rock Festivals website. 2011. '1967 Windsor Festival', http://www.ukrockfestivals.com/1967-windsor-festival.html [accessed 14 September 2012].

Uglow, J. 2007. *Nature's Engraver. A Life of Thomas Bewick.* London: Faber & Faber.

Venness, T. 1962. *School Leavers. Their Aspirations and Expectations.* London: Methuen.

Vulliamy, G. and Lee, E. 1976. *Pop Music in School.* Cambridge: Cambridge University Press.

Wald, E. 2009. *How the Beatles Destroyed Rock 'n' Roll.* Oxford: Oxford University Press.

Warner, A. 2002. 'A long time ago in a galaxy far, far away … Some personal reminiscences', http://www.emimusicpub.com/worldwide/music/catalog_jtf_a-lomg-time-ago.html [accessed 14 September 2012].

Watkins, C. 2011. 'Watkins electric music history', http://www.wemwatkins.co.uk/history.htm [accessed 14 September 2012].

Waymark, P. 2004. 'Grade, Lew, Baron Grade (1906–1998)'. *Oxford Dictionary of National Biography.* Oxford: Oxford University Press, available at: http://www.oxforddnb.com/view/article/71387 [accessed 14 September 2012].

Weber, W. 2004. 'From the self-managing musician to the independent concert agent', in W. Weber (ed.), *The Musician as Entrepreneur, 1700–1914.* Bloomington: Indiana University Press, 105–29.

Webster, I., Leib, J. and Button, J. 2007. *The Concise Guide to Licensing.* Leicester: Troubador.

Williams, A. 1976. *The Man Who Gave the Beatles Away.* London: Coronet.

Williamson, J. and Cloonan, M. 2007. 'Rethinking the music industry'. *Popular Music,* 26(2), 305–22.

Wills, A. 2004. 'Cotton, William Edward [Billy] (1899–1969)'. *Oxford Dictionary of National Biography.* Oxford: Oxford University Press, available at: http://www.oxforddnb.com/view/article/57665 [accessed 14 September 2012].

Wilmer, V. 1989. *Mama Said There'd Be Days Like This. My Life in the Jazz World.* London: The Women's Press.

Willmott, P. 1966. *Adolescent Boys of East London.* London: Routledge & Kegan Paul.

Wilmut, R. 1985. *Kindly Leave the Stage: The Story of Variety, 1869–1960.* London: Methuen.

Witts, R. 1998. *Artist Unknown: An Alternative History of the Arts Council.* London: Little, Brown and Company.

Wolf, B. 2010. 'Promoting new music in London, 1930–1980'. PhD Dissertation, Royal Holloway, University of London.

Wolfe, T. 1968. 'The noonday underground', in *The Pumphouse Gang.* New York: Bantam, 75–87.

Woods, F. 1979. *Folk Revival: The Rediscovery of a National Music.* Poole: Blandford.

Woodward, C. 2009. *The London Palladium: The Story of the Theatre and its Stars.* Huddersfield: Northern Heritage.

Workers Music Association. 1945. *A Policy for Music in Postwar Britain.* London: WMA.

Wyman, B. 1991. *Stone Alone*, London: Penguin.

Index

Printed in France by Amazon
Brétigny-sur-Orge, FR